VEGAN TACOS

VEGAN TACOS

Authentic & Inspired Recipes for Mexico's Favorite Street Food

Jason Wyrick

Vegan Heritage Press

Woodstock • Virginia

Vegan Tacos: Authentic & Inspired Recipes for Mexico's Favorite Street Food by Jason Wyrick
(Copyright © 2014 by Jason Wyrick)

ISBN 13: 978-0-9854662-7-5

Second printing, September 2014
10 9 8 7 6 5 4 3 2

Vegan Heritage Press, LLC books are available at quantity discounts. For information, please visit our website at www.veganheritagepress.com or write the publisher at Vegan Heritage Press, P.O. Box 628, Woodstock, VA 22664-0628.

Library of Congress Cataloging-in-Publication Data

Wyrick, Jason, author.
  Vegan tacos : authentic & inspired recipes for Mexico's favorite street food / Jason Wyrick. -- First edition.
     pages cm
  Includes index.
   ISBN 978-0-9854662-7-5 (paperback)
  1. Tacos. 2. Vegan cooking. I. Title.
  TX836.W97 2014
  641.84--dc23
                                2014018384

Photo credits: Cover photo by Jeff Wysocarski; styling by Erin Wysocarski. Interior photos and styling by Jason Wyrick. Incidental stock photos.

Disclaimer: Allergies can be a serious threat to one's health. If you know you have food allergies, please take necessary precautions whenever you cook. Also, gloves and eye protection are recommended for handling hot chiles. If you require a medical diagnosis, or if you are contemplating any major dietary change, please consult a qualified health-care provider. You should always seek an expert medical opinion before making changes in your diet.

Vegan Heritage Press, LLC books are distributed by Andrews McMeel Publishing.

Printed in the United States of America

Dedication

This book is dedicated to my loving wife Madelyn Pryor and my daughter Gaia, who comes into this world nearly the same day as this book. May she grow up in a world where tasty vegan eats and compassionate living are the norm for everyone.

Contents

Introduction

Food has always been in my blood, though I didn't recognize it until I was older. Growing up, my tools were a microwave, packaged food, and scissors to open the package. Cooking ramen in a pot was about as adventurous as I would get, but there was always something lurking in the background that kept calling to me. I finally heeded the call when I was in my last year of college and began to learn how to cook. The skills came quickly, but I had no idea where they came from. I wondered if I was unique in my family. It turns out I wasn't. After talking with my mom, her aunt, and my grand-

José Arámbula (Pancho Villa)

mother, I discovered that there was a long history of food in my family. They told me plenty of stories, many of which sounded outlandish at the time. The first time I heard the story I am about to tell you, I didn't believe it. You see, my great-grand uncle Hector Gonzales was a damn good cook. Cooking even saved his life.

In their youth, Hector's brothers were sold off as farmers. When he was old enough, he set off in search of them. During his travels, he was set upon by Pancho Villa's gang. I am not sure how or why they captured him, but they took him prisoner and planned on executing him. Thinking quickly, Hector told Pancho Villa that he was the best cook he would ever come across. Pancho Villa, being the nice gentleman fighter that he was, made Hector dig a grave—Hector's grave. He then staged a cook-off between his current cook and Hector. The loser would get a bullet and the grave. Hector went on to become Pancho Villa's cook for a time, until he could escape and continue the search for his brothers—or so the story goes.

I tend not to put much stock in such wild tales, but my family has so many of them: attempted assassinations, relatives being smuggled across the border in baskets to escape vengeful husbands, powerful politicos in the Mexican government, and a patrician family that lost their fortune—I do wonder if it's all true. Hector's brother Al, one of my favorite relatives, who passed away a few years ago, thought so. Certainly, the talent for and love of food in my lineage has proven true, passed down to me from generation to generation.

Food always spoke to me, though I didn't know how to make anything good until I was in my twenties. I could look at a picture of a meal and know how it should taste, but I hadn't yet turned my attention to the craft of it. Then I had my first good meal at an Egyptian restaurant in Fort Worth, Texas, and I was hooked. I wanted to have meals like that every day, but I was too poor to afford it. That's why I learned how to cook. I spent hours in the kitchen making meals just to make them. I would search out authentic recipes and talk to people from different cultures to learn the essentials of their regional cuisines. It wasn't long after that I discovered my first real culinary love: Mexican.

I went from the kid fearing a pickled jalapeño to searching out guajillo chiles, anchos, serranos, habaneros, poblanos, mulatos, and anything I could get my hands on. I loved them all, and I loved the excitement of Mexican cuisine. It is still my absolute favorite food in the world. I would research recipes to discover the flavor profiles of the different regions of Mexico. I would dream about the food and plot my meals days ahead. And then I saw my first real taco. Not those hard shells filled with junk that we far too often see in the U.S., sadly the tacos I grew up with. These were slow-cooked tacos spiced with chiles, Mexican oregano, fresh ground cumin, and epazote. They were served on warm hand-made corn tortillas with a variety of salsas and fresh condiments. They were warm and inviting, and the food was so *present*. I don't know any other way to describe it. Those tacos refused to be ignored. Ironically, I was already vegan at that point, and had been for many years, so I did not actually eat the tacos, but I knew from seeing them, being around them, and what they smelled like to know exactly how they should taste. Thus began my taco journey.

Alfonso "Uncle Al" Gonzales

I set out to explore as many different tacos as I could find, by talking to people about their family recipes, by discovering my own family's recipes and history, by visiting taquerías, by research, and mainly by making tacos and sharing them with people. If you have ever tried to serve native food to a person from that food's culture, you know pretty quickly whether or not you hit the mark. Fortunately, most of mine were successes right away. I wanted to get my vegan versions as close to the original as possible. However, there are certain techniques that don't translate well from a traditional meat version to a vegan version. That's why you may find some of the techniques in this book don't exactly match the traditional techniques. Sometimes it's because the traditional techniques rely upon specialty methods only found in dedicated taquerías, but more often, it's because I wanted to create an end result, not a process, that was as close to the traditional taco in spirit as possible.

All of this is because I fell in love with tacos. For me, the taco is the ultimate blend of comfort and excitement. It's immediate with its flavors, yet the warm corn tortilla feels soothing when I hold it in my hand. A taco is a meal all packaged up in a folded tortilla, but it has the complexity that you find in any fancy restaurant meal. Tacos manage to be both intellectual and soul-satisfying, a myriad of flavors contained in a single delicious bite. For me, a good taco instantly takes away the stress of the day. I can't help but smile when I eat them. I hope you have the same experience, because if you do, you, too, will be hooked. Thank you for reading this book. This is a book about fun and excitement, experiencing something off the beaten path, learning new techniques and new ingredients, comfort, history, philosophy, and ultimately good food. It's my love letter to tacos. I hope you end up loving them as much as I do.

Tacos al Gusto

Tacos on the center plate (clockwise from top left): Chayote al Carbon
Taco Rápido; Taco al Pastor. Surrounding plate clockwise from left: a
molcajete with chiles de árbol; tortillas in a terracotta warmer, wilted
chard in mojo de ajo; pickled onions, limes, cilantro; Salsa Verde,
Guacamole, and Guajillo Chile Salsa.

Tacos 101

"Everything you need to know about tacos."

In this book, I provide everything you need to know to make vegan versions of authentic Mexican tacos, from homemade tortillas to your own vegan queso fresco. At the same time, you are always at liberty to use storebought components, leaving only the job of preparing your filling and assembling your tacos.

The taco recipes in this book range from simple to complex. Whenever possible, I include tips on how to take time-saving shortcuts. To reduce the time even further, I suggest keeping some of your favorite salsas and hot sauces on hand. This is what I do. That way, you don't have to make the filling, the condiments, and the salsas, not to mention the tortillas every time you're hungry for a taco. Speaking of which, I strongly suggest making your own tortillas. It doesn't matter how good the taco filling is, the tortilla will make or break the taco, and there is nothing like a thick fresh corn tortilla toasting on the skillet to round out the taco experience. If you don't make your own, get a good thick corn tortilla from the store. Flimsy tortillas tend to fall apart. Even better, you may have a local tortilla factory near you where you can purchase fresh-made tortillas. Your tacos will thank you for it.

Taco Components Explained

Tacos are a modular experience. They are comprised of the tortilla, the filling, the condiments, and the sauce. You can have one type of taco in many different ways, just by changing out the condiments and the sauces and even by pairing it with one of the flavored tortillas included in the book. They are all variations on a theme. That doesn't mean I've left you on your own, though.

I have also organized the taco components for you into separate sections. With each taco, I have noted my favorite condiment and salsa/hot sauce pairings. Where there are traditional pairings, such as with the radish and cabbage that go with the Carnitas de Michoacán, I have noted that as well. Don't feel obligated to use those pairings, though. Once you get in the kitchen, these tacos are yours. Make of them what you will, and have fun doing it. If that means taking some extra shortcuts, do it. To me, food is about the overall experience, from buying ingredients to making the food and finally to eating it. Whatever brings you the most joy during the process, I encourage you to do it. If it's the difference between deciding to make a taco or not, take the shortcut and make it! I will be happy that you did. Consider me a taco enabler.

How to Assemble and Eat a Taco

Tacos are assembled from the tortilla up and are usually served in twos or threes, sometimes with a small side dish, to make a complete meal. When you make your own tortillas, you will notice a very gentle curve to one side of the tortilla. This is the face of the tortilla. Mass produced tortillas do not have this curve. Fill the tortilla with just 2 to 4 tablespoons of filling, then the condiments, and finish it off with the salsa. The salsa helps hold loose ingredients in place. A few tablespoons of filing don't sound like much, but the typical tortilla for a taco is only five to five and a half inches in diameter and it doesn't take a lot to fill it. Plus, you need to leave room for the condiments. Don't overstuff your tacos or some of the filling and salsa will fall out the sides of your tortilla. It's a messy experience. That's my best advice. In actual practice, however, I totally overstuff my tacos.

As Quick As You Like

Because of their "component" nature, preparing tacos allows for a time flexibility not found in most other recipes. For example, if you're in a hurry, you can buy many of the taco components ready-made, such as tortillas, salsas, and other toppings. If you choose a quick filling, you can have tacos on the table in 15 minutes. If you want to make everything from scratch, you could conceivably spend the better part of a fun day making tacos. It's a good idea once in a while, because if you do, you'll have fresh components for the next time you make tacos, and your from-scratch tacos will go much more quickly.

I suggest that whether you make your tacos the easy way or the classic way, read through the entire recipe. Sometimes, you may want to make certain ingredients a day ahead. Certain steps may require an hour or two of resting or marinating—these are all things you'll want to know before you begin.

When I make tacos just for me, I often buy the fresh salsas I find at my local Mexican market rather than making my own. When I make everything from scratch, it's usually when I'm entertaining guests. I generally make the salsas and other toppings the day before and then just make the filling and tortillas the day of the event.

Another aspect of speeding up your prep time has to do with your equipment and skills in the kitchen. I made all the recipes in this book using good quality pots and pans and a very nice knife. Your own cooking gear will probably differ in brand, size, etc., so it is far more important to learn how to cook by sight, smell, and instinct rather than adhering to specific times in recipes.

When you make tacos with on-hand or ready-made ingredients, it can be the ultimate fast-food meal. If you make all the taco components from scratch, it can be a relaxing and rewarding experience.

Recipe Features

Each recipe features helpful information, including:

Region(s): Because I am very interested in food history and anthropology, I included the name of the region associated with each recipe (those of my own creation are from *Casa de Jason*). If you're also into food history, I suggest researching where these recipes come from. Whenever possible, I'll steer you in that direction. There are some truly fascinating stories behind many of these recipes. If that doesn't pique your interest, and you just want to eat some good tacos, then just dig right into the recipes!

Heat Index: For each taco recipe, I have included a very subjective heat number for the spiciness of each taco, salsa, and hot sauce. These are on a scale from 1 to 10, with 1 being mild and 10 being very hot. I like very spicy food, so a 4 for me may be an 8 for you. For me, eating a fresh jalapeño by itself is only a 3. I tried to keep in mind that not everyone can handle the same amount of heat, but like I said:

it's subjective. You have been warned! Also, some salsas will be hot on their own, but the overall heat experience will be toned down when they are integrated with a taco.

Make It Simple: Even though I am a taco aficionado and a lover of fine food, I sometimes cheat in the kitchen to save myself some time or expense, and I know a lot of other people do, too. With many of the recipes, I have included instructions to greatly simplify and hasten making the tacos, without compromising too much on their flavor or texture. Keep in mind that there is some compromise involved, but you will be able to make a less labor-intensive version of the recipe that doesn't require advanced cooking techniques. Vegan tacos are for everyone!

Make It Low-Fat: My strongest commitment is to not harm other creatures, but very close to that is my commitment to health. As a former diabetic and someone who was very overweight, I think it's important to showcase health-promoting recipes. Many of the recipes in Vegan Tacos have alternate versions that do not use oil and are based solely on whole foods. That's why you'll see some of the recipes call for seitan, or for example, mushrooms, and instructions are included for cooking both. Not all of the recipes have these versions. In some instances, they were not necessary and in others, the traditional recipe would be compromised so much with the alternative that the end result would be unrecognizable.

Note: Nutrition information on all the tacos, salsas, guacamoles, sides, and drinks can be found at www.thevegantaste.com, as well as additional photographs and even more taco recipes!

How and When to Prepare the Ingredients

The recipes will instruct you how to prepare your ingredients. However, some ingredients are best prepared during the later stages of a recipe, while some should be prepared well ahead of time. I have placed these preparation notes with the ingredients that need them to make your taco-making experience the best it can possibly be. If you don't see a preparation note on an ingredient, go ahead and prepare it before you start cooking as you normally would.

About Ingredient Measurements

Each of the recipes in this book has been tested and honed with the measurements listed, and I encourage you to try the recipes for the first time as written. That said, don't feel like the ingredient measurements are rigid rules to which you must adhere! When I am cooking these recipes for myself, I never measure ingredients. For example, the taco I make today might have just under a teaspoon of chile powder, and the same one I make tomorrow might have just over a teaspoon. As long as you can approximate a teaspoon, tablespoon, and so on, your tacos will come out just fine. True taco-making includes a bit of improv in the process, and your own creativity (and personal taste preference) should be part of the taco-making experience.

What Is a Taco Exactly?

The answer to this question is hard to pin down! Tacos are the quintessential eats of one of the most diverse food cultures in the world. Mexico is truly a melting pot cuisine, and its tacos are no different, but I will try to answer the question anyway. A taco is, at its heart, a hand-sized tortilla, usually corn and almost always soft, wrapped around another set of ingredients. Think about how broad that is for a moment and then imagine the enormous amount of variations on the taco that you can create. Of course, many of them are as far removed from Mexican food as you can get, and this book is, mostly, about authentic Mexican tacos made vegan. That means we can add a few more criteria to our definition.

Tacos are vibrant. I have had bad tacos before, but I have never had a dull taco. Even when a taco is made from a simple filling like beans, the beans themselves are rarely plain, probably having been stewed with the herb epazote, chiles, garlic, and whatever else adds a depth of flavor to them. Tacos are enlivened by bold salsas and almost always feature chiles in one way or another. There are very few exceptions to that.

Tacos are personal. Tacos, especially at taquerías, are served with the tortilla and filling, but without any salsas or condiments. Those are spread out along the taco bar, and you get to choose how you want to top your taco. There are often three or more salsas at the bar, the classic three being (1) a crushed tomato and chile-based salsa, (2) a tomatillo salsa, and (3) a smooth-textured guajillo salsa. There is usually a smooth guacamole, lime wedges, pickled onions, pickled chiles, chopped cilantro, and fried *chiles de árbol*. And that's just the very basic assortment of taco toppings.

> ## Early Taco History
> • • • • • • • • • • • •
>
> I love science, history, archaeology, and such. However, there isn't a lot of information available on the tortilla until the period of the Aztec Empire, so some of the early history in this section is my speculation based on what I know about the food practices of other ancient cultures. If you just want good eats, skip straight to the recipes, but if you want a glimpse into the history and science of tasty tacos, read on!

Tacos are social. Tacos bring people together, especially at the taquería. It's not uncommon for a taco stand to have construction workers, wealthy businessmen, and teenagers out on the town all gathered side by side at the taco bar, sharing the same food experience. I suspect that's because tacos are fun and easy to eat, making them the perfect street food. Taquerías in Mexico are prolific in the extreme, so everyone visits them. I don't think it's just that, though. I think it is also because tacos are now part of the Mexican cultural identity. Ironically, it was not always so, but I'll share more about that in my taco history section.

A Note About "Authentic" Food

I love authentic food. It's a way to capture a culture through food; a way to experience the culinary intentions of a group of people through the art of what they love to eat. It's a way to experience flavor combinations that aren't part of our everyday experience at home. A body of creations that is considered authentic is usually comprised of foods that have withstood the test of time and the approving palates of the masses. In short, it's a way to connect with other people through food and to experience food the way it was intended.

What's considered "authentic food" can sometimes be troublesome. Like language, food evolves, despite the protestations of food authorities, authors of authentic food cookbooks, and ivory tower chefs trying to make names for themselves. I will readily admit to having been all three at one point or another in my career. I honestly think those attitudes are part of the process of discovery; of trying to chase down a true cultural experience and help others do the same. It requires the expert to define what is, and what isn't, acceptable. Real authentic food doesn't care what the experts say, though. It is, at its heart, eminently practical. Iconic dishes are influenced by immigration, emigration, trade, conflict, tourism, regional produce, weather patterns, and even changes in technology. Is a tortilla inauthentic because it was made with a tortilla press instead of patted out by hand? How about one cooked over an iron griddle instead of a clay *comal*? What about the flour tortilla of Northern Mexico, a holdover from Spanish times, or the soy sauce so common at taquerías in Baja, Mexico?

Food the way a culture really experiences it is agile and adaptable to its circumstances. Your kitchen experience should be the same way. Don't feel like you must replicate everything in exactitude unless that process gives you joy in the kitchen.

The History of the Taco: Children of the Maíz

The history of the taco starts with the domestication of corn and culminates with you, the taco eater. It begins with a simple grass and a curious forager. Somewhere between 9,000 to 12,000 years ago, a form of the grass teosinte was being consumed by the people of the Balsas Lowlands of southwestern Mexico. The seed kernels of wild teosinte were not particularly easy to eat, being encased in a very hard shell. To eat it, it had to be popped like popcorn or ground into a meal. Evidence exists of both cooking methods in ancient times. That means that at some point, someone decided to take the hard seeds of teosinte grass, put them on a hot plate, and see what happened. I can imagine their excitement watching the teositne seeds explode into "pop" teosinte. If that person hadn't been curious, or desperate enough to do that, we wouldn't have domesticated corn today, and that means we wouldn't have tacos.

Food Anthropology
· · · · · · · · · · · · ·

The study of the history of plants is called archaeo-botany, and the study of food and its interplay with society is called food anthropology. I love both.

Once it was discovered that teosinte seeds were edible, the slow process of selection began, with bigger and better seeds being chosen by hungry lowlanders. This is the point where this particular strain of teosinte, which would become maíz, started to be grown purposefully as a food source. Stone mills about 8,700 years old have been discovered in the Balsa Lowlands with an early form of maíz residue found in them. From this area, maíz spread through Central America to the north of South America, becoming a staple grain of those regions where it was consumed along with beans, quinoa, potatoes, and squash. Consuming maíz with these foods was particularly important because corn that has not been specially treated with the process called "nixtamalization" has little available niacin. A lack of niacin leads to pellagra, a malnutrition disease that causes skin rash, dementia, and death. Not fun. However, when paired with the other foods mentioned above, maíz is an excellent grain. The other problem, as far as tacos are concerned, is that ground corn will not form dough without first being "nixtamalized." We're getting closer to the taco, but we're not there yet.

Nixtamalization

The history of food is the history of experimentation. The earliest record we have of nixtamalization occurred around 3,200 to 3,500 years ago in the south of Guatemala. Nixtamalization is the process of soaking and boiling dried corn kernels in a highly alkaline solution. The earliest alkaline substance used to make nixtamal (which we know as "hominy"), was wood ash. That's right. Someone decided to soak and boil dried maíz kernels in a solution of water and ash. Not my first culinary choice, but I have the advantage of cooking in a modern kitchen with ready-made food available at every street corner. Later on in history, another hungry food explorer decided to soak and boil dried maíz kernels in lime, another highly caustic alkaline compound.

What happened at those moments caused a revolution in the use of maíz forever. The reason for this is two-fold. First, nixtamalization alters the protein structure of the endosperm in maíz so that amino acids become much more bioavailable. That means maíz, along with beans, was nutritionally able to serve as the backbone of Mesoamerican societies. Because maíz became nutritionally more viable and because it is a hearty plant with efficient water usage adaptable to a wide climate range, nixtamalization techniques and maíz spread rapidly throughout the Americas. Second, the alkaline solution dissolves hemicelluloses, allowing the tough pericarp (that's the outer layer) of the maíz kernel to separate from the rest of the kernel. This tough layer can then be washed away, exposing the softer, malleable kernel underneath. It also causes the starches to swell and gelatinize, meaning that maíz can

Cinteotl, the god of Maíz (from the Borgia Codex)

be mashed into a dough that will stick together. It didn't take long for someone to figure out they could mash nixtamalized maíz into dough and pat it into a flat cake, and that meant tortillas—after a fashion.

These tortillas weren't what you would expect to see today. They were thicker than the modern thin tortillas, and they remained this way until relatively recently, when the tortilla press became widely used in the early- to mid-1900s. Before the tortilla press, tortillas were commonly patted out by hand or on banana leaves, which is why they were so thick. People, however, are industrious, and even those thick tortillas could be folded into a "U" shape. As soon as someone spread beans on that folded tortilla or tossed a piece of squash in it, the first taco was invented. Since Mesoamerican societies were primarily vegetarian, chances are the first taco was vegan! If not the first, then perhaps the second or third. Either way, a vegan taco must have been developed early on.

Different regions made their own types of corn cakes, such as sopes, arepas, tlacoyo, and tamales, but we know for certain, through glyphs and drawings in the sixteenth-century Codex Mendoza that the people of the Aztec Empire ate lots of corn tortillas. Some historians speculate that it was the Aztecs that quickly spread the hand-patted precursor of the modern tortilla throughout Central America. In the Aztec capital Tenochtitlan, tortillas were commonly topped with cactus fruit, beans, squash, chiles, honey, eggs, and turkey. We definitely have tacos now. Amazingly, most of those original ingredients were vegan. The Aztecs dipped their tortillas in chile sauces—for the wealthy, chocolate chile sauces called *moles*—and we can still see some of these methods used in modern tacos.

Chiles

Speaking of chiles, these fiery fruits have long played an important part in Mesoamerican societies and are a consistent theme throughout the story of tacos. Chiles have been part of the Mesoamerican diet for at least 10,000 years, and there is evidence of their domestication as early as 6,000 years ago in the Valley of Mexico, but that wasn't the only place wild chiles were turned into crops. It's just the earliest historical record. According to Professor Seung-Chul Kim of the University of California at Riverside, "... while beans and maíz were each domesticated once at specific locations and then spread through Central America as domesticated crops, chiles were domesticated several times independently in different regions of Central America and at different times." They were an integral part of the food culture, and thus the taco. This trend remains to this day, which is why it is hard to imagine an authentic Mexican taco without some sort of chile.

The taco changed with the coming of the Spanish. Documents describing the Coyoacan victory feast of Hernán Cortés and his native allies (groups who wanted to see their Aztec masters overthrown), and written by Cortés himself, talk about tortillas served with, sadly, pigs brought from Cuba. Decidedly not vegan, but unlike the Aztecs, the Spanish ate meat frequently, and, once they established New Spain, bad food habits trickled through the region. However, speaking from a culinary standpoint, some good also came of it, because they brought with them cilantro, cumin, olives, olive oil, citrus, and certain European and Middle Eastern cooking techniques, adding even more diversity to the food culture of Mesoamerica. You can see this diversity in our tacos today through the common use of lime, cilantro garnishes, cumin, the olives used in certain Veracruz tacos, and even adobo, though Spanish adobo differs from the Mexican version.

A Claim on Tacos

People often claim foods as their own as a way to define themselves culturally. This was particularly important for Mexicans, when they first gained independence from Spain in 1821, later from the French, and then the dictator Porfirio Díaz in the early 1900s. It was important for Catholic priests to claim wheat, not corn, as the food of choice, since it symbolized their religious differences. The upper class claimed European food as their cuisine to set themselves above the peasantry. So, it was important for the lower classes to claim tacos as their own, and then it became fashionable for all Mexicans to claim them.

From Arquebus to Silver Mine

In fact, the words "tortilla" and "taco" are Spanish. The predominant language spoken in the Aztec empire was Nahuatl, and the Nahuatl word for tortilla was *tlaxcalli,* with a derivative word *taqualli.* You'll notice they sound very similar to the word "taco."

Moreover, the story of the taco is wrapped up, pun intended, with the corn tortilla. To the Spanish, *tlaxcalli* resembled little cakes, and the Spanish word for cake was *torta,* thus they called the little cakes tortillas. The word taco has a more explosive history. Also a Spanish word, a taco was a wad that was shoved down the bore of an arquebus, a predecessor to the musket, commonly used by Spanish soldiers in the sixteenth century. The wad, or taco, held the shot in place. It came to be more commonly used as a generic name for a wad or a plug, and also for a roll of explosives designed to be shoved into a small hole for blasting. And this brings us to the silver mines of Mexico.

During the seventeenth century and onward, the silver miners of the Guanajuato area carried baskets of tacos with them to work in the mines, and this is the first time we see the Spanish word "taco" associated with, well, the taco. We are not sure exactly when the first person at the mines associated the word "taco" with their corn tortilla wrap, but these miners used gunpowder tacos to blast small holes in the mines. It likely only took one person to make a joke about their spicy lunch treats being tacos for the name to catch on. I also suspect it is because the word "taco" sounds a lot like *taqualli,* and that made the joke a terrible, groan-inducing pun. More speculation on my part, but the propensity for people to make puns is universal, as is the propensity for other people to repeat them!

The miners brought their tacos to Mexico City with them some time in the 1800s, where they quickly became a favorite street food amongst the working class. You can still see that legacy in the name of one of the most popular basket tacos sold in Mexico City today, *Tacos de Mineros.* Ironically, the only book that talks about street food in Mexico City was written in 1831 and mentions plenty of tortilla-based street food, but no *Tacos de Mineros.* It's quite possible that this style of food simply wasn't worth mentioning as street food, because it was too pedestrian, or that *tacos de mineros* didn't make it to Mexico City until the mid-1800s. Regardless, they eventually became the iconic working-class food.

¡Viva la Taco Revolución!

Like any other culture, lower class dishes were not the dishes of the upper class, especially in the highly stratified society of pre-revolutionary Mexico. To the Mexican elite, who were mostly wealthy Spanish descendants called *criollo* (a word related to Creole), indigenous food was something to be scorned, and since the taco was peasant food, it was scorned as well. Instead, wealthy people of influence tried to imitate the continental tastes of Europe, which, at the time, meant French cuisine. This became even more pronounced when the French conquered Mexico for a brief time during the 1860s and invited Ferdinand Maximilian Joseph, the grandson of the Austrian Emperor, to become the Emperor of Mexico. Being from the Austrian court, Ferdinand and his wife Charlotte indulged in French cuisine, and that meant everyone else in the Mexican court did, too. Even ambassadors from Mexico would downplay their culinary tastes abroad and try to be more European. Upper class Mexicans, who were nationalists but still wanted to appear civilized, became trapped between two culinary worlds, trying to find a balance between traditional Mexican dishes and rich French dishes. The taco was not on the list.

Taco eaters weren't going to take that lying down. For the lower class, which was the majority of the country, the taco became a symbol of revolution, a food of subversive defiance against the arrogant elite. If you were a taco eater, you were a true Mexican. It became folded up in the national identity of Mexico.

Food is one of the primary ways cultures define themselves, even more so during times of social upheaval. It's no surprise that the taco became the hero of working-class Mexico. When the working class finally won the revolution in 1920, the taco gained even more prominence. Because of that victory and the national sense of the taco as quintessentially Mexican, taquerías can now be found everywhere on the streets of Mexico.

¿What Is a Taquería?

The word "taquería" used to only refer to a taco pushcart, but now it refers to any restaurant, truck, or cart that specializes in tacos.

With the proliferation of taquerías during the 1900s, a taco explosion occurred. Regional specialties came together in Mexico City, and a myriad of taco combinations was born as ingredients and techniques cross-pollinated on the streets of the capital. There are well over 100 different types of tacos served in Mexico City, though some are clearly more popular than others. Outside of Mexico City, each region developed its own iconic tacos based on their local ingredients. Some of these were just variations on a theme while others were completely different from each other. Northern tacos used wheat tortillas as well as corn, which was unheard of in the South. Because of this taco revolution in the early 1900s, taco-making reached a fairly high level of sophistication.

The taco was also influenced by immigration and tourism in Mexico. For example, with a large influx of Middle Easterners during the early to middle of the twentieth century, *Tacos Árabes* and *Tacos al Pastor* were developed. Both of these resulted from the shwarma style of cooking that incorporated Mexican ingredients. A Japanese influence in the cuisine of Baja can be seen with Tempura-Style Tacos. New tacos are continually being carried back across the border from the United States by seasonal migrant workers, as can be seen with *Tacos Vampiros,* a creation from the south of Arizona that showcases a crispy grilled tortilla that is now served in northern Mexico. Tacos have their classics, but the taco is a living cuisine that continuously evolves.

The Mexican Revolution also caused a surge in emigration to the United States. Nearly 900,000 Mexican emigrants fled la Revolución and crossed the border into southern California, Arizona, New Mexico, and Texas. These emigrants brought their cuisine with them and adapted them to local produce and tastes as needed. The taco, however, remained an underground item in the U.S.

Glen Bell's Hard Shell

While extremely popular in Mexico, tacos remained relatively unknown in the rest of the world. That is, until Glen Bell had a *taco dorado* in the early 1960s at a Mexican restaurant in California and came up with the idea of frying a tortilla to increase its longevity. This made the tortilla shelf stable and sped up taco preparation so that tacos could be mass produced for his restaurants. Those restaurants became known as Taco Bell, and, even though Taco Bell tacos are far removed from what a real Mexican taco tastes like, Taco Bell was responsible for popularizing tacos throughout the world. (It should be noted, however, that a mechanical fryer was actually invented several years beforehand in 1947 in New York City by Mexican immigrant Juvencio Maldonado.)

I admit, Taco Bell tacos are the ones I grew up eating, and I loved them. That may be exaggerating a bit as I think "like" might be a better word, but they were some of the only tacos I knew. They didn't compare to the soft wheat tacos my mom would make. Chances are, if you enjoy hard-shell tacos, it's because of Glen Bell. Tacos remained in this state until fairly recently, at least in the U.S. In Mexico, they just kept getting better. It's fair to say that in Mexico, taquerías are as common as Starbucks, but the food is made to order from fresh ingredients at a speed that would rival any fast-food drive-through.

Mexican Food in the U.S.A.

Mexican food has been popular in the United States for decades, at least a very Americanized version of it, but over the last decade, interest in real Mexican food has surged. A burgeoning group of chefs has done quite a bit to bring authentic Mexican flavors to the American table, and diners have followed. During that time, the American palate has become more sophisticated and demand for higher quality food is greater. With this surge of interest in authentic Mexican flavors, the taco was bound to take center stage, but now the taquerías aren't just taco carts on the side of the road; they are operating as high-end taco bistros. In just the past six months, I have seen four different taco bars open in my home town of Phoenix that showcase *Tacos al Pastor* and other "big name" tacos. That doesn't count the expanding number of taco trucks that each serve a few specialty tacos from different regions of Mexico. Many of these trucks display their advertising in Spanish only and are designed to serve the Mexican immigrant community. That doesn't stop me from eating at them, though. Taco Bell tacos may not be authentic, or even resemble a real Mexican taco, but they certainly helped usher in a taco Renaissance.

· · · · ·

As I write this book, I find myself looking back to the distant past, to that first tortilla that was folded up around a spread of beans. In a way, *Vegan Tacos* brings the taco experience full circle, but it's an ever-widening circle that incorporates the flavors and techniques of the world, lovingly integrated into Mexican cuisine. *Vegan Tacos* shines a spotlight on tacos through a vegan lens to create a truly beautiful food experience for vegans and everyone else. But enough of history and romantic pontification! Tacos are ultimately about tasty eats!

Tacos Are Vegan Food Ambassadors
· ·

Tacos make great vegan food ambassadors! They are not only tasty, they're fun. When I encourage people to eat vegan, I sometimes get the "I don't know if I can do that," response. Then I feed them one of my tacos. The first response is usually, "Oh my god, that's so good!" followed by, "O.K., I can do that." I am always moved when I see that reaction. It's a joy to make someone smile and incredibly rewarding to be able to help someone move along a kinder, healthier path.

CHAPTER

2

Essential Ingredients and Equipment

"All you need for

making authentic tacos."

My goal with this book is to help you bring the authentic flavors of Mexico directly into your kitchen. This means that sometimes I may use an ingredient with which you are not familiar. In fact, I hope that I do, and that the recipes tantalize you into seeking out those ingredients. It's part of being a food explorer! However, I am also a taco enabler, and that means I want you to be able to make outstanding tacos regardless of whether or not you can find some of the more exotic ingredients. As you'll see, I provide lots of substitution options whenever possible.

Fortunately for us vegans, all of our ingredients are plant-based, hence easier to import into the country as well as to cultivate, so they are much easier to find outside of Mexico than many meat-based ingredients. It should go without saying, but I am going to say it anyway: a market that caters to the Mexican population will very likely have these ingredients. I live in Phoenix, where these ingredients are fairly common. They should be available just about anywhere in the Southwest. If you live elsewhere, you may have to order them online if you don't have a Mexican-oriented market near you, but the rewards will be well worth it.

In addition to describing these ingredients, I also provide preparation and storage notes for them so you can get the most out of them. Try using these ingredients in other Mexican dishes, and I think you'll find your kitchen transforming under the intoxicating flavors of Mexico.

At the heart of this book, and much of Mexican cooking, are chiles and corn, in particular the corn dough called masa, which is used to make tortillas. The most important chiles are anchos, guajillos, and poblanos. For making fresh tortillas, masa is essential. If you acquire only these four ingredients, you will do just fine in making the recipes in this book.

Dried Chiles

Dried chiles are available in most markets, though you may need to go to a Hispanic foods section of a store to find them. If you go to a Mexican market, you will see walls filled with bags of dried chiles. Many stores also sell them from bulk bins. They will keep for at least a year in your pantry, so I suggest purchasing a big bag of them, assuming that you have the space. That way you'll have them on hand whenever you want them.

Ancho: The ancho is the dried version of the poblano. It has a slightly caramel, sweet, fruity taste and a low heat. It looks black with red touches, a wrinkled skin, is fairly flat, and wide towards the stem. You will often see bags of dried chiles labeled ancho/pasilla. Anchos and pasillas are not the same chiles, though they are closely related in flavor. You can tell the difference because an ancho is wide towards the stem (in fact, ancho means "wide" in Spanish) and the pasilla is narrow down the entire length of the chile. It is a bit of mislabeling, but don't stress if that's how your dried chiles are labeled.

güero (banana pepper)

anaheim

poblano

jalapeños

habanero

serrano

chiles de árbol

ancho

pequins

guajillo

chipotle

Substitutions: If you don't have anchos, you can use guajillos or mild New Mexico or California chile pods as a one-for-one substitution.

Guajillo: These long red chiles are the dried form of the mirasol chile. They are low in heat and have a clean, slightly caramel, fruity flavor. Chiles guajillos form the backbone of a vast array of Mexican chile sauces. They are often rehydrated and turned into sauces.

Substitutions: If you don't have guajillos, you can use mild New Mexico or California chile pods as a one-for-one substitution.

Chile de Árbol: This means "tree chile" in Spanish. These are thin chiles about two to three-inches long and are hot. These are often toasted and ground into powder, pureed into sauces, or fried to make chiles dorados, which are used as a topping for tacos.

Substitutions: If you don't have chiles de árbol, you can substitute 1/3 teaspoon of crushed red chiles on a one-to-one basis for powders and sauces, but not for frying them.

Pequin: These tiny, reddish-orange chiles are very hot and are often ground into powder, which is used to spike food with lots of heat. They are also added to salsas, but more importantly, they make a great base for a hot sauce.

Substitutions: If you don't have pequins, you can use chiles de árbol instead. One pequin will require two chiles de árbol. If you want the full heat for this substitution, add a very small pinch of cayenne pepper along with the two chiles de árbol.

Cascabel: Cascabel chiles are round, dark cherry-red chiles that rattle when you shake them. They have a mild, caramel flavor with an undertone of sweetness and not much heat. Not only do they make great sauces, they are excellent for presentation.

Substitutions: If you can't find cascabels, use one guajillo for every four cascabels.

Chipotle: The chipotle is the dried, smoked form of a jalapeño. Chipotles are typically made from jalapeños that have ripened and turned red. There are two primary types of chipotles; the chipotle morita and the chipotle meco. Chipotles morita are dark in color while chipotles meco are tobacco brown and have a less caramelized taste than the morita variety. Chipotles have a back-end heat, so they can be a little deceptive. We don't use just chipotles in this book, but we do use chipotles in adobo, which are chipotles that have been marinated in a spicy, vinegary tomato sauce.

Substitutions: If you don't have chipotles in adobo, you can use a fresh jalapeño on a one-to-one basis to get some of the chile flavor and heat into the dish, though it will be lacking in all the other flavors chipotles in adobo bring to a taco.

Pasado: These chiles are very uncommon, but you can easily make them yourself. They are fire roasted long green chiles, usually a Hatch or an Anaheim, that have been peeled and mostly deseeded and then left to dry. They have a smoky, full-bodied flavor and are typically medium in heat, depending, of course, on the fresh chile from which they are made. To make chiles pasados, roast your chiles, either over an open flame or by pan-roasting them, and then gently peel them. Slice one side open so you can fold open the chile and remove as many seeds as possible. You can tie the stems of three or four of them together with string and hang them from a hook and you should place them directly in the sun. I cover each batch of tied chiles with cheesecloth to keep insects off of them. I live in a hot, dry climate and it takes about a week for the chiles to properly dry. Your drying time will vary. Alternatively, you can dehydrate them at 115°F for 24 hours.

Substitutions: If you don't have these, use a pasilla or ancho as a one-to-one substitution and make sure to toast the pasillas or anchos before using them. The flavor won't be quite the same, but you'll still get a great dish.

How to Dry Chiles

I grow chiles in my backyard and let my chiles dry right on the vine. I live in Phoenix where the heat and lack of humidity make this very easy to do. When I am not drying chiles that I grow myself, I still dry store-bought chiles. I just lay them outside on the brick of my patio. Because the air is so dry, they don't even need to sit in the sun. My poblanos will turn into anchos in about five to seven days. If you live in a colder climate or a wet climate, you will need to tie your chiles together using string to bind the stems together. Hang these out in the sun and they will eventually dry, though it may take you up to two weeks. Hanging them allows more air to move around the exterior of the chiles and leech away the moisture in the chile. You can also use a dehydrator set at 115°F. Smaller chiles should dry within 12 hours while large chiles will require about 24 hours. If you are planning on rehydrating your chiles to turn them into a sauce, they can be slightly pliable. If you are planning on making them into chile powder, they need to be as dry as possible. Let them sit out an extra few days or dehydrate them for another 6 hours.

How to Toast and Fry Dried Chiles

There are two ways to toast dried chiles. The first is by simply placing them on a hot (medium heat), dry pan and pressing them down onto the pan with a spatula. I find an iron skillet or griddle works the best for this type of toasting. If you are toasting a small chile like a chile de árbol, this will only take about five to 10 seconds per side. If you are using a larger chile like an ancho, it will take about 10 to 15 seconds

Protect Your Skin and Eyes When Handling Chiles

• •

Hot chiles contain a compound called capsaicin, which can burn your skin and eyes. Capsaicin will linger on your hands after handling chiles, and if you are handling very spicy chiles, a lot of it will linger. I've built an immunity to it, but for handling very hot chiles, I recommend wearing gloves and eye protection. Even if you wear gloves, don't rub your eyes! You will have tears, but they will not be tears of joy. It's also very important to wash your hands thoroughly after handling chiles.

per side. Toasting chiles with this method will give the chile just a touch of smokiness, increase the chile flavor, and make the flavor more complex by activating many of the volatile elements in the chile. It also has the added effect of making the chiles more pliable and easier to puree.

You can also fry the chiles in oil, which creates a different flavor profile than dry toasting. Frying chiles doesn't just make them richer, it deepens the flavor, making the chile very robust. It quickly caramelizes the natural sugar in the chile and also activates the volatile elements of the chile to add complexity. Not being a fan of fried food, I had not done this until recently, but I wanted to make the type of chiles de árbol found in traditional taquerías. I am now hooked and consider this one of my indulgences. They are crispy, full of flavor, and create a low rumble of heat in the chile. To fry your chiles, bring about one-half inch of corn oil or neutral-flavored oil to a medium-high heat, about 375°F. Work in batches so all the chiles in the pan are resting in the hot oil. When I fry a large bag of chiles de árbol, I usually have to do four batches. You only need to fry the chiles for about 30 seconds. Quickly remove them from the oil and drain them on a paper towel to dry.

How to Rehydrate Dried Chiles for Sauces

You can use dried chiles in sauces a couple of ways. The most common is to rehydrate the chile, then puree it and use this as the base of a sauce. In this case, you want to keep as much flavor in the chile as possible and that requires a gentle rehydration method. Snip away the stems of the chile and shake out the seeds. Place the chiles in a bowl that can withstand hot water. Bring a kettle of water to a boil, and then take it off the heat for a few seconds. Pour this over the chiles. If you have a plate or other object you can place on the chiles to hold them down, so much the better, as this will keep them submerged and cause better hydration. Let the chiles sit in the hot water for about 20 minutes, and you will have nice, soft chiles.

If you want to flavor a liquid with chile flavor, but you don't want to use the chile itself, then you want to simmer the chile in your liquid (usually water). This will pull the flavor out of the chile and transfer it to the simmering liquid. I do this when I am making chile flavored coffee, or if I want a light chile flavor added to a dish. Simmer the chile for about 10 minutes, and then remove the chile. You will usually want to use three or four chiles for a pot of liquid to get an adequate chile flavor. Use a bit more liquid than you plan on adding to your final dish since some of it will evaporate. Pour the liquid through a strainer to collect any wayward seeds or stems.

How to Turn Dried Chiles into a Sauce and Chile Powder

The easy way to turn your dried chiles into a sauce is to rehydrate them using the gentle method and then simply puree them. Add as little liquid to the blender as possible so you can get the best puree on the chiles. The more liquid you add to the blender, the more tiny bits of chile you will find in your sauce. If I need to make a thin sauce, I puree the chiles first to get them as smooth as possible and then I add the extra liquid. If you want to get fancy and get your sauce perfect, press the chile puree through a fine-meshed strainer to make it silky smooth.

If you are using dried chiles to make a sauce, like with the Chile Pequin Roasted Garlic Sauce (page 228), grind the dried chiles and any accompanying dried spices together in your blender or grinder. This will make a fine powder which will easily become incorporated in whatever liquid you add. If you add the liquid and whole dried chiles at the same time, they won't turn into powder and you'll have large dried chile bits floating around in your sauce. Of course, you can also make chile powders this way, too. Whichever way you want to use them, don't forget to toast your chiles first.

Fresh Chiles

Most markets carry at least a small assortment of fresh chiles, including jalapeños, serranos, and poblanos. When purchasing fresh chiles, make sure the skin is tight and crisp, and you don't see any black spots around the stem—a sure sign the chile is on its way out. Fresh chiles can be stored on a countertop, in a hanging basket, etc., and will retain their freshness for several days. If you want to preserve them longer, store them in the refrigerator. They will typically last up to three weeks. However, make sure you do not store them in a sealed bag. Sealing them in a bag traps moisture inside the bag which will make the chiles go bad. Some chiles will still have a bit of field dirt around the stems. Just give the chiles a quick wash and pat them dry.

If you want to remove the stem and seeds from a chile, slice down the length of the chile starting from one side of the stem. This should slice off a section of the chile. Repeat this three more times, cutting a box pattern down the side of the chile. This will leave four sections of chile and the stem with the seeds still attached to it. This works for chiles as small as a serrano all the way up to large chiles like the poblano.

Poblano: The poblano is one of the staple chiles of the Mexican kitchen. They have a full-bodied flavor and when roasted, become soft and luxurious. It is a fairly large, dark green chile with a low heat. However, if you let a poblano ripen on the

---

Healthy Capsaicin
. . . .
Going through the process of gaining resilience against capsaicin may seem like an odd culinary adventure, but capsaicin has several health benefits. It increases metabolism, helps regulate blood sugar, reduces joint and muscle pain, and has been shown to kill prostate and lung cancer cells.

---

vine to the point where it becomes dark red, it will shoot up in heat. I still wouldn't call it hot, but it's a noticeable difference. Be aware that poblanos vary in heat quite a bit. Most of them are mild, but on occasion, you will get a rather piquant surprise. For our purposes, poblanos will most frequently be roasted, peeled, and deseeded and then cut into strips to top our tacos. You can also use them to make mole poblano, stuff them to make chiles en nogadas and chiles rellenos, or chop them up to add roasted green chiles to any dish. They are named after Puebla, their region of origin.

Substitutions: If you don't have a poblano available, any large green chile will do. The flavors won't be the same, but I would rather you have roasted green chiles than none at all.

Jalapeño: Jalapeños have a medium heat and a heavy flavor, and they are typically sold in their un-ripened, green state. I'm not sure what it is, but there is something about the way the heat of a jalapeño hits my tongue that affects me more than some hotter chiles. Jalapeños are often served minced or as whole roasted chiles. They are most commonly served pickled at taquerías.

Substitutions: You should be able to find these anywhere without needing to substitute anything for them. I prefer the ripe red ones, as I think they have a fuller chile flavor and, even though they have more heat, the extra sweetness balances them out. Jalapeños are also dried and smoked to make chipotles.

Serrano: The serrano is a thin chile that has a medium heat and a very bright flavor. These are typically minced and sprinkled on top of food to add a crisp spiciness.

Substitutions: If you don't have serranos available, you can substitute a jalapeño for them on a one-to-one basis.

Güero: These are also known as banana peppers because of their pale yellow skin and curved shape. They are usually hot, but not super-hot.

Substitutions: If you don't have these, substitute a jalapeño, or even better, half of a long green chile like an Anaheim.

Habanero: These are named after Havana, Cuba, where these chiles were first encountered by the Spanish. These are very hot. If you are not used to eating spicy food, do not eat something with a habanero. Start with a jalapeño, graduate up to a serrano, and then go for the habanero. These small yellow and orange chiles are bell shaped and have a very strong chile flavor, not just heat. They are excellent in salsa and for flavoring sauces. When flavoring sauces, the seeds and veins are typically removed to reduce the heat.

Substitutions: If you don't have access to habaneros, you can substitute two serranos for one habanero.

How to Turn Down the Heat

Contrary to popular belief, most of the heat of a chile resides in the capsaicin glands (or membranes), not in the seeds. Not that the seeds don't have any heat. They grow from the capsaicin glands, so they pick up about thirty percent of the heat of a chile. However, the glands contain most of the remainder of the heat in a chile. That means you can remove most of the heat by using a small knife to trim the glands away from the inside of the chile.

Capsaicin is a compound that binds to a protein found in the membranes of both pain and heat-sensing neurons. The bound capsaicin causes a flood of neurotransmitters to release, which is why it causes a sensation of both pain and heat. Prolonged exposure to capsaicin will deplete the neurotransmitters, which reduces the level of the sensations of heat and pain. What that means for you is that the more chiles you eat, the more heat you can handle. Plus, you can challenge people to chile-eating contests and come out ahead! Also, you can eat more spicy tacos. It's a win all around.

How to Roast Fresh Chiles

My favorite way to roast chiles is over an open flame. You can do this either on the grill by placing the chile(s) over the hottest part of the grill, or you can roast them directly over the flame from a gas stove. To do so, turn your burner to a medium-high to high heat. You can purchase racks that fit over a gas stove burner to hold chiles while they roast, or you can place the chile on the bars of a gas burner that are meant to support a pan above the flame. I prefer the mini grill rack because there is more support for the chile, which means it is less prone to break open. If that happens, you get chile juice dripping onto your burner and then you have extra clean-up. Not fun. This is also why I don't hold the chile over the burner with tongs. The tongs squeeze the chile and as the chile softens, it increases the chance that pressure from the tongs will cause the chile to rupture and spill chile juice.

Regardless of whether you use a wood fire/charcoal grill or you use your gas burner, you want to blister the skin of the chile to the point where most of it is black all the way around. Once it is black, place it in a bowl and cover it with a towel or place it in a bag and close the bag. Let it sit for about 20 minutes. This does two things: First, it lets the chile cool down so you can easily handle it. Second, it gently steams the chile, further softening it, but not scorching it further, since it is no longer over a hot flame. Once your chile has steamed, gently scrape away the blistered skin and pull out the stem. The seeds will often

chiles roasting on the grill

come along with it. I'll tell you a secret, though. I usually don't have the patience to wait for the chile to steam, and I just use them right away. Also, I like the charred taste of the skin and am prone to leave it on just as often as I take it off.

Coming a close second to fire-roasting is pan-roasting. This is a simple technique that I use when I don't want to take the time to light up my grill. Take a heavy pan, like an iron skillet, and turn it to just above a medium heat. Let the pan heat up, then place your chile(s) on the pan. Your next job is to wait. The pan will blister the chile in much the same way an open flame will do. You just won't get the smoke from the grill, but this is a lot less effort. Once the chile has mostly blackened on one side, flip it over and repeat. If I have a large chile, sometimes the sides don't get blackened. When that happens, I prop the chile against the side of the pan so the unblackened edges are face down in the pan and the chile is supported by the side of the pan. Then I flip it over and blacken the other edge. If you are roasting multiple chiles, you can usually prop them against themselves.

You can also use this trick with garlic, onions, tomatoes, and tomatillos. It's one of the quintessential techniques of the Mexican kitchen that we'll talk about later. Finally, this technique will most closely resemble what an open flame or coals will do when roasting chiles, more so than roasting chiles in an oven.

Masa and Hominy

Masa is the basic ingredient for making fresh, homemade tortillas, and hominy is the basis for making fresh masa. Without hominy and masa, we would never be able to eat so many delicious tacos!

Masa: Masa is the Spanish word for dough, not just corn dough. There is *masa de trigo* (wheat flour dough), *masa de maize* (corn dough), *masa harina* (a corn masa specifically for tortillas and tamales), and a host of other masas. However, when most people say "masa," they are referring to corn dough for tortillas. I find masa an interesting dough because without the nixtamalization process, in which a highly alkaline solution (usually "cal," a food-grade lime) must be applied to dried corn, because ground corn can't be made into dough. Before someone discovered nixtamalization, there were no tortillas. Now that was a sad world.

When you are shopping for masa, head to a market that focuses on Mexican food. They will almost always have freshly prepared masa. I prefer markets where they make their own masa without preservatives. Keep in mind, however, that masa that is preservative-free will only last a couple of days before it starts to dry out and only three or four days before it starts to ferment. Masa with preservatives will last about a week. After a day or two, the masa will begin to dry just a touch, but it's enough to affect the pliability of tortillas. You can wet the masa just a bit to get some of that pliability back, but you have to be careful that the masa doesn't become sodden or you will have very heavy tortillas.

If your masa is several days old, but hasn't started to ferment yet, you can make great tostadas from it since tostadas don't need to be pliable. Make sure to keep your masa refrigerated and the bag as tightly sealed as possible to keep it from drying out early. You should purchase masa especially made for tortillas *(masa para tortillas)*, and not "prepared masa." Prepared masa is usually for tamales and has lard added to it. If you do not want to purchase masa or don't have access to it, you can also make your own masa dough from masa harina, which is sold in bags like flour.

Hominy: Hominy is corn that has been nixtamalized. Most often, it is sold fully cooked in cans, but you can find fresh hominy and dried hominy at most Mexican markets. Cooked hominy is fairly large, much larger than a regular corn kernel, and provides substantiveness to a dish. It is used in pozole and some chilis. Partially cooked and soaked hominy is used to make fresh masa. You can freeze hominy, so if you purchase a lot of it and don't know what to do with it, put it in your freezer and pull out what you need to use when you need it. It will lose some texture, but you also won't waste a huge can or bag of it.

Herbs, Spices, and Sauces

I always try to buy my spices from bulk bins instead of jars. When you buy them in jars, you are always paying for the jar, and the spices are often twice as expensive as they are from bulk. When storing spices, keep them in a container as airtight as possible. This will prolong their life. This is also true for dried herbs. When purchasing fresh herbs, I keep them wrapped lightly in a paper towel and in a partially sealed plastic bag in my refrigerator. It keeps a little airflow coming into the bag and the towel takes care of excess moisture, which causes the herbs to turn early.

Epazote: Epazote has a strong, bright, acidic flavor that is unique to the plant. It is often cooked with beans and added to dishes to give them a strong herbal note. Dried epazote can be found at many spice stores, but fresh epazote cannot. I have to go to my local Mexican market to purchase it and it will go limp after a day unless you store it in a plastic bag with a slightly damp paper towel. It will last about a week this way. Even if it looks limp, it is still fine to use when you cook. If you still haven't used all of it after a week, set it outside to dry, and you'll have dried epazote that you can crumble into your food.

Substitutions: Because of epazote's unique flavor, there is no substitute for it. If you don't have it, omit it. If you are feeling particularly industrious, you can grow it. It does not require good or deep soil and is fairly hearty.

Mexican Oregano: Although it is called oregano, Mexican oregano is not related to any of the oreganos that come from the Mediterranean. It is actually part of the same family as verbena, while Mediterranean oregano is related to mint. It is almost always sold dried and can be found in most stores that have a Mexican spice section.

Substitutions: If you don't have Mexican oregano, you can substitute dried savory or marjoram for it, preferably savory.

Achiote Paste: Achiote paste is a spice mix of Mayan origin that is prominently used in Yucatecan dishes. It is made primarily with annatto seeds, allspice, cinnamon, cloves, pepper, cumin, Mexican oregano, salt, garlic, and sometimes chile powder all ground together. The primary taste is pungent and earthy due to the annatto seeds, but it is laced with fragrant, sweet spices. The paste, which is actually more like a crumbled spice mix than a paste, isn't just used for flavor. It's also used to give dishes a deep red color. Be aware that annatto causes stains, so don't wear light-colored clothes when working with achiote paste. I made that mistake once. Once. Achiote verde is a variation on the traditional achiote paste that omits the annatto and cinnamon and increases the amount of Mexican oregano. This is excellent for using with mushrooms and anything else where you want a more herbal note. The most common brand of achiote I have found is by El Mexicano (www.elmexicano.net). It comes in a small white box and I typically find it near the moles and other quintessential Mexican spices and sauces. To store it, keep it tightly sealed, and it will last for four to six months.

Substitutions: I rarely see achiote paste outside of Mexican markets, but don't worry if you don't have one. It is very easy to make and I have included a recipe for it on page 68. You can also purchase it from Amazon.

Adobo: Mexican-style adobo is a thick marinade made from chiles, cinnamon, cloves, Mexican oregano, garlic, onion, tomatoes, salt, and vinegar. The name is derived from "adobar," which is the Spanish verb for "marinate." It's used to marinate many different ingredients and dishes, but it is most commonly known to be the marinating sauce for chipotles in adobo. When used to marinate chipotles, it softens and infuses the dried chipotles with a sweet acidic taste and pulls the smoky chipotle flavor into the adobo itself. I use this not only to marinate my own chipotles, but to add to soups and sauces.

Substitutions: Don't worry. You won't need to make your own abodo unless you want to make your own chipotles in adobo. I typically get my adobo from a can of chipotles in adobo. You can just spoon the abodo instead of the chipotles from the can.

Mojo de Ajo: Mojo de ajo is a salted roasted garlic oil that is heavily spiked with sour oranges or lime juice. This is one of the treasures of the Mexican kitchen and is used extensively throughout this book. It is very easy to make (page 62). When you store it, make sure to keep it in a dark jar or out of direct sunlight, since that will degrade the oil. You can add other elements to your mojo de ajo, like chipotles, anchos, and oregano to make mojo variations. (See photo on page 71.)

Substitutions: This is one of the essential ingredients for the recipes in *Vegan Tacos,* but if you don't want to make it, you can substitute for a tablespoon of mojo de ajo by using a tablespoon of olive oil, 1 minced clove of garlic, and a squeeze of lime from a small lime wedge.

Vegetables

Tomatoes: I generally call for plum tomatoes because they are usually of a consistently good quality, with a meaty texture, and not watery like many other varieties. Plum tomatoes are sometimes labeled as Roma tomatoes.

Nopales: Nopales are the pads of the prickly pear cactus. When they are sliced or diced, they are called *nopalitos* and are often used in salads and tacos. They are a little tart and sour, and once they are cooked they have a slimy texture like okra. If you sauté the nopales over a high heat, or if you grill them, this texture is minimized. You can purchase fresh nopales at most Mexican markets, and I rarely see them anywhere else. Some of them have the spines still attached. You will need to pare the spines away. I strongly suggest holding the nopales with tongs while you do this so you don't get any of the thorns stuck in your fingers. Once you pare away the spines, remove the entire rim of the nopal, because it is generally too hard to cook. I usually cheat and get nopales that already have the spines removed. You may also find fresh-cut nopalitos, which can save you even more trouble. When you purchase fresh nopales, make sure they are firm. If they are bendable, they are on their way out. You can keep fresh nopales in your refrigerator for about a week before they start to turn. You may also find jarred nopalitos in many stores. For me, these are a bit too sour, and I don't like the texture much, but they make an acceptable substitute if you can't find fresh ones. Just rinse them thoroughly before cooking them to get rid of as much of the jarring liquid as possible.

Substitutions: If you can't get nopales, it would be better to skip those tacos that call for them.

Chayote Squash: The most common form of chayote is an oblong, firm squash, four to five inches long, with a light green skin and a pinched look where the stem grows. You may also encounter a dark green, fuzzy version, and if you travel to Central America, you'll discover a host of different types of chayote in the markets. It has a very mild flavor that I liken to a pear without the sweetness. The seed of the chayote is a light cream color, almost the exact color and texture as the rest of the interior. Although the seed is usually discarded (you can scoop it out with a spoon), it is completely edible. If you leave a chayote out for several days, it will start to sprout and you can plant it. My favorite way to eat chayote is to cut it in half, brush it with mojo de ajo and salt, and grill it.

Substitutions: If you don't have chayote available, you can substitute zucchini in the taco recipes and still get a great taco. Because zucchini is softer than chayote, reduce the cook times by about one-third.

Jackfruit: Jackfruit is a gargantuan tropical fruit with a fibrous interior that harbors very large seeds. Technically, these large seeds are a covering for the real seeds that lie within, but for practical purposes, these are considered the seeds. Ripe jackfruit is soft, yellow, and slightly sweet. Unripe jackfruit is dense, fibrous, and needs to be cooked thoroughly. To remove the seeds from fresh jackfruit, just scoop them out with a spoon. Don't discard them, as you can roast them and eat them as a snack. Jackfruit is often used as a meat alternative, and the fibrous nature of the fruit can make it feel like shredded meat. The unripe jackfruit is said to taste a little like meat, though I don't find this to be true. You will need a large, heavy knife to cut open a fresh jackfruit if you buy one whole. Keep in mind that whole ones are very, very large and heavy. Many places that sell jackfruit also sell jackfruit wedges, which are much easier to handle.

Substitutions: An alternative to fresh jackfruit is canned jackfruit, though I find the taste of the canned jackfruit to be a little tinny and slightly sour. When buying canned jackfruit for the recipes in this book, be sure to buy the kind packed in brine or water, not packed in syrup. If you want to use jackfruit, I strongly suggest trying to find it fresh. Where I live, that always means my local Asian markets. To store it once you cut it open, wrap it in plastic wrap and keep it in your refrigerator, where it will last up to two weeks. One final note: jackfruit does not easily absorb flavors, so you need to cook it a very long time to get it to absorb any spices or sauces in which you cook it and even then, it will still not be highly absorbent.

Plantains: Plantains are starchy cousins of the banana. When unripe and green, they are hard and have little sweetness, but as they mature, they develop more sugar content to the point where they become soft and sweet, perfect for dessert. In their unripe state, they are frequently sliced and fried like potato chips. As they age, the skin turns yellow and then starts to blacken. Once the skin is black and the plantain is soft, it is often sliced into large pieces and fried for dessert. Personally, if I am using them in a savory dish, I prefer them just turned yellow. They are just a bit sweet, but still very firm at this point. They can be used in place of a potato in any of the taco recipes. If the skin has a few black splotches on it, it can still be used this way, but if it is a quarter black or more, it is best used for dessert.

Substitutions: If you don't have plantains available, you have two options for substitutions. The first is to use the greenest banana you can find. It should be very firm and not that sweet. The other option is to use two Yukon Gold or other waxy potatoes. The potatoes will give you a similar texture to an unripe plantain while the green banana will give you a similar flavor.

Sour Oranges: Sour oranges, called *naranja agria* in Spanish, are used extensively in Mexican cuisine. They are also known as bitter oranges. A sour orange is a small orange with a light colored skin splotched with red. It has a high acid content and low sweetness. It is used as a marinade, as a component to sauces, and cooked with some foods to give them a distinctive flavor. They are a key component of mojo de ajo, one of the essential ingredients used in this book, and they are used to flavor our Michoacán-Style Carnitas (page 144). Sour oranges are not the easiest orange to find. If you're trying to locate them, look for sour oranges, bitter oranges, or Seville oranges for the best chance of finding them. I ended up having to plant a sour orange tree in my backyard to get them. Fortunately, there is a great substitute for them.

Substitutions: When you see sour orange juice called for in a recipe, do two parts orange juice, two parts lime juice, and one part grapefruit juice. Alternatively, you can do a mix of half orange juice and half lime juice. If you see a recipe that calls for sliced sour oranges, use sliced Valencia or Navel oranges and add a squeeze of lime juice to the dish.

Mushrooms

Mushrooms make a great addition to nearly any taco. They are my second favorite ingredient, just behind chiles, which means I use them a lot in this book. They each have their own texture to impart, with some being substantial enough to carry the taco on their own and others being more appropriate for an accent. They absorb flavors well and are particularly good on the grill.

When purchasing fresh mushrooms, make sure they look firm and tight. If they look dried out or have limp, discolored parts, pass on them. To store fresh mushrooms, I've found a couple of methods that work exceedingly well. If you purchase packaged mushrooms, store them in the original packaging. It is designed to keep those mushrooms fresh. Just cut open a small area of the plastic and remove what you need. These packages usually have containers that are slightly moisture absorbent and have holes in the plastic to allow a modest amount of airflow into the packaging. If you end up taking all the plastic off, you can place the mushrooms and the container into another plastic bag. Leave it partially open. If you purchase mushrooms in bulk, store them in a partially opened plastic bag with a small paper towel in the package. Use them within a week, and keep in mind that the thicker the mushroom, the longer it will last and the thinner the mushroom, the faster it will turn.

Finally, I generally get the best price on my mushrooms at Asian markets, which also tend to have the freshest mushrooms, too. This is important because good fresh mushrooms can be expensive. If you happen to live near a mushroom purveyor, don't tell me. I'll get jealous.

Substitutions: You can substitute dried mushrooms for fresh ones, although you may not always end up with the same volume or texture, so be aware of that. Also, the earthy flavor of the mushrooms will be intensified. To rehydrate dried mushrooms, bring a kettle of water to the point where it steams, place the mushrooms in a bowl, and pour the water over the mushrooms. They should be rehydrated within seven or eight minutes at most. Save the liquid because you can use it as stock to flavor other dishes.

Hen-of-the-Woods: You may also know this mushroom by its Japanese name, *maitake*. These are large, hearty mushrooms that have a thick base and "fans" emanating from the base. They do not need to be cooked very long and should be left in large pieces to get the best texture from them. When I grill them, I don't even chop them. I just brush them with oil, dress them with a little salt, and put them right on the grill. Only after that do I chop them. They have an earthy flavor that goes particularly well with chiles and smoke. Older hen-of-the-woods mushrooms get tough and are said to be inedible, but you can slice up an older hen-of-the-woods mushroom, simmer it in a sauce, and get a satisfying chew from it, so don't throw away those old hens!

Substitutions: If you don't have hen-of-the-woods, choose any other hearty mushroom that will give you the same volume. You will not get the exact same flavor, but you will still be able to make the recipe. I have to drive across town to find these, so I sometimes substitute either king trumpets or shiitakes.

King Trumpets: Also called king oyster and king oyster trumpet, these are hearty mushrooms with a very tall and very thick stalk culminating at a fluted cap. These mushrooms have a mild flavor and a good shelf-life. Because they are so hearty, they do not lose a lot of their volume when they are cooked and because they are so thick and long, you can place them directly on a grill rack. They also make a great scallop alternative. I like to slice them into thick medallions and soak them with a little kombu and a very tiny touch of sugar to add an oceanic flavor to a taco.

Substitutions: If you don't have these available, any sort of thick mushroom will do.

Oyster Mushrooms: While oyster mushrooms can grow very large "fans," most cultivated varieties have a thick, clumped base with one- to two-inch fans. They will reduce in size quite a bit as they cook, so if you want them to retain most of their volume, they must be cooked quickly. They have a mellow flavor and absorb surrounding flavors quickly. I use them two primary ways: when I want a flakey texture, an example of which you can see in Tempura Tacos (page 182), or if I want a slightly bacon-like flavor. To achieve that, I bring oil to a high heat, salt the mushrooms, and fry them until they are brown and crisp.

These mushrooms are prone to wilting, so take care to store them well using the instructions outlined above and do not buy small oyster mushrooms that are dried out.

Substitutions: If you do not have these fresh, you can use rehydrated oyster mushrooms in their place.

Shiitakes: Fresh shiitakes are among my favorite mushrooms. They have a robust, but not overpowering flavor and a medium-firm texture. They cook quickly, but if you cook them for more than a couple minutes, they will lose a lot of volume. Fortunately, that's all the time they need to cook. Look for firm caps with no wrinkles. If the stems are soft, you can use those, too. If they are woody, tear them off and use them to make shiitake stock. You can use dried shiitakes in place of fresh, but be aware that the flavor of a dry shiitake is greatly intensified. You will need to remove the stems from dry shiitakes. Whole Foods often has good quality fresh shiitakes, and they are on the large side. Trader Joe's and Asian markets usually sell smaller caps.

Substitutions: If you don't have shiitakes, rehydrate 1/4 cup of dried wild mushrooms in place of 4 small shiitakes.

Lobster Mushrooms: Called *orejas de puerco* in Spanish, these are not true mushrooms, but are actually a parasite that grows on mushrooms. They are thick and hearty with a very meaty texture. They have a ruddy, rust-colored outer layer and the interior is whitish. They lose very little volume when cooked and they have a hint of an oceanic flavor. Lobster mushrooms are very expensive, so I use them sparingly. They are not always easy to find fresh, but can be found dried, though you will have to go to a higher-end market to find them.

Substitutions: Flavor-wise, there isn't an appropriate substitute for them. When I want the heartiness of a lobster mushroom, I am more prone to use a chewy alternative such as seitan than a substitute mushroom.

Huitlacoche: Huitlacoche is a fungus that grows on corn. It is a delicacy of the Mexican kitchen that sometimes goes by the name "Mexican truffles," and by the more unfortunate name "corn smut." It also happens to be packed with good nutrition, especially amino acids. It has a gray, bulbous look, but an amazing pungent, earthy flavor. Be warned, though. The texture is slimy. This is a love-it or hate-it ingredient. Fresh huitlacoche is hard to find. Check with a corn grower or at a large farmers' markets in your area. More commonly, it is sold canned at Mexican markets.

Substitutions: There is no substitute for this ingredient.

Meat Alternatives

I used to spurn meat alternatives, proclaiming that real vegan chefs didn't need to rely on them. I was pretentious about it, especially when you consider that when I first went vegetarian, I relied heavily on meat alternatives. They were comforting and made the transition to vegetarian very easy. At some point, though, I decided they were limiting my creativity, and I didn't need these "crutches." There were always a few exceptions, like soy chorizo and Tofurky-brand sausages, but for the most part, I stayed away from them. However, I've come to feel that these ingredients are good in their own right, and I don't think of them as lowly substitutes any longer. Each one has its own unique traits and cooking requirements, and they serve to create different textures and flavors.

Throughout the book, when the recipes call for "seitan," you can feel free to substitute other plant proteins. Seitan is a wheat-based protein created over a thousand years ago by Buddhist monks in China. It is fashioned from the protein strands in wheat and has a strong *umami* quality. Many of the plant proteins on the market are similar in texture to seitan, though they may be made with different ingredients.

Substitutions: For a tender plant protein other than seitan, I prefer the brands at Trader Joe's. For a firm one, Beyond Meat® is a good brand, though I find it gets tough on the grill. You can also use the Gardein products. If you must avoid gluten altogether, check the labels carefully to make sure they don't contain wheat gluten. Otherwise, you can instead substitute pressed extra-firm tofu, tempeh, or reconstituted Soy Curls, depending on the recipe.

I provide two recipes for seitan that I find work very well in tacos. The first is for a thin, pounded seitan. The second is really the same recipe, but without the pounding. Many of the recipes offer a seitan and a whole-food option, such as mushrooms, eggplant, or jackfruit, so you can decide which version you want. In a few cases, seitan is such a superior choice that I only included the seitan version.

Chorizo: Mexican chorizo is a crumbly sausage flavored with chiles, vinegar, salt, garlic, Mexican oregano, and several sweet and aromatic spices. It pairs well with potatoes and tofu scrambles. There are several vegan chorizos on the market, and I even found a few versions at my local Mexican market.

Substitutions: If you can't find chorizo, or don't want to make your own, I provide a recipe for chorizo made from ground dried mushrooms, ground tempeh, or soy crumbles (see page 67).

Taco Gear

Your taco making will be faster, more precise, and more flavorful with the right equipment. Fortunately, none of it is expensive and some items are more necessary than others, although I love them all. Most of these items can be found online at www.mexgrocer.com. Aside from the gear I've listed below, I cannot stress enough how much a good quality, heavy, sharp knife and a good cutting board will go towards speeding up your time in the kitchen.

For Tortillas

Tortilla Press: Known as a *tortilladora* in Spanish, this is essential for making your own tortillas. The most common tortilla presses are made of aluminum and are very inexpensive. However, they don't have a lot of pressure, so you won't be able to get thin tortillas with them. They'll still be great tortillas, just not thin. These are typically six inches in diameter and will comfortably make four- to five-inch tortillas. They are excellent for making thick tortillas because it is difficult to press them too hard. This is the tortilla press with which I started out, and I used it for years before graduating to the cast iron press.

The next grade of tortilladoras are made of cast iron. These tortilla presses, which usually come in two sizes, are typically six inches or seven-and-a-half inches in diameter. Because these have a greater weight than the aluminum presses, you can make thin tortillas with them. I prefer the larger cast-iron press, because it gives me a little more room to play, so I can make different sizes of tortillas. These are a little more expensive, but you can still find them for around $30.

Finally, there are some very beautiful wooden presses available. These also have a good weight to them for making thin tortillas, but are just as much for show as they are for making great tortillas. A cast iron one will do the job just as well. If you want to purchase a wooden press, look for ones made from mesquite or some other hardwood and make sure the seller is reputable. Ones made from pine are often warped and older ones may be missing pieces.

Comal or Cast-Iron Griddle: Traditional comales are made from clay. They are perfect for cooking tortillas and they tend to cook very evenly. However, most people now use thin metal comales. These are really just flat oblong pans large enough to cook several tortillas at once. You can get these very inexpensively at most Mexican markets. However, I would recommend a cast-iron griddle or a cast-iron comal instead. They cook more evenly than the thin metal comales, duplicate what the traditional clay comal does, and you can get them for around $30 to $45. Make sure you get one that is at least 9-inches wide and at least 15-inches long so you can cook multiple tortillas at once. If you go with cast iron, make

Clockwise from top left: metal comal, tortilla press (tortilladora), tortillas in a taco warmer, a molcajete and tejolote, molino, (center) a clay comal, and a cazuela.

sure you wipe it dry after you use it and take a towel and wipe a thin coat of olive oil onto it to preserve it. If you do happen to get a clay comal (they are not easy to find outside of Mexico), you will need to slowly bring up the heat on it instead of cranking it up all the way. The clay needs time to slowly expand over the heat or it will crack, and then you'll have a cracked comal and tears to go with it. You don't want that. Start it at a low heat and bring the heat up a notch every two to three minutes. To clean, do not let it sit in soapy water or run through the dishwasher. Just wipe it down with warm water and soap and give it a rinse. Also, clay comales are usually concave, which means they work better over an open flame, for example, with a gas stove, than with electric coils. Finally, there are also round comales which are used to cook food other than tortillas, so know which one you are ordering.

Knives: I can't encourage you enough to purchase a good knife and cutting board. When I got my first good knife, it made the kitchen experience less stressful, way more fun, my chopping more even, and my prep time much quicker. I still use that knife as my primary knife and because I take good care of it, I'll be able to pass it down to my child. I use a Shun Classic 8" Chef's Knife and my cutting board is a laminate cutting board by Epicurean. My cazuelas are made by La Tienda and my cast-iron gear is made by Lodge Logic. None of these companies endorsed me. I just want you to have the best equipment you can get at affordable prices.

Wide Spatula: This may seem like a small thing to list in the equipment section, but a spatula that has at least a 4-inch-wide surface will make tortilla flipping very easy.

Tortilla Warmer: Most of these are made from very thick plastic to trap heat inside them, but you can find some nicer ones made from clay. These are handy because you can place your tortillas in them and keep the lid closed. They do the same thing that wrapping tortillas in cloth will do. They're not necessary, but handy to have around.

Molino aka Manual Plate Grinder: If you get serious about making your own masa, you will need one of these grinders to grind your nixtamal into masa. The smaller versions attach to your countertop and have a funnel with the grinder and a crank for you to manually turn the grinder. They typically cost around $60 to $70, though I have seen some as low as $35. There are also electric molinos and those with larger funnels and grinding mechanisms, which cost significantly more. Those that feature stone grinders will generally give you the best texture for your masa.

For Pan-Roasting

Cast Iron Skillet: A cast iron skillet is perfect for pan-roasting chiles, garlic, onions, tomatillos, and tomatoes.

For Tacos de Asador

A Wood-Fire/Charcoal Grill: This is the ideal grill for making *tacos de asador.* There's nothing like smoky wood and the char of an open flame to give tacos a primal taste. If you use a gas grill, make sure you have a wood chip smoker so you can get some of the flavors into your tacos that you would normally get from wood. I also think it's fun to host a taco party and have everyone hanging out and having a good time on my back porch while I grill taco fillings to order, so I am a bit prejudiced. Even if you don't have a large wood-fire or charcoal grill, you can still make lots of tacos on a hibachi and they are inexpensive.

Grill Pan: These are perforated pans designed to keep your food from falling onto the coals while still allowing smoke to penetrate the food and for flames to directly cook your grilled food. Most of these are coated aluminum and need oil to keep the food from sticking to the grill pan. I suggest stainless steel if you can find one simply because it is healthier.

Plancha: A plancha is simply a metal plate that you can put on your grill to cook various ingredients. It's handy when some of your ingredients are grilled and some are griddled or sautéed because you place the plancha on your grill and do your grilled foods and your foods *a la plancha* at the same time. Whenever I use one, I tell my wife that I am the Man of La Plancha. I usually get hit for that.

For Tacos de Guisados

Cazuela: A cazuela is a clay cooking pot that is perfect for stewing and simmering taco fillings. Because they are made of clay, they cook very evenly and they hold their heat for a long time. They also do not react with acids, so they don't leach flavors into the food. Like the clay comal, they should not be soaked in soapy water or run through the dishwasher. Just wash them clean under running water. They also need to have the heat slowly adjusted up to the appropriate level. They come in vastly different sizes from 6-inch cazuelas on up. I have a 15-inch cazuela, and it holds enough food for about thirty tacos! I also use my cazuela for lots of other dishes besides tacos, and this has been one of my best kitchen investments. I strongly suggest ordering these online from either La Tienda or The Spanish Table. Many cazuelas are glazed with lead, but these are not. If you go to Mexico and bring one home, chances are it was glazed with lead.

For Tacos de Canasta

Basket and Large Cloth: These are used to make tacos de canasta. I don't use a large basket because I don't make that many "basket tacos" at one time, but you do need a cloth big enough to rest in the basket and also fold over the top of the tacos while they steam.

A Taco for Everyone
· · · · · · · · · · · · ·

"There are well over a hundred classic, regional tacos, a host of non-Mexican regional tacos, and far, far more that are spontaneous creations. There is, I like to think, a taco out there for everyone."

For Guacamoles and Salsas

Molcajete and Tejolote: The molcajete and tejolote are a rough-carved stone mortar and pestle. Traditionally, these are made from basalt, though there are less expensive versions now being made from concrete. The rough texture of the molcajete makes it easy to turn chiles and garlic into pastes. This is also used to make crushed salsas and guacamoles. You will need to rinse your molcajete several times before use to remove any residual grit. Because of the porous nature of the stone, they are impossible to thoroughly clean, so they will season over time. In fact, older molcajetes are said to develop their own personalities in a way, each one unique. You can also keep food warm or even cook it directly in your molcajete simply by heating the molcajete in the oven. When you remove it, it will hold the oven's heat for a very long time. It's a cool presentation piece as well as one of my most used kitchen implements. You can also use a mortar and pestle in place of a molcajete, but it won't be as rough and won't make pastes quite as quickly. Molcajetes usually cost around $40.

Tortillas, Masa, Nixtamal, and You

*"All about tortillas
and how to make your own."*

The tortilla is a simple food. At its heart, it's just corn, water, and sometimes salt. It has a rustic elegance that keeps drawing me back to the griddle to make more. When I am craving something late at night, I am prone to head out to my patio kitchen, heat up my griddle, cook some fresh tortillas, spread some beans on top, and dip them in salsa. Not only do they have a sensual taste, they make me feel invigorated and comfortable at the same time.

The tortilla is also loaded with nutrition. While low in the essential amino acids lysine and iso-leucine, they have a notable amount of the other essential amino acids. They have a moderate amount of fiber, are 10 percent protein, and are low in fat. A taco-sized tortilla is about 60 calories. When coupled with beans, their amino acid profile becomes very high in all 20 essential amino acids. This combination of ingredients is filling, nutritious, and easy to make. No wonder corn and beans were a staple of the Central American diet.

The tortilla makes the perfect vessel for holding a variety of ingredients. It's thick enough to hold even saucy ingredients without falling apart; it's pliable enough to wrap around those ingredients; and it's perfectly sized to fit in the hand. Plus, they taste great on their own, melding with the flavors of the filling to create bites of soulful perfection. I should note that the standard tortilla size for a taco is 5 1/2 inches in diameter. I'll tell you a secret, though. I usually make mine a little bigger. I like to eat!

Tortillas are the foundation of any taco. They carry the flavors of the rest of the taco. They are the vessel that holds the filling, condiments, and sauces, and they are the first thing you taste when you bite into a taco. While the tortilla is often the component of a taco that gets ignored in most kitchens, for me, it is the most important element. Without a good foundation, the entire taco is diminished. This is why I spend the extra few minutes to make my own tortillas when I make tacos, instead of resorting to packaged tortillas. The fresh tortilla is a star!

With that said, however, while I next show you how to make your own excellent corn tortillas from scratch, you can make most of the tacos in this book with storebought corn tortillas.

Making Corn Tortillas from Masa Dough

Let me be candid with you. I purchase my masa more frequently than I make it from scratch. I am fortunate enough to have Mexican markets within a few minutes away, so I just head to the store and get my masa for the next couple of days. Not everyone has that luxury, though. Then again, there are times when I just want the feel of the dough mashing together in my hands, or I want a flavored masa, which requires making it myself. Those are the moments where it's time to bust out the masa harina flour, get some warm water, and make my own masa dough.

Make Your Own Masa Dough from Corn Flour

Masa harina is a type of ground corn flour specially made for tortillas and tamales. It's made from corn that has gone through the nixtamalization process, which makes the corn more nutritionally sound and enables it to be turned into a dough. Do not try substituting corn meal, polenta, grits, or corn flour. Masa harina is your one-and-only friend here. At most stores in the U.S., masa harina will be found near the wheat flour or in the Mexican section of the grocery market. Bob's Red Mill (see Resources) makes a great organic masa harina, though Maseca is the most well-known brand. To make your own masa dough for tortillas from masa harina flour, all you need are:

2 cups masa harina flour
1 1/2 cups warm water

1. Place the masa in a mixing bowl.

2. Heat the water until it is just starting to steam. Pour the water into the bowl. Mix it together with the masa harina so it's evenly distributed. Hang out and wait for 5 minutes.

3. The masa harina needs time to absorb the warm water before it can be turned into dough. Once that time has passed, work the wet masa with your hands until you have a thick, smooth dough.

Make Your Own Masa Dough from Nixtamal

If you are lucky enough to have a Mexican market near you, chances are you can find fresh nixtamal (usually located next to the bags of prepared masa) and can make masa from nixtamal instead of dry masa harina flour. Tortillas made from nixtamal freshly ground into masa have a depth of flavor unmatched by even tortillas made from premade masa. Nixtamal is corn that has been treated with a highly alkaline solution to remove the outer chaff, break down cellular walls, and make the niacin in the corn more available. Some markets will cook nixtamal to the point where it is fully cooked and ready to grind into masa right away, basically making hominy. They've done all the work for you. You just need to grind. To make masa from fresh nixtamal, you will need a bowl and a molino (grinder).

4 cups nixtamal

Add the nixtamal to your grinder in two batches and grind it to a smooth dough. Yes, that is all there is to it. Masa made from fresh nixtamal will start to spoil within a couple days, so just make what you need and no more. If you end up with leftover nixtamal, you can freeze it.

Storing Masa

To store your masa dough, place it in a plastic bag and press out as much of the air as possible. Keep this in the refrigerator. When you want to use it again, let it warm up to room temperature before working it into tortillas. If you try to press the dough cold, the tortilla will be prone to falling apart. Ideally, you should use your masa within a day of making it. It will generally last four or five days before it starts to turn (it sours, though not in a good way). It loses some of its plasticity after a day, making the tortillas less light and fluffy. Despite that, I hate wasting food, and I still use my masa after a day of being in the refrigerator. If the tortillas don't puff up quite as much, so be it.

Working with Older Masa

If your masa is more than a day old, chances are it has dried out just slightly. It's enough to make the tortilla a little dry, but there is a work-around for it. Before grabbing a chunk of masa, dip your hands in a bowl of water. The residual amount of water on your hands will get into the masa as you form it into a ball, and this will be just enough water to bring your masa back to the right consistency.

Masa Dough from Masa Harina vs. Nixtamal
• •

Important: These recipes assume that you are making masa from masa harina. If you are making them from fully cooked nixtamal or your own homemade nixtamal, *omit the water in the recipes.* Add in about 1/4 cup of masa harina to the mix to make sure it binds with the additional liquid introduced by the flavoring ingredients.

Want to Make Your Own Nixtamal?

What's that, you say? You want to make your own nixtamal, too? I approve of your dedication.

Important: When using homemade nixtamal, it will take practice to get the tortillas to come out right, so don't get frustrated if they don't turn out perfectly the first time. Nixtamal is finicky and nuanced. Each batch comes out slightly different, so practice until you get a feel for it. It will also help to rub oil onto your metal comal or griddle to give you some leeway with your technique. Alternatively, use a clay comal, which is by nature more forgiving on homemade nixtamal.

To make your own nixtamal, you will need a bowl, colander, non-reactive enamel or stainless steel pot, a molina (grinder), and patience.

   4 cups organic dried corn
   2 1/2 tablespoons cal (see below)
   2 quarts water

Rinse the corn in a colander for about two minutes, moving the corn around with your hand as you rinse to remove the chaff. In a non-reactive pot, combine the cal and water and bring to a boil. Add the corn and boil for 5 minutes, turn the heat off, and let the corn rest in the water for at least 8 hours. Pour the corn into a colander and rinse for 3 to 4 minutes, while rubbing the corn with your hands. Get your hands in there and vigorously rub the whole batch of corn. This will remove the pericarp of the corn, which is not very digestible. Don't worry about getting this perfect. The pericarp comes off easily and rinsing it will wash away the bits. Now it's time to grind your corn.

Nixtamal being ground into masa with a molino.

Transfer the corn to a molina (grinder) and grind away. Once you have the loose dough in the bowl beneath the grinder, knead the dough until thick and smooth. Then, congratulate yourself because you just made fresh masa from nixtamal you made yourself, and that makes you the king or queen of the vegan Mexican kitchen! Now that you have your masa, it's time to make tortillas.

You Can't Make Nixtamal Without Cal

"Cal," short for calcium hydroxide (aka pickling lime or slaked lime), is essential for making nixtamal. It is highly alkaline and dissolves the hemicelluloses of the corn, breaking down the cellular walls and separating the hull from the kernels. Without that breakdown, the corn would not stick together and form into dough. The process also makes the niacin in the corn bioavailable. I usually purchase cal at my local Mexican market, although it is available in specialty stores and online. It's fairly cheap, so I get enough for several batches of nixtamal. The leftover liquid from nixtamalization, called *nejayote*, requires careful disposal since it is environmentally disruptive.

Making Fresh Corn Tortillas

I accidentally spoiled myself. When I made my first fresh tortilla, I thought I was making something that would be a step up from using the storebought versions I had used my whole life. What I didn't expect was that the fresh tortillas would be so much better than the storebought variety that the fresh ones would make the other ones taste like corn-flavored cardboard forevermore.

Fresh tortillas feel like home to me. They are warm and inviting, and nothing beats holding a tortilla that just came off the griddle, filling it with beans or grilled veggies and salsa and chomping down. They also have a complex flavor, slightly sweet, a little bit toasty brown, and full-bodied. They absorb flavors from the ingredients placed on them, but they don't become soggy messes. Instead, the tortilla incorporates those other flavors, which accent the rich flavor of the tortilla instead of dominating it. It's such a simple food, but it has such a beautiful impact. Have I convinced you yet to make your own tortillas?

To make your own corn tortillas, you will need:

- a tortilla press
- plastic sheets or wax paper
- a hot griddle (whenever I call for a griddle, you can use a comal or iron skillet.)
- a wide spatula
- a towel
- practice

Before you start working the masa, heat your griddle to just above medium heat. That way, as soon as you are done pressing your masa into proto-tortillas, you can put them on the griddle right away. Have a towel near the griddle so you can place your tortillas on it as they come off the griddle. Take a chunk

The balls of masa that get pressed into tortillas are called testales. (My wife thinks an angry Mexican housewife named them.)

of masa and roll it in your hands into a ball about 1 1/4 to 1 1/2 inches in diameter. If you need to take or remove masa from the ball, do so and then just re-roll it. Next, flatten this out into a disk between your hands. Lay a sheet of plastic wrap or wax paper on the bottom part of your tortilla press. (See step-by-step photos opposite.) Place the disk on the plastic slightly off center towards the hinges. This is important, because when you close the press, the masa will be pressed away from the hinges. By placing it slightly toward the hinges, the tortilla will be centered when you are done pressing it. Lay another sheet of plastic or wax paper on top of the masa, making sure the plastic covers the entirety of the tortilla press, bottom plate, as well. Press the tortilla press closed, flattening the masa. The harder you press, the thinner your tortilla will be. If you want very thin tortillas, you will need a heavy press, like a cast-iron press. Peel away the top sheet from the flattened masa. Gently lift the plastic and flattened masa off the press and flip

From Masa to Tortillas

Step 1: Place the testale and cover with plastic.

Step 2: Press the testale and peel off the plastic.

Step 3: Place on the griddle or comal to cook.

Step 4: Flip to cook on both sides.

Step 5: A finished tortilla ready to enjoy.

the flattened masa into your palm. The raw flattened masa should now be in your palm, and what was the bottom sheet of plastic should still be stuck to it, though now on top of the masa. Peel this away. One word of caution before you peel away your masa and put it on the griddle. If you are using masa made from stone ground nixtamal, lime, and water and nothing else (you can tell because bits of rough nixtamal will still be in the masa), you need to be careful when handling it or it will break. The flavor of this pure masa is amazing, but the texture requires extra practice and skill to get it to work properly.

Gently lay the tortilla onto your hot griddle. After about 30 seconds, you will see the edges turn color. Tease your spatula gently underneath the tortilla and flip it over. Let it toast for about a minute or so, then flip it over again. This time, you will toast the tortilla for another 30 seconds. If you've done everything right, your tortilla will puff up. If you like your tortillas a little extra toasty, you can go 2 to 2 1/2 minutes per side to get a little char on them, though they will lose some pliability. Transfer the tortilla to the towel and then fold the towel over it to keep it warm and pliable while you make the other tortillas.

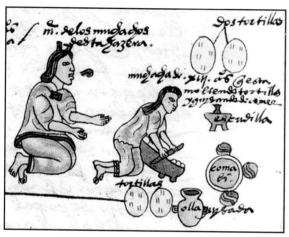

An Aztec woman teaches her daughter how to make corn tortillas. You can see the Aztec glyph used for corn tortillas. (from the Mendoza Codex)

If you have a griddle big enough to cook several tortillas at once, press out all the masa into ready-to-be-made tortillas that you plan to cook before laying any of them onto the griddle. That means that if your griddle can handle cooking four tortillas at once, press out all four before placing them on the griddle. Now work quickly. Lay them on the griddle. By the time you lay the last one down, it's probably time to flip the first one. This is why you should get the masa pressed out before you start cooking it because the tortillas cook fast. It takes a little practice, but you will find a rhythm and the tortillas will come together effortlessly. It took me about four times before I could get my tortillas to puff and another four or five times before I developed a good tortilla-making rhythm.

Once you have made your tortillas, keep them wrapped in a moist, warm towel to keep them pliable. You can easily keep them this way for an hour. After that, you should warm them using one of the techniques below.

Warming Corn Tortillas (storebought and fresh)

Fresh tortillas should ideally be eaten right away, and if not right away, kept in a moist warm towel. If you have time constraints that dictate you have to serve them later, all is not lost.

There are three ways to warm your tortillas. First, bring a dry pan to a medium heat. Place the tortilla in the pan for about 5 seconds per side. You can also do this on a grill. Your tortilla will be pliable at this point and can be filled with delicious taco fillings. Another option is to gently steam the tortillas. They only need to steam for about 30 seconds. Once you steam them, place them in a tortilla warmer and they will stay pliable for about 10 minutes. If you have a thin, dry tortilla, you will only need to steam them for about 15 seconds. If you steam longer than that, you risk them falling apart. The final technique is to lay your tortilla over a hot pot of taco fillings that are moist, but not wet. The residual heat and moisture will warm and steam the tortilla. You'll need about 30 seconds on one side with this method. My preferred method is warming them in a dry pan, while I prefer steaming them if I am serving lots of tortillas.

Taco Heresy: How to Make Wheat-Flour Tortillas

The corn tortilla has always been, and still is, the preferred tortilla for tacos. Taco aficionados will spurn any taco served with wheat and declare it unpalatable. However, the northern states of Mexico and the American Southwest still show a heavy influence from the agricultural legacy of the Spanish, who preferred wheat. That's why quite a few tacos served in the north of Mexico are served with wheat flour tortillas. Baja, Mexico also features a number of wheat flour tacos, though these are more due to a California influence.

Unlike corn tortillas, you will have a hard time simply pressing wheat dough into a tortilla shape. Instead, you will need a rolling pin and a little extra flour on your work surface. You will also need a bowl, a hot griddle or comal, a wide spatula, and a towel.

- 1 1/4 cups all-purpose flour (I actually prefer whole wheat, but your tortilla will be a bit chewier)
- 1/2 teaspoon salt
- 1/4 teaspoon baking powder
- 2 tablespoons vegan shortening (you can omit this, but the tortillas will be a little tougher)
- 1 cup hot water

In the bowl, combine the flour, salt, and baking powder. Incorporate the shortening and use your hands to work it into the flour. The dough should be crumbly at this point. Slowly pour hot water into the flour, 1/4-cup at a time. After each addition, work the water into the dough with your hands. After doing this, you should have a smooth dough. Knead until the dough no longer sticks to the kneading surface and your hands. Divide the dough into 10 balls. Cover them with a damp cloth and let them rest for 45 minutes. This is very important. This is the time where a gluten web in the dough forms. If you don't do this, the dough becomes very hard to roll into disks.

Preheat the griddle to a medium heat. Very lightly flour your working surface. Flatten a dough ball into a small disk. Roll this out into a tortilla about

Tortilla-Making by Hand
• • • • • • • • • • • • •

Tortillas used to be formed by hand, patting them back and forth between the palms to create a perfectly round, flattened masa cake. The tortilla press, which requires little practice, has made this a vanishing art.

5 to 6 inches in diameter. To do this, roll the rolling pin forward, then back, and then adjust the angle slightly and repeat. Continue this until you have your flattened tortilla disk. You need to be firm, but not forceful, with the rolling pin. If you push too hard, it smashes the dough too much and makes the tortilla

tough. If you push too lightly, it will take forever to roll into a disk. It takes a bit of practice, so don't worry if they don't look perfect the first time.

Place the tortilla on the hot griddle. These cook very quickly. After 30 to 45 seconds, flip the tortilla. After a minute, flip it again. If you got everything right, the tortilla should puff up. As soon as it puffs after the second flip, take it off the heat. Cover it in a towel while you make the rest of the tortillas, repeating this process.

Hard Shell Tacos

The hard taco shell was made famous by Glen Bell, the founder of Taco Bell. After eating at the local Mexican restaurant in California, he figured out how to bring the *taco dorado* to market. Though far removed from authentic Mexican tacos, here's how to make your own. You will need:

- A deep fryer or heavy large pot like a Dutch oven
- Enough corn oil for 5 inches in your pot
- Tortillas
- A taco form (or a can, see variation)
- Plate and paper towel
- Courage

"(Tortillas are) extremely wholesome, and when fresh (are) made of a good taste, (but) become disagreeable when stale." – Father Francesco Saverio Clavigero, from his 1710 treatise *The History of Mexico*

1. There are frying baskets specially designed for frying tacos, which is the taco form. This is by far the best implement to use because it is sized properly and has a handle designed to keep your hands away from the hot oil.

2. Pour 5 inches of oil into your pot and bring the oil to 350°F. Make sure your tortillas are pliable enough to lay over the taco form and not break. If they are not, warm your tortillas using the dry pan method described earlier. Do not use the steaming method since this introduces water back into the tortillas. Lower the tortillas into the pot and fry them for 2 minutes. Remove them and gently slide them off onto a paper towel or rack. Repeat until you are tired of frying tortillas, or you run out of them!

Variation: You can also use an empty can as a taco form, but you will need something to safely dip it into and out of the pot, like tongs. Just grab the edges of the can with the tongs to lower and lift the can. Make sure you remove both ends of the can using a can opener that makes a clean cut, not a jagged one.

Baked No-Fat Hard Taco Shells

If you're really in the mood for a crunchy taco, but don't want to use any oil, baking will do. To make baked, no-fat hard taco shells, you will need:

- An oven
- Oven mitts
- Storebought packaged tortillas
- A plate
- A really strong desire to eat baked, hard tortillas

1. Place the oven rack you want to use away from the heating element. Usually that's on the bottom of the oven, so you'll be placing your rack towards the top. Turn the oven to 375°F. Make the tortillas pliable. My preferred method is to warm them in a dry pan, but you can get away with a quick 10-second steam. If you steam them longer, the excess moisture will make them stick to your oven rack.

2. Drape a tortilla over two of the bars of the oven rack. This will ensure the tortilla is concave enough to hold lots of filling. Repeat this until you are out of tortillas or oven room. Bake them for 10 minutes. Bake these to the point where the tortillas are hard enough to crack. Otherwise, they will come out tough and leathery.

Warming Crispy Tortillas (handmade and storebought)

Be aware that even though packaged corn tortilla shells have been sealed, they have been sitting on the store shelf long enough for the oil in the tortilla to start to turn. That's also true with your homemade ones, if you are keeping them around for weeks on end, but chances are, if you have been making fresh crispy corn tortillas, that's not the case. Regardless, as soon as the shells come to room temperature, they need to be rewarmed to get the most flavor out of them.

To do so, bring your oven to 325°F and place the rack away from the heating element. Gently drape the hard tortilla over one of the bars on the rack and warm it for 2 to 3 minutes. It's just enough time to bring out the toasted corn flavor.

Flavored Tortillas

Now that you've got some experience making fresh masa and tortillas, you can start to make different flavors of tortilla. The key to making flavored tortillas is keeping the amount of liquid used the same as if you were making unflavored tortillas. Also, keep in mind that masa harina and nixtamal are flavor dampeners. They will significantly cut the flavor of whatever you mix into them, so if you want to create your own flavored tortillas, go heavy on the flavoring ingredients.

Remember, with all of these recipes, you need to let the masa rest for five minutes once you add the wet mixture to the dry masa harina, so the masa harina can fully absorb the liquid. After that, you can work it into dough.

Chile-Flavored Tortillas

Taco Pairing: These tortillas go well with just about any taco, but they are particularly delicious when used with Tacos de Asador. There are three ways you can make these, each with its own flavors and intensity.

Method 1: Chile Powder

You can add plenty of chile flavor to a tortilla by mixing chile powder directly into your masa harina. For every 1 cup of masa harina, use 2 tablespoons of your favorite chile powder. I like using my own ground mild chiles such as ancho or guajillo. If I want to spike the chile powder with some heat, I first grind ground chiles de árbol or ground chipotles and mix it into the chile powder before measuring my 2 tablespoons. A little of this heat goes a long way in the tortilla, so use sparingly. If you don't want to grind your own chiles, you can instead use your favorite storebought chile powder. Because you're adding the chile powder to the masa harina dry mix, you will need to add an additional teaspoon of water when you make the dough. Use the same proportions of masa harina to water you would use if making your own masa. Just remember to add 1 teaspoon of water for every 2 tablespoons of chile powder.

Method 2: Chile Water

When making chile water, you want as much chile flavor to seep into the water as possible. This happens when you simmer it. This will give you a light, very smooth chile flavor accent, rather than a dominant flavor. All you have to do is rehydrate the chiles in water and then use the rehydrating water in place of the water in the regular recipe. For every 2 cups of water you need for making masa, you will want to add 3 to 4 large dried chiles, like the ancho or guajillo.

If you want some heat, you can add a dried chipotle, habanero, or a couple of chiles de árbol to the pot. Use more water than you want to end up with at the end because it will evaporate as you simmer the chiles. For example, if you want to end up with 2 cups of water, add 3 cups of water to the pot and 3 to 4 chiles. You'll have a little excess liquid left over, but it's better to have too much than too little. Simmer the chiles over a medium heat for about 10 minutes. Place a bowl underneath a strainer and pour the water through the strainer. This ensures that you catch all the seeds and chile bits so they don't get in the masa. Use this chile water for making your masa dough.

Method 3: Chile Puree

> 4 ancho or guajillo chiles, stems removed, seeds taken out
> Water for rehydration and mixing
> 3/4 teaspoon salt
> 1 1/2 cups masa harina

1. When making chile puree, you want as much flavor to seep into the pulp of the chiles as possible, which is why a gentler rehydration method is used. This method will give you a much more intense chile flavor since you are using the pulp of the chile to flavor the tortilla. It's a little more finicky, because there isn't a straight one-to-one water substitution.

2. Toast the chiles over a medium heat in a dry pan for about 30 seconds per side. Cover the chiles with enough very hot water and rehydrate them by letting them sit for 20 minutes. Drain, reserving the liquid. In a blender or food processor combine the chiles with 1 cup of the water used to rehydrate the chiles. Puree until smooth. Press the chile puree through a sieve and collect it in a bowl below the sieve.

3. In a separate bowl, combine the salt with the masa harina and mix well. Combine the masa harina mixture with the chile puree and mix well. Because the size of the chiles vary, you will need to practice to find the optimum consistency of the masa.

Guajillo Garlic Tortillas

Taco Pairing: These tortillas go well with just about any taco, but they shine with Tacos de Asador and Tacos de Canasta. Suggested tacos are My Family Tacos (page 85), "Cecina" Tacos (page 86), Charred Chayote Tacos (page 77), Mushroom Tacos (page 117), and any of the Tacos de Canasta (page 157).

This works best with Method 3. Start by removing the stem and seeds and toasting the chiles. Rehydrate them using Method 3. When you puree the chiles, add 8 cloves of raw garlic to the blender. Combine 1 teaspoon of salt with 1 1/2 cups of masa harina and then add the chile garlic mix to the masa. Work the masa with your hands until you have a tight, smooth dough. Try making this with pan-roasted garlic, too!

Black Bean Tortillas

Taco Pairing: These tortillas have a heavier flavor and texture, but they go well with most tacos. I would not use them with tacos that utilize beans already or with tacos that have a lighter, brighter flavor profile. Suggested tacos are Bricklayer Tacos (page 132), Tacos with Sweet Potato and Chard (page 97), Michoacán-Style Carnitas (page 144), and Tacos with Hominy and Seitan Tacos in Roasted Garlic Cascabel Sauce (page 106).

I love black beans. I love the texture, the flavor, and the health benefits they possess. They happen to make a great flavoring agent for tortillas, too. You will need 1/2 cup of cooked black beans. If you are using canned, save the liquid. If you are using beans you cooked yourself, save the liquid. Save the liquid! You will need a total of 1 1/2 cups of liquid. Use your bean liquid and make up the rest of the amount with water. Puree the beans, liquid, and 3/4 teaspoon of salt into a bean sauce. If you want to get really fancy, you can use a smoked salt. Mix this with the masa harina. Let it sit and form your dough.

Beer Tortillas

Taco Pairings for Dark Beer: Tacos with Pintos Borrachos (page 100), Tacos with Yucatecan Barbecue (page 92), Mole Tacos (page 103)

Taco Pairings for Light Beer: Tacos Veracruz (page 98), Basket Tacos with Potatoes and Chorizo (page 160), Cactus Tacos (page 124), and Tacos with Purple Potatoes and Roasted Poblanos (page 123)

Beer-flavored tortillas are very easy to make. As a rule of thumb, dark beers go best with tacos that have a deep, heavy flavor, while light beers work best with tacos that have fillings that taste light, themselves. Use your beer of choice with this recipe, but my favorite beer for these tortillas is a nut-brown ale (not really a beer, but close enough for this recipe) by Samuel Smith. It's vegan, and it tastes great. I also like Black Toad and Minerva Imperial Stout. For light beers, I usually go with India Pale Ale. If you want to go truly Mexican, both Tecate and Negra Modelo are both vegan. Use the beer as a one-to-one replacement for water in any of the tortilla recipes.

Salted Lime Tortillas

Taco Pairing: These have a very bright, acidic flavor that pops as soon as you bite into the tortilla and they should be paired with tacos that have fresh, crisp flavors. Some of my favorite pairings include Tempura Tacos (page 182), Charred Chayote Tacos (page 77), and Hominy and Seitan Tacos in Roasted Garlic Cascabel Sauce (page 106).

When you fill these tortillas, fill them on the unsalted side. That way when you bite into the taco, the first taste you get is the salted side of the tortilla. Cooking them this way may seem tedious, but if you mix the large salt crystals directly into the masa, they can cause the tortilla to break when you press out the dough. Plus, you don't get quite the same effect when you bite into the taco.

    1/2 cup fresh lime juice
    1 cup warm water
    1 1/4 teaspoons coarse salt

1. The 1/2 cup of fresh lime juice replaces 1/2 cup of water used in the original recipe, meaning you will need 1/2 cup of fresh lime juice combined with 1 cup of warm water to make a total of 1 1/2 cups of liquid. You will also need 1 1/4 teaspoons of coarse salt. Don't use regular fine ground salt. Use one that has a large crystal, such as kosher salt. Combine the lime water with the masa and make your dough.

2. Before you start making your tortillas, sprinkle 1/4 teaspoon of salt onto a clean countertop and spread it out. You are going to be pressing about four tortillas into each sprinkle of salt. Make sure the salt is near your griddle.

3. Cook the tortillas, but not all the way. Cook the first side for 30 seconds, then the second side for 1 minute. Take the tortilla off the griddle and flip it so the first, less-cooked side is face down towards your countertop. Gently press it into the salt.

4. Return the tortilla to the hot griddle, salted side down, and cook it for another 30 seconds to 1 minute (or more if you want them toasty).

"For me, making masa and tortillas is a meditative process. I get lost in the feel of the dough and the rustic aroma of toasting corn."

Tacos Aquí

Tacos de Asador	Los Otros Tacos
Tacos de Guisado	Tacos de Canasta
Tacos de Comal	Tacos Mañaneros
	Tacos Dulce
Tacos Dorados	Fusion Tacos

¡Tacos Aqui!

I still remember the moment when I held my first homemade corn tortilla

fresh off the griddle. I could feel the soft warmth permeating the tortilla and smell the comforting aroma of toasted corn. I could tell how the salsa was going to drip down and meld with the tortilla, how it was going to gently fold around the pintos borrachos and fresh avocado I had prepared. It was a promise of taco ecstasy, and that promise was about to be fulfilled. My wife still laughs about it. Evidently, my eyes glazed over for a moment as I lost myself in the possibilities of just what I could do with these new, magical tortillas. Of course, whenever I make fresh tortillas now, she always asks for some, too. We are both thralls to beautiful food.

• • • • •

With their succulent texture and bold flavors, it's no wonder that tacos are the greatest food invention of Mexico and that country's greatest culinary ambassador to the world. They can be as simple as a tortilla filled with beans and salsa or as complex as the multi-component tacos de canasta. They are eminently versatile. Anything that can be folded into a tortilla can be turned into a taco and probably has been. It's another reason why tacos are so popular. There are well over a hundred classic, regional tacos, a host of non-Mexican regional tacos, and far, far more that are spontaneous creations. There is, I like to think, a taco out there for everyone.

You can see that diversity reflected in this book just by looking at the different styles of tacos that are included. It is by no means an exhaustive list. How can it be? The story of tacos is the story of Mexico—vast and a little chaotic, but with certain themes that tie it all together. For tacos, that theme is tortillas folded around bold ingredients, a handheld meal, and a lively soulfulness. If you're enjoying all those elements, you have a true taco.

How the Recipe Chapters Are Organized

I divided the tacos in this book mainly by cooking technique, though a few sets are based around when the tacos are eaten rather than how they are prepared. I also listed the recipe names in Spanish. Even if you don't speak Spanish, you'll know what they are and who knows, maybe learn a little Español along the way!

First, we have some foundation recipes and ingredients that will help you build better tacos. They are core ingredients, like spice mixes, *mojo de ajo*, homemade chorizo, achiote paste, and other similar goods. Most of these can be purchased at a store, but a few should be made at home. Following that are the taco chapters, which break down as follows:

Tacos de Asador: Perhaps my favorite style of taco, these are tacos where the filling has been cooked over an open flame on a wood-fire grill. Smoky, a little charred, and perfect for long summer days and cool winter nights.

Tacos de Guisado: Guisados are stews and *tacos de guisado* represent the most diverse category of tacos. These are tacos with stewed fillings, typically served in clay cazuelas dishes at taquerías. They are easy to make and can be made in large batches. In a way, guisados represent the best of Mexican homestyle cooking.

Tacos de Comal: These are tacos where the filling is cooked on a comal, which is really just a flat pan. Think of them as tacos with sautéed fillings.

Tacos Dorados: These tacos are rolled closed and fried to a crispy golden color, hence the name. You've probably seen them under the names *taquitos* or *flautas.*

Tacos de Canasta: *Tacos de canasta* are the classic breakfast taco in Mexico. Carried around in baskets, from which their name derives, these tacos are suffused with a sauce and steamed by closing up the basket. In a way, they are the "slider" version of tacos.

Los Otros Tacos: This just means "the other tacos." These are the tacos that don't quite fit into one of our categories. Some of them, like the *tacos de mixiote* and *carnitas* are categories unto themselves, but since we only have one version of each, it made more sense to place them here.

Tacos Mañaneros: Additional breakfast tacos. Some of these are more of a Texas invention, while the tacos with *chiles rellenos* and *quelites* (edible field greens) are less common authentic Mexican breakfast tacos.

Tacos Dulces: Dessert tacos. These run the gamut of complexity from ultra-simple to fancy gourmet, but all are uniformly sweet and tasty. Unlike other tacos, which are usually served in twos or threes, these are meant to be a decadent finish to a meal, so one of them should do.

Fusion Tacos: These tacos are an obvious melding of one culture's food with Mexican cuisine. Although many of these are tacos found outside of Mexico, some are tacos in which Mexican cooks have incorporated other culture's dishes, like with the Tacos Tempura. Fusion tacos are the result of creative taqueros (taco makers) around the world.

When I wander into the markets of Mexico, or even to the small markets of U.S. border towns, it is not the colorful sights or the passionate buzz of the crowd that captivates me, it's the heady aroma of corn and chiles and smoke. When I smell that combination, I know a taco is waiting for me somewhere around the corner. I fell in love with that experience, and I ended up bringing it into both my professional kitchen, home kitchen, and this book. Tacos inspire me. I hope they inspire you, too.

CHAPTER

4

Foundation Ingredients and Techniques

*"Good ingredients
build good tacos."*

Making great tacos means having the right ingredients and mastering a few essential techniques. First and foremost is learning how to make good tortillas, which we covered in Chapter 3. Aside from that, your taco-making experience will be greatly improved by making a few of the core ingredients at home since they are not commonly available at stores that don't focus on Mexican ingredients. The two most important ingredients to learn how to make yourself are *Mojo de Ajo* (a citrus garlic sauce) and Flattened Seitan. (I've also included three bonus recipes at the end of this chapter for vegan chorizo, red achiote paste, and chiles in adobo.) In addition to these basic ingredients, this chapter includes instructions for pan-roasting, an essential (and easy) technique to get the most flavor out of vegetables, as well as instructions for fire-roasting, another terrific flavor-enhancing technique.

Mojo de Ajo

Mojo de Ajo is a roasted garlic citrus-infused oil that will make any taco pop with flavor. It's complex, rich, and zesty, and it's one of the essential ingredients of the Mexican kitchen. This is the secret weapon of Mexican cuisine. Mojo de ajo means "garlic sauce," and it's a salted, roasted garlic oil, heavily flavored with sour orange juice or other citrus when sour orange isn't available. You can also make variations by flavoring it with different chiles. The only reason I don't call for mojo de ajo for every taco in this book is to avoid turning it into the mojo de ajo cookbook! I always keep this kitchen treasure around in my pantry, and if I start to run out, I make more. (See photo page 71.)

Note: For this recipe I recommend using storebought peeled garlic—it saves a lot of time.

MAKES 4 CUPS

> 4 cups olive oil (I prefer a fruity olive oil)
> 2 cups peeled whole garlic cloves (see Note)
> 2 teaspoons coarse sea salt
> 1 cup sour orange juice or lime juice

Preheat the oven to 325°F. Combine the oil, garlic, and salt in a large baking dish and roast for 45 minutes. Carefully remove the baking dish from the oven, stir the juice into the oil, and return it to the oven for another 20 minutes. Remove the baking dish from the oven again and mash the garlic using a masher or the back of a large heavy spoon. Allow the mixture to cool and pour it into a jar with a mouth wide enough that you can reach in and spoon out some of the garlic bits. This will keep for up to three months at room temperature or up to six months if stored in a cool, dark place.

Flattened Seitan

Flattened seitan is seitan that has been pressed thin. Not only does it create a more ideal texture than you would get with thick seitan strips, but it has a larger surface area which can be exposed directly to the flames of a grill. That translates into more smoke and char flavors. This recipe has several different stages and takes a while to make, but it is well worth the time. I usually make triple or quadruple batches and freeze them. As long as the seitan is sealed, it will last for months and won't pick up wayward freezer odors. These flavors accentuate *umami* and caramel flavors, and the texture stands up well on the grill. You can add other flavoring agents to the mix, such as achiote paste, to create different flavor profiles, or you can add them to the simmering broth to create a gentler flavor. Play around with the recipe so you can find your favorite flavor combos. I designed this recipe to be soy-free for those who want to avoid soy.

MAKES 3 (6 X 6-INCH) SHEETS

5 large cremini mushrooms, quartered

1 teaspoon olive oil

1 cup cooked black beans, rinsed

2 tablespoons vegan shortening (Spectrum organic is my preferred choice)

1/2 teaspoon brown sugar

1/2 teaspoon apple cider vinegar

1/2 teaspoon bitters, optional (available at liquor stores)

1 1/2 cups warm water

2 cups vital wheat gluten powder

2 teaspoons onion powder

1 teaspoon salt

1/4 teaspoon Indian black salt, optional

Enough water to cover the seitan sheets plus 1/2-inch

1/4 cup Basting Ingredient(s), optional (see below)

1. Preheat the oven to 450°F. Combine the mushrooms and oil in a baking dish and toss to coat. Roast the mushrooms for 20 minutes. They should shrink quite a bit and develop quite a bit of browning and some charring.

2. Transfer the mushrooms to a blender or food processor. Add the black beans, shortening, sugar, vinegar, bitters, if using, and warm water (be sure the water be warm so the sugar can melt). Puree until smooth, then set aside.

3. In a large bowl, combine the wheat gluten, onion powder, salt, and black salt, if using. Stir in the black bean mixture and knead for about 10 minutes. Cover and let it rest for 1 hour. Uncover it and knead it for another 10 minutes.

4. Pull the seitan apart into three separate chunks. Place a large piece of parchment paper on your counter top and tear off another sheet of equal dimensions. They should both be about 10 inches long.

Flatten your first chunk of seitan into a flat rectangle as best you can. Place this on the parchment on your counter. Place the other parchment on top of it. Gently pound the seitan flat until it is about 1/4 inch thick. Don't worry if it's not exact.

5. Preheat the oven to 325°F. Place a sheet of parchment at the bottom of a baking dish or oil it very well (this will keep the bottom sheet from sticking to the baking dish). Layer the seitan sheets onto it. Pour enough warm water in the dish to rise about 1/2-inch above the seitan sheets. Add basting ingredients, if you are using them. Give the water a gentle stir to evenly distribute the flavoring ingredients. Bake for 1 1/2 hours. Every 30 minutes or so, rotate the seitan sheets in the pan. The liquid should mostly be gone by the time you are done. Let the seitan rest for at least 30 minutes before using it. You now have flattened seitan sheets that can be added to the grill or cut up and sautéed or even just eaten as is.

BASTING INGREDIENTS: Add any of the following basting ingredients, in whole or in combination:

> 1/4 cup achiote paste
> 1/4 cup chipotles in adobo
> 1 teaspoon liquid smoke
> 1/4 cup tamari or Braggs Amino or Better than Beef Bouillon, and
>   sprigs of oregano

Most often, I add a combination of achiote paste and Better than Beef Bouillon.

VARIATION: SEITAN STRIP OPTION: You can use the exact same ingredient list as above to make seitan strips instead of flattened seitan. To make them, press the seitan into a sheet about 3/4 inch thick and cut strips out of it about 3 inches long and 3/4 inch wide. Cook the strips in the same way as for flattened seitan.

Alternative Flavors
· · · · · · · · · · · ·

You can add other flavors to the seitan by incorporating spice mixes like achiote paste, chile powders, garlic powder, and other powdered spices and herbs directly into the dry mix. My general rule is to add 2 tablespoons of the dried ingredients and an additional tablespoon of water. If you're using something particularly spicy, like chipotle powder or ground *chiles de árbol,* use less, unless you want a very fiery food, and don't add the water. You can also add wet mixes, like adobo or chile purees or even liquid smoke to the seitan. If you do that, I usually add about 1/4 cup, unless it's super powerful like liquid smoke (just 1 teaspoon will do), and you won't need any additional liquid. When adding these flavorings, just keep in mind that if you are eye-balling it, you should always add extra, as the beans and wheat gluten will try their hardest to mute whatever flavors you add to them.

How to Pan-Roast

In addition to making your own tortillas, mojo de ajo, and a few other ingredients, your taco-making experience will also be greatly improved by learning how to pan-roast. I discovered this technique a few years ago, and I am completely hooked.

Pan-roasting is a simple technique used to roast chiles, tomatoes, tomatillos, garlic, and onions in a dry pan and letting the item sit until it blackens. This is particularly important because it mimics what fire-roasting does without having to light your grill or turn on your oven. In fact, it creates a better roasted flavor than your oven will make. I only use my oven for these ingredients if I don't want to light my grill, and I need to thoroughly soften an ingredient.

Pan-roasting is an important technique for getting maximum flavor from ingredients without a lot of effort. This is a great technique for making rajas, roasted garlic, and getting tomatoes and tomatillos ready to be turned into salsa.

Not only does pan-roasting soften and char a vegetable in a manner similar to roasting over an open flame, but it also gives the ingredient some of the flavor profile it would obtain if it were being sautéed. That means if you pan-roast garlic, it's going to taste like a cross between oven-roasted garlic, fire-roasted garlic, and sautéed garlic. Note that you can do this in any sort of pan, but it really works best on a cast-iron skillet, griddle, or on a clay comal. If you don't have one of those, use the heaviest pan you have. It will heat more evenly and keep your ingredients from burning before they soften.

Note: In most cases, turn the heat to medium and let the pan heat up before adding ingredients.

Pan-Roasting Vegetables

Roasted chiles, garlic, onions, tomatoes, and tomatillos are some of the most common, delicious ingredients of the Mexican kitchen. The sugars in the veggies caramelize, giving them a richer, more complex flavor, they pick up some charring, and they prime the veggies to be turned into outstanding sauces and additions to just about any taco. Here's how to pan-roast the primary ingredients used in the recipes in this book. Be sure to set your heat on medium for all the vegetables, unless otherwise specified.

Garlic. Ideally, you should keep the paper intact around the individual cloves of garlic. This will protect the garlic from burning. However, if I am pan-roasting fifty or sixty cloves of garlic, I cheat and use the garlic that is already peeled. You need to pay a little more attention to make sure it doesn't burn, but you also don't have to peel all those cloves. Once your pan is hot, scatter the garlic cloves onto the pan. After about five minutes, start checking the garlic. The paper should have a generous black splotch on it where it was touching the pan (or a dark brown one if you are using peeled garlic). Once the cloves gain that black splotch, flip them over. Some of the cloves will roast faster than others, so you'll just need to check them every minute or so after that first five minutes. Once the other side of the garlic has done the same, remove it from the pan. After you have removed all the garlic and it has cooled, peel it.

Chiles. You can pan-roast any chile. When I am pan-roasting chiles, I generally turn the heat up just a notch above medium. The flatter the chile, the better as more of the surface area of the chile will be exposed to the direct heat of the pan. Just lay the chile flat on the hot pan and wait until the bottom fully blisters and most of the skin blackens. Flip the chile and repeat. If the chile is thick enough, you can also lay it on its side to make sure the thin sides also blister. Another trick you can do is to prop the chile against the side of the pan or against other chiles. You usually won't have to worry about this with chiles like serranos and small jalapeños because they are so small, but fatter chiles like a poblano should be propped up so that as much of the chile is blistered as possible. Once you are done, just rub off the black- ened part of the skin with your fingers and you have a nicely roasted chile. This will take around 10 to 12 minutes for the larger chiles and about half that for the smaller chiles.

Onions. Peel your onion and cut it into disks about 3/4-inch thick. Don't separate the rings, but keep the disks of the onion intact. Like the chile, heat the pan to just above medium and lay the onions on the pan. The bottom of the onion will blacken. When about half the bottom of the onion has blackened, flip it over and repeat. Once both sides have blackened about half way, you are done. This will take about 10 to 12 minutes.

Fire-Roasted Chiles
• • • • • • • • • • • • •

When it's chile season at home in Phoenix, I can smell the Hatch chiles and poblanos being fire-roasted in great rotating cages at the markets as soon as I step out of my car. Even if I don't need them, I usually buy a bag of fire-roasted chiles. The aroma is too hard for me to resist.

Tomatoes and Tomatillos. For these, the pan should be at a medium heat. Remove any stems from the tomatoes and the paper from the tomatillos, but leave the tomatoes and tomatillos whole. Place them on the pan and leave them alone. The bottom will blacken and some of it will probably end up stuck on the pan, but that's ok. After the bottom blackens, flip it over and repeat this process. Once that is done, do the same to the sides of the tomatoes and tomatillos. This will take about 15 minutes to finish.

How to Fire-Roast

Like pan-roasting, fire-roasting is another simple way to roast your vegetables. The flavor you can get from roasting vegetables over an open flame is absolutely incredible. It will add char, smoke, and a rich flavor to your ingredients, particularly chiles.

On the Grill: You can use a wood fire or gas grill to fire-roast your ingredients, though I prefer a wood fire grill since the ingredients will also pick up some smoke flavor. Chiles, onions, tomatoes, and tomatillos should go directly over an open flame, while garlic, because of its small size and high volatility, should be set aside from the hottest part of the grill. Chiles and onions should be placed directly on the grill rack while tomatoes, tomatillos, and especially garlic do best when they are fire-roasted in a perforated grill pan. For preparation, just leave your chiles whole, remove the stems from tomatoes, and remove the paper from tomatillos. Prepare your onion the same as for pan-roasting. Garlic should be peeled and lightly tossed in oil to keep it from burning. Your ingredients should turn out the same way they would as if you were pan-roasting them. The chiles should blacken while tomatoes and tomatillos will have black- ened skin that will most likely peel away and stick to the grill pan. Onion should be about half blackened and garlic should be lightly browned.

On a Gas Stovetop: You can also fire-roast ingredients on a gas stovetop, though I would avoid doing garlic, tomatoes, and tomatillos. Stick with chiles and onions. Turn your gas burner up to high and gently grip your chiles or sliced onion with a set of metal tongs. Make sure they are metal so they don't melt and be sure to grasp the tongs with some sort of protective gear. You don't want the heat of the flame to transfer up the tongs to your hand! As above, blacken the chile and rotate it until all sides are blackened and half-blacken the sliced onion. This works adequately, but expect your gas burner to get dirty as sometimes the chiles will erupt and spill chile juice over the burner. That's why I prefer to use a special grill rack designed to fit over a gas burner. I can just lay my chiles or onion slices on it and not touch them. Since I don't have to put pressure on the chiles by grasping them with tongs, it reduces the amount of times chiles erupt and keeps me from having to clean up a bunch of spilled, dried out chile juice! Plus, you can use these special racks to toast bread and grill other veggies and still get nice grill lines on them.

pan-roasting vegetables

Three Bonus Recipes

I'm ending this chapter with three "bonus" recipes for ingredients that most people buy ready-made: Vegan Chorizo, Red Achiote Paste, and Chipotles in Adobo. I provide these recipes both for those who really want to delve into artisan taco making and also for those of you who want to discover just what goes in to some of these quintessential Mexican ingredients.

Vegan Chorizo

Mexican chorizo is a ground sausage flavored with vinegar, chiles, and aromatic spices. It has a flavor reminiscent of both adobo and achiote paste. This is not surprising, considering that both those ingredients pretty much contain all the spices and flavors found in chorizo. What differentiates Mexican chorizo from Spanish chorizo is the crumbly texture of the sausage (Spanish chorizo is a hard sausage) and the extravagant use of chiles. There are plenty of variations on the spice mix for chorizo, so feel free to play around with this recipe. The core elements are chiles, a little vinegar, and some sort of aromatic spice, whether that be cinnamon, allspice, cloves, or something similar. Everything else is negotiable.

If you don't want to make your own, you may purchase ready-made vegan chorizo. The commercial vegan chorizo that I've seen is all made from TVP, an acronym for textured vegetable protein. It's a hard, dry crumble that absorbs liquids and spices quite readily. If you go to a Mexican market, you will often see bags of it, where it will be called carne de soya (this translates to soy meat). I prefer to make mine from ground seitan and if I want a nutty flavor, I make it from ground tempeh. For a more exotic version, I pound dried wild mushrooms in my molcajete. They will all give you very different flavors and are all excellent. Traditional Mexican chorizo is stored in casings to form links. However, my version skips that part and simply stores it in a sealed container.

MAKES 4 CUPS

The Spice Mix/Marinade
3 chiles guajillo, toasted and rehydrated or 3 tablespoons chile powder

2 chiles ancho, toasted and rehydrated or 2 tablespoons ancho powder

1/2 tablespoon ground cumin

1 teaspoon ground coriander

1/2 teaspoon ground cinnamon

1/2 teaspoon ground allspice

1/2 teaspoon dry marjoram or Mexican oregano

1/3 teaspoon ground black pepper

1/4 teaspoon ground cloves

2 tablespoons salt

1/4 teaspoon Indian black salt, optional

4 cloves garlic

1/4 cup olive oil or vegan shortening (omit for a low-fat version)

1/4 cup apple cider vinegar

1 teaspoon grated piloncillo or brown sugar

Chipotle powder or chile de árbol powder, optional (to bring some heat)

The Sausage

4 cups of one of the following: ground tempeh, ground seitan, TVP, or ground dried mushrooms

In a dry skillet, toast the chiles for about 30 seconds on each side. Place them in a bowl and bring a kettle of water to a boil. Pour the hot water over the chiles and let them sit until they are soft. Remove the stems from the rehydrated chiles, but keep the seeds. Puree the chiles along with the other ingredients for The Spice Mix/Marinade. Note: if you are using piloncillo instead of brown sugar, you will need to grate it with a microplane grater or other such implement. Also, the vegan shortening in the recipe will give the chorizo a fatty flavor while the olive oil will give it a smooth, cleaner flavor. Use whichever you prefer.

While the chiles are rehydrating, grind the sausage component. Each one works a little differently. See below for how to make them and how to use The Spice Mix/Marinade with them.

Prepare your choice of options for the sausage:

Tempeh: Place the tempeh in a food processor and pulse it several times until it grinds into very small crumbles. Do not fill the food processor all the way to the top or you will probably end up with ground tempeh on top and tempeh paste on the bottom. Not good. Fill it half way and work in batches if you need to do so. The tempeh needs to sit in the marinade for a day to fully develop.

Seitan: If you are using storebought seitan, treat it just like you would the tempeh. If you are making your own, you can cheat with this recipe by making the marinade and using it as the wet mix for your home made seitan. This is a one to one replacement, so if you have one cup of marinade, you can replace one cup of liquid in your seitan. Just keep the proportions the same. Save 1/4 cup of the spice mix/marinade to the side so you can toss your finished ground seitan in it to keep it moist. If you do it this way, your chorizo will be ready as soon as you grind your seitan.

TVP: Once you puree the spice mix/marinade, add 2 cups of warm water to it and then toss the TVP in it. It only takes about an hour for the TVP to fully absorb the chorizo flavoring and then it will be ready to use.

Ground Wild Mushrooms: This version of the recipe is expensive, but also incredibly good. You will need a molcajete or a mortar to make this. I find that when I try to grind the dried mushrooms in a food processor, they turn to powder too quickly. I typically use a mix of dried mushrooms, but you can use dried cremini, dried shiitake, or whatever else you have available. The dried cremini and shiitake will make the recipe much less expensive. If you are using dried shiitakes, you will need about 8 cups of whole dried shiitakes. If you are using other mushrooms, you will need about 12 cups (that's why I use dried shiitakes most often). Working with just a few at a time, gently bash them in your molcajete or mortar to pieces about 1/4-inch thick. None of these will be uniform, so don't worry about getting it perfect or else insanity will become part of this recipe. Transfer them to a large bowl and repeat until you have about 4 cups of crushed dried mushrooms. Add 1 cup of warm water to the marinade and pour it over the mushrooms. Toss immediately. After about 1 hour, the mushroom chorizo will be ready.

MAKE IT SIMPLE: Make a quick version of this by using the dried chile powders, the salt, and 1/4 cup of storebought achiote paste combined with either 1/4 cup apple cider vinegar or fresh orange juice.

Red Achiote Paste
Recado Rojo

Achiote (named for the shrub from which it is made) is a specialty of the Yucatán that is used all across Mexico. You can easily purchase it at a Mexican market or make it at home. Achiote is used for color as well as for its earthy flavor, giving dishes an intense red hue. Achiote paste isn't really a paste, despite the name. It's actually a crumbly block of spices that can be used as a rub, like we use with Tacos al Pastor, or cooked directly into a dish the way with do with the Achiote Rice recipe on page 240. Achiote paste is primarily comprised of (you guessed it) achiote, but it includes a few other aromatic spices as well. It's one of those spice mixes that was unique to each household, though most people now purchase it at a market. The recipe that follows is my own household's version of achiote paste. If you prefer to purchase yours either at a market or online instead of making it, you can find it under the names achiote paste, Recado Rojo or Recado Colorado.

MAKES 1/2 CUP

The Dry Mix (Makes about 7 tablespoons)
1 tablespoon cumin seeds or 2 teaspoons ground cumin
1 tablespoon coriander seeds or 1 1/2 teaspoons ground coriander
10 to 12 black peppercorns or 1 1/2 teaspoons finely ground black pepper
10 allspice berries or 1 1/2 teaspoons ground allspice
2 cloves or a pinch of ground cloves
1/4 teaspoon ground nutmeg
2 teaspoons salt
1/4 cup ground achiote (annatto)

The Wet Mix (Makes about 6 tablespoons)
10 cloves garlic, pan roasted
1/4 cup sour orange juice (or use 2 tablespoons orange juice and 2 table-
    spoons lime juice)

In a dry skillet over medium heat, toast the cumin and coriander seeds for one minute, then remove them from the skillet. Toast the peppercorns, allspice, and cloves for about one minute. Grind the spices in a spice grinder or with a molcajete or mortar and pestle. Combine the cumin, pepper, allspice, cloves, nutmeg, salt, and achiote in a jar with a tight-fitting lid. Stored in a cool dry place (no need to refrigerate), it will keep for up to three months.

When you are ready to use it, pan roast the garlic, then puree the sour orange juice and garlic, and combine this with the dry spice mix to make the achiote paste. If you are not using all of the spice mix, you will need to proportion the wet mix accordingly. In other words, if you use half the dry mix, you only need to make a half portion of the wet mix.

Important: Adding the wet mix to the dry mix will barely increase its volume, so if you see a recipe that calls for two tablespoons of achiote paste, for example, you only need to combine a couple of tablespoons of dry mix combined with just under a couple of tablespoons of wet mix. It may seem counterintuitive, but the dry mix will absorb the wet and condense.

MAKE IT SIMPLE: Don't worry about toasting and grinding the spices or pan roasting the garlic. Just combine already ground spices together in the proportions listed above. Even easier, just buy red achiote paste at the store.

Green Achiote
. . . .

There is a green version of achiote paste called Achiote Verde or Recado Verde, which is made primarily from Mexican oregano as opposed to achiote/annatto. It has a very herbaceous flavor that goes well when cooked with rice or used to flavor lighter dishes.

Chipotles in Adobo
Chipotles en Adobo

Chipotles in adobo are widely availble, even in supermarkets, but you can make it at home for a fun food experiment. Adobo is the Spanish word for marinade, and this particular one is the marinade used for those oh-so-delicious chipotles in adobo. Most of the time, I purchase my chipotles in adobo at the store, but sometimes I get in the mood to make my own fresh homemade adobo and add chipotles that I make from the jalapeños growing my garden. It has such a deep, rich, and clean flavor. What I think is particularly fun about this recipe is that you are using chiles to marinate other chiles! You can also use the adobo as a wet mix to flavor your own homemade seitan or even as a marinade for other chiles or veggies. **Note:** A piloncillo is unrefined brown sugar compacted into a "little pylon." It's sold in rack bags at Mexican stores or online for about $3.00.

MAKES JUST OVER 4 CUPS

40 to 50 dried chipotles morita (or 20 to 25 chipotles meco), rehydrated
2 plum tomatoes
2 ancho chiles
1/2 cup olive oil
1/2 large white onion, roughly chopped (about 1/2 cup)
1 large carrot, roughly chopped
5 cloves garlic
1/2 teaspoon dried marjoram
2 teaspoons coarse salt
2 ounces piloncillo (a medium-size cone) or 5 tablespoons brown sugar
1 bay leaf
3/4 cup apple cider vinegar

1. To rehydrate the chipotles, bring a kettle of water to a boil. Place the chipotles in a heatproof bowl. Add enough of the hot water to cover them. Set them aside to soften.

2. Add the tomatoes and anchos to a saucepan with enough water to cover them. Bring the water just to a boil. Reduce the heat to a simmer and simmer the tomatoes and anchos until they are soft, about 10 minutes.

3. Heat the oil in a large skillet over medium-high heat. Add the chopped onion and carrot and sauté until the onion just starts to brown, about 3 minutes. Add the garlic and sauté for 2 more minutes, then remove the pan from the heat.

4. Transfer the simmered tomatoes and anchos and about 1/2 cup of the cooking liquid to a blender. Transfer the onion, carrot, and garlic to the same blender. Add the marjoram and salt and puree until smooth. If you are using brown sugar instead of piloncillo, add this to the blender as well to puree.

5. Add the puree to the pan in which you cooked the onion and carrot and add the piloncillo and bay leaf to the sauce. Simmer over medium heat for about 10 minutes, allowing time for the puree to caramelize a little and the piloncillo to dissolve. Stir in the vinegar. Drain the chipotles and add them to the sauce. Simmer for 5 minutes longer.

6. The chipotles in adobo are now ready to use in recipes. Once they are cool, transfer them to a jar and seal it. Let them sit for a day to achieve the best flavor before using them. Stored in your refrigerator, they will keep for six months to a year, but in my house, they get eaten well before that! You can prolong their storage life even longer by freezing them.

chipotles in adobo (recipe opposite) and mojo de ajo (page 60)

vegetables charring on the grill

5

Tacos de Asador

*"Tacos with fillings
charred over an open flame."*

Tacos de asador

Tacos de asador are simply tacos in which the filling has been grilled or cooked on a spit. They also happen to be my favorite style of taco. I cannot resist the char of the grill and the intoxicating smoky flavor imparted by my local desert mesquite. It's a primal quality that makes the taco thrum with excitement. Actually, it's me that thrums with excitement, but I always imagine the taco humming with a fiery energy. To me, they speak of an evening standing over a grill and making tacos for my friends and family on my backyard patio. In Mexico, especially in the major cities, taquerías fire up the night with the heady aromas of grilled ingredients and toasting tortillas. It is truly a magical experience.

Grilling Over a Wood Fire

There are a few tricks to getting the most out of your *tacos de asador* experience. Paramount to the experience is getting a good char over an open flame. Almost as important is the smoke flavor from the grill. That means that the best tacos de asador are made on a wood-fire grill.

My two favorite woods are mesquite and pecan. Both of these are hard enough to burn evenly and for a long time. The flavor they impart to the food is perfect for most types of veggies (particularly mushrooms) and seitan. You don't want your ingredients to cook too fast, or they won't pick up much smoke, so let your wood or coals get to a point where they are hot, but not at the height of their burn. If using

coals, make sure they are spread evenly under the cooking area of your grill, but still pressed into a tight spread a couple layers deep. If you are using wood, stack the wood together to get it lit properly.

Once the pieces are burning well, spread out the wood like you would with coals. If the pieces are large, you should end up with one jumbled layer. If the pieces are small (four to eight inches across), make a tight spread with a few layers of small wood pieces, if possible. You can control how long your ingredients remain on the grill by moving them towards or away from the hottest flames. I do a hand-check to find the hottest—meaning too hot for me! (I have developed the mutant power of heat resistance by doing this, so do the hand-check at your own risk.) The safer method is to use an infrared heat scanner.

Remember, the longer you are willing to keep your ingredients on the grill, the more smoke they will pick up. Here's the secret trick: I cook my ingredients over one of the cooler areas of coals for 10 to 15 minutes, allowing them to pick up a good smoke flavor. Then, to get a good char, I move them over to the hottest part of the grill for just a couple minutes per side. It's the best of both worlds.

If you are grilling small ingredients or shredded seitan, a perforated grill pan will prevent anything from slipping through the grill grates. You can pick these up at most kitchen stores. They are designed with small holes to allow smoke to permeate the food and for the flame to get to the grilled ingredients, but the holes are small enough that food won't slip through them. Keep in mind, though, that if you do use one, I highly suggest oiling it, even if you are oil-averse. Nothing makes food want to stick more than an open flame. It's no fun to remove food that has stuck to a grill pan and the stuck the food often fall apart during the process. The pans are no fun to clean. Once you have cleaned the pan, dry it, and rub some oil onto it to keep it from rusting.

Grilling on a Gas Grill

If you do not have a wood-fire grill, but you have a gas grill, you can still make great tacos de asador. Get a smoking box and use mesquite chips with it. Be sure to soak the chips for an hour so they smolder instead of fire. (Follow the directions for the smoking box.) Once the chips are smoking, you can start grilling. Start with your grill at just below a medium heat. This will allow the food to be on the grill for about 10 to 15 minutes. Once your food has smoked and mostly cooked, crank the grill up to high so your food can get a good char. As with a wood-fire grill, this should only take a few minutes per side.

Tacos de Asador Without Grilling

If you do not have a grill, you can still make a variation of tacos de asador by sautéing the ingredients in a skillet on top of the stove. Technically, this makes them into *tacos de cazo* or *tacos de comal* since they aren't grilled, but the flavors will be similar. In general, you only need 1 to 2 teaspoons of oil in your sauté pan, and you will want to bring the pan to a medium-high heat. Sauté the ingredients until they develop some blackened spots and then remove them from the pan. They won't have the smokiness from the grill, but they are still going to taste great.

Tacos de Asador Using a Spit

Finally, if you want to take it to the ultimate level and use a spit or rotisserie for those tacos that traditionally call for it, namely the *Tacos al Pastor* and the *Tacos Árabes,* I commend you. That is a dedication to food that I can appreciate. I urge you to make your own seitan to do this, as even very hearty veggies don't hold spice rubs or texture very well under long periods of heat unless you treat them with great care. You will want to make enough to create a 6-inch diameter log of seitan that is at least 1-foot long. If you need to feed a lot of people or just want a hoard of leftovers, make the seitan longer, not thicker. Keeping it at six inches in diameter maximum allows for greater permeation of smoke. When you make it, mix two batches of the appropriate rub into the seitan for every foot you make. We have an advantage over non-vegan cooks because we can place our spices directly into the seitan. Take advantage of that. Cook the seitan over a low heat for at least three hours. You will need to spritz the seitan with water or brush it with oil every 30 minutes or so. The longer it cooks, the better it gets. When you serve the taco, use a very sharp knife to slice thin slabs of seitan off the spit. Also, please invite me over.

A Note on Tortillas for Tacos de Asador

Tortillas for tacos de asador tend to be a bit thicker than normal. If you are making your own, don't press your tortillas all the way down in the tortilla press. Back off just a touch to make the tortilla thicker. It's only about a one-sixteenth difference in size, but the extra-thick tortilla will hold together with the juices from vegetables, rubs, and marinades that are often found in tacos de asador. If using storebought tortillas, go for the thickest ones you can find at the store or use two tortillas for one taco.

The Set-up for Tacos de Asador

Tacos de asador beg to be assembled right near the grill. Once the ingredients come off the grill, they should be placed in a tortilla and topped immediately for the best experience. Make sure your tortillas are warmed and pliable and kept in a covered basket next to the grill so you can grab a tortilla with one hand and place ingredients into the tortilla straight from the grill with the other. Set up the salsas and condiments nearby so your diners can go directly from the grill to the condiment area and eat their tacos while they are fresh off the flame.

Convert Your Tacos to Tostadas and Enchiladas

This book may be about tacos, but you can easily turn it into a tostada or enchilada book!

Tostadas

To make crispy tostadas without having to fry them, heat a griddle to a medium heat. If you are making your own tortillas, after the first flip of the tortilla, leave the tortilla on the griddle for about 4 minutes, then flip it over and leave it on the griddle for another 3 to 4 minutes. You may need to adjust this, depending on the type of masa you are using, but the key is to get the tortilla crisp. Do the same for storebought tortillas, but don't cook them quite as long. The tortillas should show some charring. If you want to fry your tortillas, it's best to use day-old homemade or storebought tortillas. Heat 1/2-inch of oil in a skillet to 375°F. Add the tortilla and fry for about 1 minute, then flip it and fry for another 30 seconds. You now have fried tostadas. You'll need about double the amount of filling for a tostada than for a taco.

Enchiladas

For enchiladas, make a double batch of Guajillo Chile Salsa (page 217). Dredge the tortillas through the salsa. If you want to bake them, spread a thin layer of sauce on the bottom of a baking dish. Roll the dredged tortillas around the filling directly in the baking dish. Once you have rolled all the enchiladas, cover the dish with foil and bake at 325°F for 30 minutes. If you want to fry your tortillas, which is more traditional, bring a thin layer of oil to 350°F and fry the dredged tortilla in the oil for about 10 seconds on both sides. Then roll it around the filling, and you're done. Use the same amount of filling as you'd use in a taco. Be sure to cook the filling before it gets rolled in the tortilla, even if you are baking them.

Charred Chayote Tacos

Tacos al Carbón de Chayote

Tacos al carbón are the classic grilled tacos. These are cooked specifically over wood, although if you want to use coals or a gas grill, I won't tell. They are designed to cook quickly, with a predominant charred flavor from the open flame, so unlike other tacos de asador, I put these guys on the grill on the hottest part I can find for only a few minutes, just long enough to blacken the exposed area of the chayote squash. Try these with some other semi-hard veggies like zucchini or eggplant, or even a quartered onion so you can make charred onion tacos.

Note: If you omit the minced serrano chiles, this is a great taco for those who don't like spicy food.

REGION: EVERYWHERE | HEAT LEVEL: 4 | MAKES 8 TACOS

The Filling
2 chayote squash, cut in half with the seed scooped out
1 medium sweet onion, cut into 1/4-inch strips
2 tablespoons Mojo de Ajo (page 60)
1/2 teaspoon coarse sea salt

The Tortillas
8 (5 to 6-inch) corn tortillas

The Toppings
4 serrano chiles, deseeded and minced
Salsa Verde (page 218)
Chopped fresh cilantro
1/2 cup Queso Fresco (page 205) or toasted pepitas
1 lime, cut into 8 wedges

1. Toss the chayote and onion separately, each in half of the mojo de ajo. Keep the vegetables separate from each other. Toss only the chayote with the salt. Place the onion in a grill pan, and transfer it to the grill. You won't need a grill pan for the chayote, just place them directly on the grill rack over the hottest part of the grill. Once one side of the chayote has blistered and mostly blackened, flip it over and repeat with the other side. Stir the onions every minute or so until they are well browned and partially blackened. Remove the chayote and onion from the heat. Cut the chayote into strips, then combine them with the onion.

2. Fill each tortilla with a generous amount of chayote and onion, then garnish with minced serrano, salsa verde, fresh cilantro, and vegan queso fresco, Serve with a lime wedge.

Arabic Tacos

Tacos Árabes

Both Mexico City and Puebla State have large Middle Eastern populations, and the Tacos Árabes highlight the fusion between these cultures. In fact, this taco isn't even served on a corn tortilla; it's served on pita bread and topped with a yogurt sauce! Tacos Árabes are traditionally cooked shwarma-style—slow-roasting the fillings on a spit—but since most people don't have spits in their backyards, I have created a much more home-friendly version.

REGION(S): PUEBLA, MEXICO CITY | HEAT LEVEL: 4 | MAKES 4 TACOS

The Rub
2 ancho chiles
5 cloves garlic
2 serrano chiles, stems and seeds removed
1 chipotle in adobo
1/2 teaspoon ground cumin
1/2 teaspoon dried Mexican oregano
1/2 teaspoon black pepper
Pinch of cinnamon
Pinch of nutmeg
Pinch of cloves
1/2 teaspoon salt
Juice of 1 lemon
Water, as needed

The Filling
1 large eggplant, cut into 4 slabs or 2 cups thinly sliced seitan
1 medium yellow onion, sliced into 1/4-inch thin strips (prep this just after you light your grill)
4 cloves garlic, minced (prep this just after you light your grill)
1 tablespoon olive oil
4 (7-inch) whole-wheat pitas

The Toppings
Yogurt Sauce (page 227)
Hot sauce or adobo sauce

1. Bring a small pot of water to a simmer, add the anchos, and simmer for 10 minutes to soften. Drain the anchos, then remove and discard the stems and seeds.

2. In a blender or small food processor, puree the rehydrated anchos, garlic, serranos, chipotle, cumin, oregano, pepper, cinnamon, nutmeg, salt, lemon juice, and 2 tablespoons of water into a smooth paste. This is your rub. If you need to add more water to smooth out the paste, add 1 tablespoon and puree it again. Repeat as necessary. Transfer the pureed rub to a shallow bowl and add the eggplant or seitan, then toss them in the rub to coat. Set aside.

3. Light the grill, preferably with mesquite wood, and let the heat die down a bit so that the food slow-cooks. Combine the onion, garlic, and oil in a bowl and toss to coat. Transfer all the filling ingredients in a grill pan positioned just off the hot part of the grill. Close the lid. The filling will take about 30 to 40 minutes to properly cook and you will need to flip the ingredients every 10 minutes or so, depending on how hot your grill is. If the filling starts to cook quickly, move it farther away from the heat or let your grill die down some more. Quickly warm the pita on the grill, about 5 seconds per side, and fill each one. Top the tacos with the jocoque sauce and either hot sauce or the adobo sauce, but not both.

MAKE IT ON THE STOVETOP: Bring a pan to about a medium-high heat. Add the onion, oil, and pinch of salt. Sauté the onion until it is heavily browned. Add the garlic and sauté 2 more minutes. Remove the onion and garlic from the pan and turn the heat down to medium. Add the rubbed seitan or eggplant to the pan and cook these for about 10 minutes, stirring the seitan or flipping the eggplant every 2 to 3 minutes. Do not constantly stir them because you want the sauce to sit on the direct heat of the pan to tighten up. While you are doing this, warm the pita in the oven at 300°F for about 2 minutes. Fill the pita with the seitan or eggplant, then the onions and garlic, and top it with your sauce of choice.

MAKE IT SIMPLE: Puree all the ingredients for the rub and set it aside. Over a medium heat, sauté the onion, garlic, and seitan or eggplant in the oil for about 2 minutes. Add the rub and cook another 6 to 7 minutes, slowly stirring. Warm your tortilla, fill it, and top it with hot sauce. You won't have the complexity of flavor you get from the main recipe, but you also just made Tacos Árabes in about 10 minutes.

MAKE IT SPECIAL: If you can let the seitan or eggplant sit in the rub for six or more hours, it will be even better, but I rarely have the patience for that. If you have a smoker at home, you can make this really outstanding by smoking the eggplant or seitan for about 4 hours before finishing it off on a hot grill for 8 to 10 minutes.

Food Anthropology Is Fun!

During the 1920s and 1930s, Puebla State had a large influx of immigrants from Lebanon, Syria, and Iraq. Like many cultures on the move, they brought their culinary tastes with them. It was in 1933 that the Tabe family, immigrants from Iraq, first took shwarma-style ingredients and methods, fused them with Mexican ingredients, and served the first Taco Árabe. Now there are hundreds of taquerías in Puebla serving Tacos Árabes.

Shepherd-Style Tacos

Tacos al Pastor

Like Tacos Árabes, Tacos al Pastor are influenced by Middle Eastern cuisine. Traditionally, they are cooked on a spit shwarma-style with a pineapple above. The filling is sliced off into thin strips. Tacos al pastor are red because of the achiote paste used in the rub as well as all the delicious dried red chiles. What makes this taco particularly interesting is the pineapple, which is also found in the rub. Pineapple has an enzyme, called bromelain, that tenderizes the protein in the veggies and making the filling incredibly soft and lush in texture. The longer you let the marinade do its job, the more this process will continue. This recipe looks complex because of the long ingredient list, but it's actually fairly simple, so don't let the length intimidate you. These are some of the best tacos I've ever had.

REGION: PUEBLA | HEAT LEVEL: 3 | MAKES 10 TACOS

The Marinade
4 guajillo chiles, rehydrated
4 ancho chiles, rehydrated
2 chipotles in adobo
2 tablespoons adobo sauce
2 tablespoons achiote paste (page 68 or storebought), optional but recommended
6 cloves garlic
1/2 cup chopped pineapple
1/2 teaspoon salt
1 teaspoon ground cumin
1/4 teaspoon ground cloves
1/2 to 1 cup water

The Filling (choose either the seitan or eggplant)
4 cups seitan strips or 3 large eggplants, cut into 3-inch x 1-inch strips
2 medium red onions, cut into 1/4-inch strips (prep this after your seitan or eggplant has marinated)
3 cups chopped pineapple (prep this after your seitan or eggplant has marinated)
1 tablespoon olive oil
1/4 teaspoon salt

The Tortillas
20 (5 to 6-inch) corn tortillas (or 10 very thick corn tortillas)

The Toppings
Salsa Verde (page 218) or storebought
Fresh cilantro

1. In a blender or food processor, puree the rehydrated guajillos and anchos with the chipotles, adobo sauce, achiote paste (if using), garlic, pineapple, salt, cumin, cloves, and enough water to make a very thick marinade. Transfer the marinade to a large shallow bowl. Toss the eggplant or seitan with the marinade to coat and let it sit for at least 2 hours.

2. Preheat the grill. In a bowl, toss the onion, pineapple, oil and salt together, then transfer to a well-oiled grill pan. Transfer the marinated seitan or eggplant to a different well-oiled grill pan.

3. Transfer the grill pans with the filling and the onions and pineapple to the grill. The onions should caramelize and the pineapple should develop a slight charring. Stir every 2 to 3 minutes. If you are using seitan, stir every 2 to 3 minutes. If using eggplant, stir it every 2 minutes until it starts to soften. At this point, stir it every minute. As soon as the eggplant is soft, get it off the grill. Do not overcook.

4. If using very thick tortillas, you only need one tortilla. If using regular tortillas, you will need two stacked on top of each other. If I am using handmade tortillas, I take them from my tortilla basket and warm them on the grill for about 5 seconds and only on one side. Then I immediately fill them. If I'm using storebought tortillas, I don't warm them on the grill because they tend to be too fragile. Fill a tortilla with seitan or eggplant, then the onions and pineapple. Top with salsa verde and a sprinkle of cilantro.

MAKE IT ON THE STOVETOP: Make the marinade and marinate the filling the same as above. Toss the onion and pineapple in the oil and salt as above. Sauté the onion and pineapple in a wide saute pan over medium-high heat until the onion is caramelized. Remove from the pan and set aside. Add 2 more tablespoons of oil to the pan. Add the filling and sauté for 7 to 8 minutes, stirring a few times. Do not constantly stir the filling, or it will take longer to cook. This is more important than adhering strictly to the cooking time. When the filling begins to darken, remove from the heat and fill the tortillas.

Vampire Tacos

Tacos Vampiros

I first saw these tacos at a taco truck parked in a dirt lot in Tucson, and instantly had to find out what they were. It turned out that this particular taco truck didn't have anything vegan, but I got to watch them make their *tacos vampiros* and see how the corn tortilla edges folded up on the grill. This is supposedly the origin of the name, because the edges look like bat wings. It's sort of a cross between a tostada and a taco. Traditionally, they are made with *carne asada* (thin-sliced beef), but I make mine with charred beans.

REGION: SONORA/SOUTHERN ARIZONA | HEAT LEVEL: 5 | MAKES 8 TACOS

The Filling (choose either the beans or seitan strips)
2 cups cooked, rinsed pinto beans or 2 cups seitan strips
1 tablespoon olive oil
1/2 teaspoon salt
1 1/2 cups shredded Queso Oaxaca (page 207) or your favorite white melting
   vegan cheese
2 serrano chiles, sliced very thin

The Tortillas
8 (5 to 6-inch) corn tortillas

The Garnish
Minced white onion
Minced cilantro
Crushed Red Salsa (page 212)
Basic guacamole (page 234)

1. Light your grill. Toss the beans or seitan strips with the oil and salt and transfer to a well-oiled grill pan. Place the grill pan on the grill and slowly stir while they grill until blackened. This should only take a few minutes. Remove from the grill and set aside.

2. Place the tortillas on the grill. When the edges start to curl from the heat, sprinkle the queso on the tortillas, leaving a rim around the edge. When the tortillas are hard and crunchy, remove them from the grill. Top the tortillas with the beans or seitan strips, followed by the onion, cilantro, salsa, and guacamole.

MAKE IN THE OVEN: Dress your beans or seitan the same way, but place them in a baking dish and leave them uncovered. Roast them at 400°F for 15 minutes, opening the oven to stir them every 5 minutes. While they are baking, place your tortillas in the oven on the lower rack. When they begin to curl, slide the lower rack out, dress them with the queso, and return them to the oven. Once the queso melts, remove them from the oven and set them aside. Dress them just as you would above.

Vegan Options at Traditional Taquerías

. . . .

A taquería is a fun experience, however, be aware that some ingredients that look vegan are not. This is usually true of the beans, to which lard or bacon are often added. Vegan-friendly choices are nopales, rajas, and other grilled veggies, which are usually just dressed in oil and spices. Those will often be grilled on the same grill as meat, however, so you will have to decide whether that is acceptable.

On occasion, you will find a non-vegan salsa. Fried chiles are usually fried in oil, but sometimes may be fried in lard. My rule is, if they glisten, they were probably fried in oil, and if they look glazed, they were fried in lard.

Flour tortillas usually have lard added to them, but corn tortillas do not. However, if the corn tortillas are fried, they may be fried in lard. This is why I avoid tacos dorados when I am traveling, unless I can talk to the cook or see the tacos made myself. My safe bet is a taco of grilled veggies to which I add salsas, guacamole, and fried chiles. I usually ask for "tacos con sólo verduras," which means tacos with vegetables only. Also, make sure to order them "sin queso" (without cheese), just in case.

My Family Tacos

Tacos de Mi Familia

Whenever my mom talks about the food her grandmother used to make, this is the taco she's referring to. Simple grilled veggies with pinto beans and a little bit of salsa all wrapped up in a fresh tortilla. These are very easy to make and the veggies used in them are just suggestions. In reality, they were made with whatever veggies that grandma Rachel had on hand. You may not immediately use all the grilled veggies in your tacos, but that's O.K. They make great leftovers for a midnight taco snack.

REGION: CASA DE JASON | HEAT LEVEL: 3 | MAKES 8 TACOS

The Filling
2 zucchini, cut into 3 to 4-inch long strips
1 large red onion, cut into 1/4-inch thick strips
2 poblano chiles, deseed and cut into 1 inch thick strips
4 plum tomatoes, cut in quarters
1 tablespoon olive oil
1/4 teaspoon salt
1 1/2 cups cooked pinto beans, rinsed

The Tortillas
8 (5 to 6-inch) corn tortillas

The Toppings
Pico de Gallo (page 216)

In a bowl, combine the zucchini, onion, chiles, and tomatoes with the oil and salt and toss to coat. Wrap all the vegetables in foil to make a large packet and pierce it with a fork a few times. Transfer the packet to the grill. About every 2 to 3 minutes, flip the packet over. Prod the packet every few minutes to check if the veggies are soft. Once they are soft, remove the packet of vegetables from the grill. Unwrap the packet and fill each tortilla with the vegetables and pinto beans. Garnish with pico de gallo and eat.

MAKE ON THE STOVETOP: Prep the veggies just as above, but don't toss them in oil or salt. You will only need 1 teaspoon of oil for this instead of 1 tablespoon. Bring a wide pan to just above a medium heat and add the oil. Sauté the onion in this until it just starts to brown. Add the zucchini, poblano, and salt and keep sautéing until the zucchini browns. Add the tomatoes and beans and sauté 3 to 4 minutes longer.

Cecina Tacos

Cecina is a lightly dried variation of jerky. My version of these tacos is made with a thin cut of veggies or lightly dried seitan marinated in a chile sauce laced with aromatic spices and finished off on the grill. The most famous version comes from the village of Yecapixtla, south of Mexico City. The taco should have a chew and saltiness to it, but shouldn't be tough. Top with some avocado tomatillo salsa and a minced onion and cilantro mix, and you have a flavor powerhouse of a taco. I've provided several different versions of the recipe, all close variations on a theme.

REGION: MORELOS | HEAT LEVEL: 5 | MAKES 6 TACOS

The Marinade
8 guajillo chiles, toasted or 1/4 cup chili powder
1 teaspoon dried oregano
1/4 teaspoon ground cinnamon
1/4 teaspoon ground cumin
1/4 teaspoon ground black pepper
Pinch of cloves
1 teaspoon salt
4 cloves garlic
2 tablespoons white vinegar

The Filling (choose one of the following)
1 (8 x 10) sheet flattened seitan or 2 eggplants, cut into 1/2 inch thick slabs, or 2
  white sweet potatoes, cut into 1/8 to 1/4-inch thick slabs
1 tablespoon olive oil

The Toppings
1 small white onion, minced (prep this just before grilling)
1/4 cup minced fresh cilantro (prep this just before grilling)
1 serrano chile, deseeded and minced (prep this just before grilling)
Juice of 2 limes (prep this just before grilling)
Green Salsa with Avocado (page 214) or 1 cup storebought tomatillo salsa
  blended with 1 avocado

The Tortillas
6 (5 to 6-inch) corn tortillas

1. Toast the chiles in a dry pan over a medium heat, 30 seconds per side. Remove the stems. Grind the chiles, oregano, cinnamon, cumin, pepper, cloves, and salt. Transfer this to a mixing bowl. Smash the garlic using the back of a large knife, or even better, a molcajete. Add this to the mixing bowl along with the white vinegar and stir it into a paste.

2. Prepare your choice of filling. Rub the chile paste over the filling. Place the filling on a plate or in a bowl, cover it, and place it in the refrigerator. If you are using flattened seitan or eggplant, you will only need to let this sit for about 4 hours. If you are using sweet potatoes, you will need to let this sit for at least 12 hours. The sweet potatoes are very hard and they resist being marinated.

3. Prepare the toppings before you start grilling so the flavors have time to meld. In a bowl, combine the onion, serrano, cilantro, and lime juice and toss to coat. Set aside. Prepare the salsa. Set aside.

4. If you are using the flattened seitan, cook it an extra 30 minutes to dry it out. If you are using the eggplant or sweet potatoes, use them as normal.

5. Preheat the grill. If you are using a gas grill, don't worry about using wood chips. The filling won't be on long enough to smoke. Toss the filling in the oil. Place the filling on the hottest part of the grill. You will only need to grill the filling for about a minute or two at most per side. Transfer this to a cutting board and cut the filling into strips.

6. Warm the corn tortillas. Fill them with the grilled filling. Top with the salsa and then the onion-cilantro mix.

MAKE IT SIMPLE ON THE STOVETOP: Use chili powder instead of toasting and grinding the chiles and just mince the garlic instead of smashing it into a paste. Combine all the ingredients for the marinade, then set it aside. Take your filling of choice and slice it according to the recipe above. Then slice the filling again into strips. Bring the oil to a medium heat and sauté the filling until it is soft (the seitan only takes 3 to 4 minutes per side, and the eggplant and sweet potato strips only take about 8 minutes total). As soon as the strips are soft, stir the marinade into the pan and cook for another 2 minutes. Remove the pan from the heat, prep the toppings as above, and you're done.

Baja-Style Tempeh Tacos

Tacos de Tempeh Estilo Baja

This is a riff one of several Baja-style tacos that features the pop of chiles de árbol, but using tempeh instead of seafood. Even though it is a grilled taco, it has a bright, fresh, spicy flavor to it from the lime, avocado, and fresh cabbage, and is incredibly easy to make. Because of the influence of California tourists in Baja, tacos from this region are also served with wheat flour tortillas. I prefer corn tortillas for this taco, but a toasted flour tortilla won't let you down.

REGION: BAJA | HEAT LEVEL: 5 | MAKES 6 TACOS

The Filling
16 ounces tempeh, cut into 1-inch wide strips
2 cups apple cider vinegar
1/2 teaspoon sugar
2 pieces kombu
20 chiles de árbol, ground or 2 tablespoons chili powder
1 tablespoon Mojo de Ajo (page 60) or olive oil
3/4 teaspoon salt

The Tortillas
6 (5 to 6-inch) corn or flour tortillas

The Toppings
1 1/4 cup Chopped Guacamole (page 234)
12 Grilled Spring Onions (page 197)
3/4 cup shredded red cabbage

1. Place the tempeh in a heatproof bowl. In a saucepan, combine the vinegar, sugar, and kombu and bring to a simmer. Simmer for 5 minutes, then pour the hot marinade over the tempeh. Let the tempeh marinate for about 4 hours. Remove the tempeh from the marinade. Toss it with the mojo de ajo, then toss it with the ground chiles and salt.

2. Preheat the grill. Place the tempeh pieces on the grill over some of the lower heat coals or wood (or place them in a grill pan and put the pan on the grill). Close the grill and let them smoke for about 10 minutes. Transfer them to the hottest part of the grill and finish them off, about 2 minutes per side. You will need to work quickly to get all your tempeh strips flipped. As soon as they begin to blacken, take them off the grill and place them in a bowl or on a plate. Add green onions to the grill and grill for about 30 seconds. Remove them from the grill and slice them.

Corn Tortillas: Fill the tortillas with the tempeh, then the guacamole (about 3 tablespoons per taco), sliced onions, and cabbage. Fold and eat.

Flour Tortillas: Fill the tortillas with the tempeh, then the guacamole (about 3 tablespoons per taco), sliced onions, and cabbage. Fold them closed. Place the tacos on the grill and grill each side for about 1 minute per side. Serve and eat.

MAKE IT ON THE STOVETOP: Instead of grilling these, bring a wide sauté pan up to a medium heat. Slice the green onions while the pan is heating up. Add an additional tablespoon of mojo de ajo or oil to the pan. Add the tempeh and sauté it until the strips are browned. Add the sliced green onion and sauté about 2 more minutes. Fill the tacos just as above. If you are using flour tortillas, you can toast them in a dry pan over a medium heat, about 3 minutes per side.

grilled tempeh

Tacos with Smoked Mushrooms, Jalapeño, and Lime

Tacos de Champiñones Ahumados, Jalapeño y Limón

This recipe combines my love of so many things: mushrooms, chiles, tacos, and the grill. It's a very simple grilled taco. Although I use an exotic mushroom in the recipe, you can substitute plenty of other hearty mushrooms for it. The key to the recipe is getting a good smoky flavor from the grill.

REGION: CASA DE JASON | HEAT LEVEL: 4 | MAKES 8 TACOS

The Filling
1 pound hen-of-the-woods (maitake) mushrooms left as whole as possible (see tip)
1 tablespoon Mojo de Ajo (page 60) or olive oil
1/4 teaspoon salt
4 to 8 whole jalapeños (use 8 if you want a spicier taco)

The Tortillas
8 (5 to 6-inch) corn tortillas

The Toppings
1 lime, cut into 8 wedges
1/2 cup Queso Fresco (page 205)
Salsa Verde (page 218)
Chopped fresh cilantro

1. Preheat the grill with mesquite wood or mesquite coals. If you are using a gas grill, use soaked mesquite chips. Brush the hen-of-the-woods mushroom with the mojo de ajo and sprinkle it with salt.

2. Place the whole jalapeños on the grill rack directly over the flames and the hen-of-the-woods mushroom in a grill pan set off center of the hottest part of the grill. As the jalapeños blacken, rotate them until the skin has blackened and blistered all around. Remove them from the grill, set them in a bowl, and cover them. As the hen-of-the-woods mushroom browns, rotate it until it is soft and grilled all the way around. Ideally, you want this on the grill for 15 minutes or so to pick up some smoky flavor.

3. Chop the mushrooms into bite-size pieces. Peel the jalapeños, remove the seeds, and give them a rough chop. Combine the mushrooms and jalapeños together. Fill each tortilla with the mushroom jalapeño filling, give the filling a squeeze of lime, sprinkle on the vegan queso fresco, and finish it off with salsa verde and fresh cilantro.

MAKE IT ON THE STOVETOP: Pan-roast the jalapeños. Chop the hen-of-the-woods mushroom(s). Bring the oil to a medium-high heat. Add the hen-of-the-woods mushrooms and salt to the pan and sear this until it is browned. Peel, deseed, and chop the jalapeños and combine them with the mushrooms. Fill the tortillas and add the toppings.

HEN-OF-THE-WOODS TIP: Hen-of-the-woods mushrooms are often found at market as a baseball-size mass of little mushrooms growing off a mushroom "stem." The stem is edible and you should use it in this recipe. You may find one gigantic hen of the woods or you may need three or four different masses to get one pound of mushrooms.

MUSHROOM SUBSTITUTIONS: You can also use oyster mushrooms if you don't have the heartier hen-of-the-woods, though you may need a little more oil to brush them since they have a larger surface area to weight ratio. If you don't have either of those, go with quartered cremini mushrooms.

Tacos with Yucatecan-Style Barbecue

Tacos de Barbacoa Estilo Yucatán

These tacos are based on the Yucatan's famous *cochinita pibil* style of barbacoa. Traditionally, this is cooked in a fire pit dug into the ground and filled with super-hot stones. The pit is covered with maguey leaves. Now that's rustic. However, I am not sure if my wife would allow me to dig a fire pit in our yard (actually, she might), and I know I can't find maguey leaves anywhere close to home, so I came up with the next best thing. Plus, to be honest, I would probably dig a fire pit, use it once, and then use my grill from then on. The key to this recipe is getting the filling to slow-cook in the marinade so it turns super soft. It's actually fairly easy to put together, it just takes a very long time to cook. The optional vegan shortening will create a more authentic flavor, but there is no pretending that it is healthy.

REGION: YUCATAN | HEAT LEVEL: 3 | MAKES 12 TACOS

The Marinade
1/4 cup achiote paste
12 cloves garlic
1 cup sour orange juice or 1/2 cup orange juice and 1/2 cup lime juice
1 teaspoon salt

The Filling (choose either the seitan or jackfruit or do a mix of half and half)
4 cups seitan, cut into very thin strips or 5 cups fresh jackfruit or canned (see page 30)
3 tablespoons vegan shortening, optional

The Tortillas
12 (5 to 6-inch) thick corn tortillas

The Toppings
Pickled Onions (page 203) (prep this before you start making the marinade)
Dog Nose Sauce (page 223) or Habanero Tequila Hot Sauce (page 230)

1. In a blender or food processor, combine the achiote paste, garlic, orange juice, and salt and puree into a thick sauce. Transfer the marinade and the filling to a pot that can withstand the grill, such as a Dutch oven or a large iron skillet.

2. When you place the coals in the grill, place them to one side of the grill. Light your grill and let the coals get hot and the flames die down. Alternatively, if you are using a gas grill, use pecan wood chips (or whatever ones you have on hand) with the grill and turn it to a medium low heat. Place the pot away from the coals. Pierce a sheet of foil with a fork and then lay the foil over the pot. This will trap in lots of moisture, but still allow the smoke from the grill to penetrate the filling and marinade. Cook this for about 4 hours. If you are using a charcoal or wood-fire grill, you will need to add some more coals to it every 20 to 30 minutes.

3. When you serve the tacos, warm the tortillas for a couple seconds on the grill. Lift out the filling directly from the pot using a large fork or tongs and fill the tortilla. Top with pickled onions and salsa.

MAKE IT IN THE OVEN: Place the filling and marinade in an ovenproof pot and cover it tightly with a lid or foil. Roast this at 300°F for 4 hours. You won't get the smoky flavor from the grill, but it's a no-hassle way to make this taco.

Hominy and Seitan Tacos in Roasted
Garlic Cascabel Sauce (page 106)

CHAPTER

Tacos de Guisados

"Tacos made with stewed fillings."

Tacos de guisados are made with a stewed filling. I love them because they are easy to make in large batches and they keep well. A guisado (that's the actual stew) will keep for days in the refrigerator. I suspect those are the very reasons why tacos de guisado are the most common type of taco and the most varied. They certainly are the most common type of taco served at my house.

Many Mexican taco stands specialize in tacos de guisado. They close up around mid-afternoon, since these are mainly eaten for breakfast and lunch. Some of the vendors will also serve a few fillings that aren't stews, such as chiles rellenos, but for the most part, the fillings for tacos de guisado are stews cooked to perfection. The tacos are almost always served with rice, beans, fresh or pickled chiles, and, of course, salsa. Tacos de guisados taquerías typically use a host of cazuelas, those beautiful wide clay pots, with different guisados in them sitting out for you to choose from. When I say a host, I mean a host. Seeing a tacos de guisados taquería with twelve or more cazuelas, each with a different filling, is not uncommon. Sadly, most of them are not vegan, but now you have the opportunity to set up your home taquería of tacos de guisado!

If you want to start with something easy, go with the Tacos with Sweet Potato and Chard, the simple version of the Tacos Veracruz, or the Tacos with Pintos Borrachos and Rajas Poblano (skip the vegan *queso fresco*). The Tacos with Purslane in Salsa Verde are also quite simple to make, although it's not always so easy to find the purslane: but they're also great made with another hearty green such as kale or chard.

Tacos with Sweet Potato and Chard

Tacos de Camote y Alcegas

This taco is like comfort food for me. The sweet potato and wilted chard have a very homey feel, and they make for a very soft taco that just melts in your mouth. The sweet potato is so flavorful, I just used a bit of salt to accent it, and that's it. It's also a simple taco with just a few ingredients; exactly what I want on a day when I just want to hang out and relax. If you want a heartier taco, add some cooked pinto beans or just serve them on the side.

REGION: CASA DE JASON | HEAT LEVEL: 0 TO 5 (DEPENDING ON TOPPINGS) | MAKES 8 TACOS

The Filling
1 large orange sweet potato, peeled and cut into 3/4-inch dice
Water
3/4 teaspoon salt
Wilted Chard in Mojo de Ajo (page 199)

The Tortillas
6 (5 to 6-inch) corn tortillas (Chile Flavored Tortillas on page 50 are excellent here)

The Topping
Crushed Red Salsa (page 212)
Rough Salted Chile Powder (page 199)

1. Add the sweet potato to a saucepan with just enough water to cover them. Add the salt and give it a quick stir. Bring this to a simmer and simmer until very soft, about 10 minutes. While the sweet potato is simmering, make a batch of Wilted Chard in Mojo de Ajo (or just cook some greens down with a couple minced cloves of garlic and a pinch of salt).

2. Warm the tortillas by laying them on the hot sweet potatoes, one at a time, for about 10 seconds each. Fill the tortillas with the sweet potato, then the chard, and finish it off with a little salsa, rough chile powder, or both.

Tacos Veracruz

Tacos Estilo Veracruz

This taco is named after the classic Veracruz tomato sauce. You can see the Spanish influence here with the use of green olives and capers. Coupled with chipotles in adobo, this taco has a glorious zing! Veracruz tacos often feature seafood, so I used my "scallop" hack in this recipe. It's meant to evoke, not duplicate, the oceanic taste often found in this diverse region. **Note:** You can skip the scallop hack, but I wanted to give you a "best practice" version. This hack works because king trumpets can be sliced into scallop-like medallions that stand up well to the pan. Fresh scallops have a touch of sweetness, so the marinade uses kombu for the ocean flavor and a little sugar and lemon juice to brighten the sweetness.

REGION: VERACRUZ | HEAT LEVEL: 3 | MAKES 12 TACOS

The "Scallop" Hack

3 king trumpet mushrooms (or 3 cups chopped oyster mushrooms)

2 cups water

1 teaspoon sugar

1/2 teaspoon lemon juice

1 (3-inch) piece kombu

1 tablespoon Mojo de Ajo (page 60)

1/3 teaspoon coarse sea salt

The Sauce

2 cups crushed fire-roasted tomatoes

8 to 10 pitted green olives, sliced (I really like ones stuffed with garlic)

2 chipotles in adobo, roughly diced

1 tablespoon fresh oregano or 1 teaspoon dried

3 tablespoons capers

1/2 teaspoon salt

The Filling (choose either beans or vegan chorizo)

1 Yukon gold or other waxy potato, cut into 1/2-inch dice

1 cup cooked pinto beans, rinsed or 1 cup crumbled vegan chorizo (page 66 or storebought)

The Tortillas

12 thick (5 to 6-inch) corn tortillas

The Condiments

Fried Chiles de Árbol (page 201)

Basic guacamole (page 234)

Wilted Chard in Mojo de Ajo (page 199)

1. Slice the king trumpet mushrooms into 1/4-inch thick medallions. Warm the water in a small saucepan and add the sugar, stirring to dissolve. Add the lemon juice and kombu and give it a quick stir. Add the mushroom medallions to the water. Remove the saucepan from the heat and set it aside for at least one hour, then drain, discard the kombu, and pat the mushrooms dry.

2. In a large saucepan or cazuela, combine the fire-roasted tomatoes, olives, chipotles, oregano, capers, and salt. Bring this to a low simmer, then add the potato and continue simmering until the potatoes are al dente, about 10 minutes. Add the beans or vegan chorizo and continue simmering for 2 minutes longer.

3. While the sauce is simmering, heat a sauté pan to just above a medium heat. Add the mojo de ajo, then add the mushroom medallions and salt. Sauté until the medallions are lightly browned around the rims. Remove from the heat.

4. Warm the tortillas. Fill them with the potato Veracruz sauce filling, then the mushroom medallions, and finally any of the toppings you want to use.

MAKE IT LOW-FAT: Instead of sautéing the mushroom medallions in mojo de ajo, add them directly to the sauce when you add the potatoes and let them simmer in the Veracruz sauce. Skip the guacamole, too.

MAKE IT SIMPLE: Skip the "scallop" hack and you can make this in 10 to 15 minutes with a minimal amount of work.

Tacos with Pintos Borrachos, Poblano Strips, and Queso Fresco

Tacos de Pintos Borrachos, Rajas, y Queso Fresco

These are my staple tacos. I usually have cooked beans in my refrigerator and the *rajas poblano* is easy to make. If I have no vegan queso fresco ready, I just skip it. Using my pintos borrachos cheat, these can be ready in about 15 minutes. If I already have some made up, it takes about 10 minutes. They are flavorful, filling, and soul satisfying; the perfect taco in my opinion.

REGION: EVERYWHERE | HEAT LEVEL: 3 | MAKES 8 TACOS

The Pintos Borrachos

4 cups water

1/2 medium-size yellow onion, cut into 1/4-inch dice (about 1/2 cup)

3 cloves garlic, minced

2 plum tomatoes, chopped

1 1/2 cups dried pinto beans (or canned beans: see "Make it Quick")

1/2 tablespoon dried epazote, optional but recommended

3/4 teaspoon ground cumin

2 tablespoons ancho powder or chili powder

1 (12-ounce) bottle dark ale or beer

3/4 teaspoon salt

1/4 cup vegan shortening, optional (for very creamy beans)

The Tortillas

8 (5 to 6-inch) corn tortillas

The Rajas Poblano

2 poblanos, pan roasted, stem and seeds removed, and cut into strips

---

Ale or Beer?
• • • • • • • • •

I prefer using ale with this recipe because it has some extra sweetness and a nice smooth flavor. If I don't have ale on hand, I will use dark beer instead. The light ones just don't have enough flavor and are often too hoppy. My favorite brand of ale to use is Samuel Smith's Nut-brown Ale, but I've also had good success with Black Toad, both of which are vegan as of the writing of this book.

The Toppings
Crushed Red Salsa (page 212)
Queso Fresco (page 205)

1. Bring the water to a boil in a saucepan. Add the onion, garlic, tomatoes, beans, epazote (if using), cumin, and ancho powder. Return the water to a boil, then turn the heat down to a simmer. Cook until the beans are tender, about 1 1/2 hours. You may need to replenish some of the water, making sure the beans stay barely covered with water. As soon as the beans are soft, turn the heat up to cook away most, but not all, of the water. Turn the heat back down to medium. Smash the beans, but don't worry if every single bean doesn't get smashed. Add the ale or beer, salt, and optional vegan shortening, stirring just to combine. Cook for 30 minutes at a low simmer, stirring them every 5 minutes or so.

2. Spread 3 to 4 tablespoons of pintos borrachos on each tortilla, then add the poblano strips, then the salsa, and finish it off with the vegan queso fresco.

MAKE IT QUICK: Add two cans of pinto beans to a pot with the onion, garlic, tomato, epazote, cumin, ancho powder, ale, and salt and simmer until there is only about an inch of liquid at the bottom of the pot. This will take about fifteen minutes. Once you've got that, smash the beans. You now have quick pintos borrachos. While they are simmering, go ahead and pan roast the poblanos and make the tortillas. Everything should come together at about the same time using this method.

Use Your Cazuela!
• • • • • • • • • • • •

A cazuela is a great vessel for making these tacos because the fillings tend not to stick to the glazed cazuela surface. Also, cazuelas heat fairly evenly. They also retain heat for quite a while, so you can cook your guisado in the cazuela, leave it out for an hour, and it will still be warm. Don't worry if you don't have one, though. I didn't get one until a few years ago, and I had been able to make great guisados in my regular pots just fine. If you need to let the guisado sit, just cover it with a lid and it will stay warm for quite a while. One other great thing about tacos de guisado is that most of the guisados are easy to make and don't require a lot of actual labor, even if they do require a lot of time.

Tacos with Shiitake Chorizo and Fresh Shiitakes in a Chipotle Tomato Stew

Tacos de Tinga Poblana

Tinga Poblana is a famous dish out of Puebla, Mexico. It can be served on its own or used in a taco. The tinga itself refers to the chipotle tomato sauce, while my version of this classic uses a shiitake chorizo and sliced fresh shiitakes. It has a spicy, deep, earthy taste accentuated by the heady herbs in the sauce. The smoky flavor and back-end heat remind me of late summer nights.

REGION: PUEBLA | HEAT LEVEL: 4 | MAKES 8 TACOS

The Filling
1 tablespoon olive oil

1 medium onion, cut into 1/4 inch thick strips

2 cloves garlic, minced

5 plum tomatoes, chopped

2 chipotles in adobo, roughly chopped

2 tablespoons adobo (use the sauce from the can)

1 teaspoon dried Mexican oregano

1 teaspoon dried thyme

2 bay leaves

1/2 teaspoon freshly ground black pepper

3/4 teaspoon salt

1/2 cup water or dark beer

2 cups vegan chorizo, storebought or homemade (shiitake version, page 66)

12 large or 20 small fresh shiitakes, stems removed, sliced into thin strips

The Tortillas
8 thick (5 to 6-inch) corn tortillas

The Topping
Sliced avocado

Heat the oil in a large saucepan over medium heat. Add the onion and sauté until lightly browned, about 5 minutes. Add the garlic and sauté 1 minute. Stir in the tomatoes, chipotles, adobo sauce, oregano, thyme, bay leaves, pepper, and salt. As the tomatoes soften, press them, then add 1/2 cup of water or dark beer. Continue pressing the tomatoes until they turn into a rough sauce. Add the chorizo and shiitakes. Simmer 10 minutes. Fill the tortillas with the filling and top with avocado.

MAKE IT SIMPLE: Use a large can of crushed fire-roasted tomatoes instead of cooking your own tomatoes. If you do this, just combine everything in the pan at the same time and simmer for 10 minutes.

Mole Tacos with Seared Zucchini, Wilted Chard, and Pepitas

Tacos de Calabacín en Mole Poblano, Alcegas y Pepitas

This taco packs a lot of deep flavors, partly from seared caramelized zucchini, but primarily from the mole sauce, which contains a lot of ingredients. For me, making mole is meditative, and I don't mind spending the time making it on a lazy afternoon in my patio kitchen. If you are passionate about food and cooking, though, I strongly urge you to try making your own mole at least once! If you don't want to spend all that time, or work with a page of ingredients, you can easily use a storebought version and turn this into a super quick taco recipe. **Note:** The most commonly available vegan mole is the Doña María brand. Be aware that in other brands the "natural ingredients" can mean chicken stock.

REGION: CASA DE JASON | HEAT LEVEL: 3 | MAKES 12 TACOS

The Filling
1 tablespoon olive oil
4 medium zucchini, cut into 3-inch x 3/4-inch strips
1/2 teaspoon salt
1 cup mole (see headnote)

The Tortillas
12 (5 to 6-inch) corn tortillas

The Toppings
Roasted and salted pepitas
Rough Salted Chile Powder (page 199)
Wilted Chard in Mojo de Ajo (page 199)

1. Heat the oil in a large skillet or sauté pan over a high heat. Add the zucchini and salt. Sear the zucchini, stirring it every 15 to 20 seconds, until it is very well browned. Reduce the heat to medium. Add the mole and stir for about 2 minutes. Remove the pan from the heat.

2. Warm the tortillas. It is particularly important to make sure your tortillas aren't dry, or else the mole will make them fall part. Fill the tortillas with the zucchini and mole, then top with the chard, pepitas, and chile powder.

MAKE IT LOW-FAT: Dice the zucchini into 3/4-inch cubes and sauté it in a dry pan over medium-high heat until well browned. As soon as it is browned, add in 1/4 cup of water and give everything a quick stir. Allow the water to cook out. Reduce the heat to medium. Add the mole and simmer for about 2 minutes.

Tacos with a Durango Stew

Tacos de Caldillo Durangueño

These tacos are based on a *caldillo Durangueño,* a stew from Durango that features a sauce made from chiles pasados, poblanos, and tomatoes. Chiles pasados are fire-roasted green chiles that are then dried and used in sauces and chile powders. They have the smoky flavor from the grill and an intensified sweet flavor from the drying process. It's an interesting spin on the classic dried red chile, and it makes for a vivacious taco.

REGION: DURANGO AND NORTHERN MEXICO | HEAT LEVEL: 4 | MAKES 8 TACOS

The Filling (choose either pinto beans or seitan)

1 poblano chile, pan-roasted or fire-roasted

3 pasado chiles, stemmed and rehydrated or 6 dried large red chiles

3 plum tomatoes, roughly chopped

1/4 cup chopped onion

2 cloves garlic

1/2 teaspoon salt

1/2 teaspoon ground black pepper

2 tablespoons olive oil

2 cups cooked pinto beans, rinsed or 2 cups chopped seitan

The Tortillas

8 (5 to 6-inch) thick corn tortillas or 16 tortillas (2 for each taco)

The Toppings

Shredded cabbage

Sliced radish

Fried chiles de árbol (page 201)

Taco Guacamole Salsa (page 215)

1. Remove the seeds and stem from the roasted poblano and give it a few rough chops. Using a molcajete or mortar and pestle, smash the chiles pasados and poblano into a rough paste and set aside. Alternatively, you can pulse the chiles in a food processor until you have a rough paste.

2. In a blender or food processor, puree the tomatoes, onion, garlic, salt, and pepper. Heat the oil in a sauté pan over just above a medium heat. Add the pureed tomato sauce and fry until it tightens up, stirring slowly, 3 to 4 minutes. Add the pasado/poblano paste and the seitan or beans. Fry 2 to 3 minutes longer. You can fill your taco at this point, or reduce the heat to low and let the filling simmer for 20 minutes to intensify the flavors. Warm the tortillas, fill them, and top with any or all of the toppings.

MAKE IT SIMPLE: Instead of chopping and smashing the pasados and poblano, just puree them with the tomatoes, onion, etc.

MAKE IT LOW-FAT: Don't fry the sauce. Simply add the pureed tomato/onion mix to the pan along with the chiles and the seitan or beans and simmer over medium-low heat for about 10 minutes.

Hominy and Seitan Tacos in Roasted Garlic Cascabel Sauce

*Tacos de Pozole y Seitan en Salsa de
Chile Cascabel y Ajo Asado*

I love using cascabel chiles in this taco for their pure red chile flavor. They are a nice looking chile, so I always put a few on the plate for presentation. The contrasting flavor of the hominy (aka *pozole),* with the chewier seitan, all work together to make a very rustic-flavored taco. This is one of my favorite taco creations. Make them low-fat by simmering the seitan and hominy in the sauce instead of sautéing in oil. If you don't want to use seitan, substitute potatoes, zucchini, chayote, mushrooms, or any vegetable that will provide a substantial texture. Just sauté the vegetables at a medium heat long enough to brown them before adding the sauce. You can even use pinto beans (but don't sauté them).

REGION: CASA DE JASON | HEAT LEVEL: 3 | MAKES 8 TACOS

The Filling (choose either seitan strips or portobellos)
10 cascabel chiles or 4 guajillo chiles
1/2 cup rehydrating liquid (after rehydrating the chiles)
10 cloves garlic, pan-roasted
1/2 teaspoon dried oregano
3/4 teaspoon salt
1 tablespoon olive oil
2 cups seitan strips or 2 portobello mushrooms, cut into 1/2-inch thick strips
1 cup cooked, rinsed hominy

The Tortillas
8 thick (5 to 6-inch) corn tortillas

The Toppings
Rough Salted Chile Powder (page 199)
A sprinkle of chopped roasted and salted peanuts per taco

1. Bring a small pot of water to a simmer, add the cascabels, and simmer until soft, about 10 minutes. Reserve 1/2 cup of the simmering liquid and remove the stems from the chiles. In a blender or food processor, puree the chiles, roasted garlic, reserved simmering liquid, oregano, and salt. Set aside.

2. Heat the oil in a sauté pan over medium heat. Add the seitan and sauté until lightly browned, about 5 minutes. Add the reserved sauce and hominy and simmer until the sauce thickens, about 5 minutes.

3. Warm the tortillas. Fill them with the seitan hominy mixture and finish them off with a rough salted chile powder to taste and a sprinkle of chopped roasted salted peanuts.

Hen-of-the-Woods Tacos with Coconut Milk and Poblano Strips

Tacos de Pollo de Bosque en Leche de Coco con Rajas

Creamy and robust, this taco is a riff on a classic Southwestern taco, but I use mushrooms and coconut milk instead of chicken and cream. It has a smooth, creamy texture that keeps inviting another bite. I am usually full on two of these tacos, but the spinach and mushrooms enrobed in garlicky coconut milk always tempt me for a third. If hen-of-the-woods mushrooms are unavailable, use oyster mushrooms or even plain white button mushrooms.

REGION: SOUTHWESTERN U.S. | HEAT LEVEL: 3 | MAKES 12 TACOS

The Filling (choose either the mushrooms or seitan strips)

2 poblano chiles, pan-roasted or fire-roasted

1 tablespoon olive oil

1 small onion, cut into 1/4-inch wide strips

4 cloves garlic, minced

2 cups unsweetened coconut milk

3/4 teaspoon salt

1 pound hen-of-the-woods mushrooms, chopped into bite-size pieces; or 4 cups chopped seitan or vegan "chicken" strips

4 cups sliced chard or 8 cups baby spinach leaves

The Tortillas

12 (5 to 6-inch) corn tortillas

The Toppings

Salsa Verde (page 218)

Chopped roasted jalapeños

1. Remove the stem and seeds from the poblanos and chop them into 1/2-inch pieces. Set aside.

2. Heat the oil in a skillet over a medium heat. Add the onion and sauté until it is just browned. Add the garlic and sauté for 2 more minutes. Add the coconut milk, chopped poblanos, and salt and give it a quick stir.

3. Add the mushrooms to the skillet, along with the greens and give everything a couple stirs to combine them. Simmer this until the greens are completely soft. If you are using spinach, this will only take 4 to 5 minutes. If you are using chard, it will take 7 to 8 minutes. If you have the time, reduce the heat to low and let this stew for another 30 minutes so all the flavors can meld.

4. Warm the tortillas, fill them, and top with salsa verde and chopped roasted jalapeños.

Tacos with Hot Dogs in Tomato Salsa

Tacos de Salchichas

I laughed the first time I saw these tacos at a taquería and laughed even harder when I discovered just how popular they are. Tacos de Salchichas are none other than hot dog tacos in a bright tomato sauce. That's right. Hot dog tacos. Not only that, there are two versions of them. One version rolls the hotdog in a tortilla and fries it, making it a hot dog taco dorado. The second version, this version, is a taco de guisado. You can, of course, use vegan hot dogs if you want, but I just couldn't bring myself to do it, so I made a slightly more refined version with Tofurky beer brats.

REGION: MEXICO CITY | HEAT LEVEL: 4 | MAKES 6 TACOS

The Filling

1 tablespoon olive oil

3 Tofurky beer brats, sliced into 1/2-inch thick disks

1/2 cup dark beer or ale (I prefer ale)

1 small white onion, halved and thinly sliced

4 plum tomatoes, quartered

1 cup chopped fresh cilantro

1 teaspoon dried Mexican oregano

3 dried chiles de árbol, crushed

3/4 teaspoon salt

The Tortillas

6 (5 to 6-inch) corn tortillas

The Toppings

Lime wedges

1. Heat the oil in a saucepan or deep skillet over a medium heat. Add the sliced beer brats and cook them, stirring occasionally, until they are browned, about 5 minutes. Stir in the beer or ale and allow it to evaporate (it will only take a couple of minutes), then add the onion and cook them until they are lightly browned, about 5 minutes. Add the tomatoes and let them cook down into a sauce, pressing on the tomatoes with a large spoon as they are cooking to help them turn into sauce more quickly.

2. Once the tomatoes cook down into a sauce, add the cilantro, oregano, crushed chiles de árbol, and salt and cook this for another 3 minutes. Fill the tortillas and serve with lime wedges.

Tacos with Vegan Sausage, Seitan, and Chorizo

Tacos de Discada Norteña

This is unabashedly a meat alternative-lover's taco. It's perfect when you want something incredibly hearty, or you have meat-eating friends coming over that enjoy meat alternatives. This taco was developed in the northern states of Mexico and gained popularity among the agricultural workers. The original *discada* was cooked on discarded plow disks, which are shaped similarly to a large wok. Discada Norteña has many variations, but it almost always features beer or cola, onions, tomatoes, salt, and pepper, with the remaining flavorings being personalized by the cook.

REGION: NORTHERN MEXICO | HEAT LEVEL: 3 | MAKES 12 TACOS

The Filling
2 tablespoons olive oil

2 links vegan sausage (I prefer Tofurky beer brats), chopped

3 portobello mushrooms, cut into 1-inch thick pieces

1/4 cup chopped white onion

4 plum tomatoes, chopped 6 cloves garlic, minced

2 chipotles in adobo, chopped

2 cups seitan strips

1 1/2 cups vegan chorizo

3/4 teaspoon salt (I prefer mesquite smoked salt)

3/4 teaspoon black pepper

1 teaspoon maple syrup

1 (12-ounce) bottle dark beer or cola (I prefer beer)

1/4 cup tequila blanco, optional

Juice of 2 limes

The Tortillas
12 thick (5 to 6-inch) corn tortillas or flour tortillas

The Toppings
Guajillo Chile Salsa (page 217) or Green Salsa with Avocado (page 214)

Whole roasted jalapeños

Basic guacamole (page 234)

Heat the oil in a wok or a large skillet over medium heat. Add the vegan sausage and sauté until it is slightly browned, about 5 minutes, then move it to the sides of the wok. Add the portobellos and sauté until they no longer look raw, 5 to 6 minutes. Add the onion, tomatoes, garlic, chipotles, seitan strips, chorizo, salt, pepper, maple syrup, beer or cola, and tequila, if using. Simmer until everything cooks down and you have a very thick sauce, about 15 minutes. Stir in the lime juice and remove the wok from the heat. When I serve these, I usually put out both types of salsa and let people choose which one they want, or even both. I only put out the jalapeños if I have time to make them and I know my guests prefer spicy food.

Tacos with Purslane in Salsa Verde

Tacos de Verdolagas en Salsa Verde

Verdologas, known in English as purslane, is commonly stewed with salsa verde for taco fillings and other dishes. In Mexico, it is part of a family of edible greens called *quelites*. I had never had it until I found some growing in my backyard, and my wife pointed it out to me. I'm glad she did, because otherwise I would have torn it out of the ground and discarded it. Verdolagas has a strong, bitter taste if you don't cook it long enough, but when cooked for about twenty minutes or so, the leaves develop a minty sweetness. They are hearty leaves that keep a lot of volume as they cook, making them a perfect taco filling. If you don't have verdolagas available, you can use other hearty greens like kale and chard. They won't taste the same, but this is basically a taco of hearty greens cooked in salsa verde.

REGION: EVERYWHERE IN MEXICO | HEAT LEVEL: 5 | MAKES 6 TACOS

The Filling
2 tablespoons olive oil
2 cups Salsa Verde (page 218)
4 cups chopped purslane (verdolagas) leaves
2 serrano chiles, minced

The Toppings
Queso Fresco (page 205) or pepitas
Basic guacamole (page 234) or chopped avocado
3 to 5 whole pan-roasted garlic cloves per taco

The Tortillas
6 (5 to 6-inch) corn tortillas

Heat the oil in a large saucepan over medium heat. Add the salsa verde and fry it for about 5 minutes. Add the purslane and serranos. Reduce the heat to medium low and stew for about 20 minutes. Prepare the toppings. Warm the tortillas, fill them with the stewed purslane, and top the taco as desired.

MAKE IT LOW FAT: Simply omit the oil and don't worry about frying the salsa verde. Just simmer the chopped purslane, serranos, and salsa verde for about 20 minutes.

How to Host a Taco Party

I love to entertain and tell stories. For me, food isn't just a tasty bite, the food experience is a story waiting to be told and a good one always gets a smile. It's fun making people happy and one of the best ways to make your friends and family happy is to host a taco party. That social experience is part of the story of food. These can be informal gatherings of just a few people on up to big events with music, lights, dancing, and more. These taco parties even have a name: taquiza.

Most taquizas are informal with just a few people standing around a grill or kitchen table with tortillas in hand, but some of them can get quite large. While it's easy to put together a taquiza for four or five people, putting one together for thirty is a big production and requires logistical skills to pull off. Here are a few tips to pull off a large taquiza.

Serve Three Fillings and Three Salsas: I generally serve three fillings, three salsas, and a variety of toppings. With just three fillings and three salsas, you can create nine different tacos. Plus, if you reserve the number of fillings you make, you'll have people asking you to do it again and you can create a completely different taquiza. My ideal choice for the three fillings is a bean filling, a taco de comal or cazuela filling, and a taco de asador so I can get my grill going.

Start a Day Ahead: Start cooking a day ahead of time. That's when I usually make beans, pickled onions, condiments that will last a day, and the salsas. The day of the event, I make my other fillings, the guacamole, and the tortillas.

Enlist Help: I used to try and pull off large events by myself, but it meant I didn't get to participate in the party as much as I would like and I denied other people the pleasure of giving back by helping out. If you have some friends that are willing to help you make a few ingredients or do some shopping, take them up on it! No one wants a stressed out host and cooking with your friends is fun. Even if they aren't perfect cooks, a joyful experience is more important than perfect food.

Ask People to Bring Drinks and Other Goodies: Cooking for a lot of people can get expensive. Don't be shy about asking people to bring drinks, beer, tequila, salsas, chips, a salad, or anything else you think will go well with your tacos. Just tell them specifically what brands you want and where to get them so you don't have something show up at your vegan taquiza that isn't vegan.

Set Your Salsa and Condiment Bar away from Your Grill or Cooking Area: Don't set up your taco "assembly" bar near your cooking area. You want to divert traffic away so you have some space to play. On a related note, you don't want a lot of other stuff going on around your taco bar. It's no fun trying to put together a taco while you're getting bumped and jostled.

Don't Use Your Best, Breakable Serving Vessels and Dinnerware: If you have a lot of people trying to make tacos, someone may accidentally drop something that you really don't want broken. This is especially true if you are serving alcohol, so don't set everything out in expensive bowls and plates.

Let People Make Their Own Tacos: It's part of the experience! Let people assemble their own tacos. Not only do they get a personalized taco, they do all that work.

Work That Grill: If you have a grill, I encourage you to use it when you are hosting a taco party. The smoke and open flames are intoxicating and you look awesome when you are working it.

Find a Friend to Make Tortillas: If you are at the grill, you probably don't have time to make fresh tortillas and there is nothing like a fresh tortilla just off the griddle to lift your taquiza to a state of soul-satisfying extravagance. Ask a knowledgeable friend to make the tortillas during the taquiza. If you need to make them ahead of time, make sure the tortillas stay moist and warm and try to make cooking the tortillas the last bit of cooking you do.

The Big Cheat: One of my local Mexican markets makes incredible salsa fresh every day. If I am going to be pressed for time, I purchase my salsa from them instead of making it. If you are in the same position, I highly encourage you to purchase your favorite salsa instead of making it.

Have fun!: As the taquiza host, your job isn't just to serve good food, it's to provide an enjoyable experience and you enjoying yourself is part of that. It rubs off on your guests, so relax, make some good food, eat some good food, and spend some time with your friends.

If you are hosting a small taquiza, many of these tips still apply. You probably won't have to worry about traffic issues and crowding, but even if I am doing a taquiza for four, I still ask people to bring drinks and help out in the kitchen. And if they're not willing to contribute? I become the Taco Nazi. No taco for you!

Baja-Style Taco with Lobster Mushrooms (at top, page 121); Mushroom Taco (page 117)

CHAPTER

7

Tacos de Comal

"Tacos made with sautéed fillings."

When tacos de comal are served at a taquería, they are referred to as "tacos a la plancha." A *plancha* is a large, smooth metal griddle. The ingredients are placed on the plancha and quickly sautéed or seared on the super-hot surface. In a way, a plancha is like a giant comal. It's just a smooth, flat cooking surface, and that's just a really long way of saying you should cook these in a large skillet.

I strongly suggest using a skillet that is at least 12-inches in diameter. Since the fillings for these tacos are cooked quickly and at a fairly high heat, you don't want to crowd the pan with ingredients. That just slows down the cook time and that won't do any favors for the texture of the food. Also, the heavier the pan, the more evenly it will cook, making a better taco.

Although these tacos require you to be at the stove the whole time, many of them cook very quickly. When I am in a rush, these are the tacos I tend to make, and I often use the "Make It Simple" options to save time. Plus, they are a lot of fun to cook! You get to see the ingredients transform immediately and, soon after, turn into delicious tacos. Just keep an eye on the ingredients so they don't burn, and you'll become a maestro taquero.

The easiest tacos de comal to make are the Tacos with Potatoes and Poblano Strips, the Mushroom Tacos (using your favorite vegan cheese alternative instead of making the ones in the recipe), and the Ten-Minute Seitan Carnitas. Tacos Rápidos are also incredibly easy and, as you can tell from the name, quick to make.

Mushroom Tacos

Tacos de Hongos

The mixed mushrooms are the stars of this taco, so I leave them fairly unadorned so their flavors can shine. Oyster mushrooms give the taco a heavily browned flavor; the shiitakes add earthiness; and the creminis a sort of mellowness, all working together to provide a complex flavor in every bite. The taco is topped off with roasted habanero crema for a piquant bite. For less bite, omit the habanero. These tacos can be a little light, so I sometimes add a cup of cooked black beans at the end of the recipe to make the filling heartier. (See photo on page 124.)

REGION: CASA DE JASON | HEAT LEVEL: 7 | MAKES 6 TACOS

The Filling
1 guajillo chile (to make guajillo powder) or 1 teaspoon chili powder
2 tablespoon olive oil
4 cups oyster mushrooms, chopped into big 2-inch pieces
10 to 12 small fresh shiitake mushrooms, stems removed and cut in half
10 to 12 cremini mushrooms, quartered
4 cloves garlic, minced
1 1/2 tablespoons chopped epazote, optional
3/4 teaspoon salt

The Tortillas
6 (5 to 6-inch) corn tortillas

The Toppings
1 cup Crema (page 204)
1 roasted habanero, optional
Queso Fresco (page 205) or raw pine nuts

1. Heat a dry skillet over a medium heat. Add the guajillo and toast it for 30 seconds on each side. Use a spatula to press it flat on the skillet to maximize the area that gets toasted. Remove the stem. Grind it into powder and set aside.

2. Heat the oil in a large skillet over high heat. Stir in the oyster mushrooms only, then let them cook for 1 to 2 minutes until they begin to brown. Stir again, and let them sit again. Continue to do this until they are greatly reduced in size and heavily browned and crispy. This will take 10 to 12 minutes. Turn the heat down to medium. Add the shiitakes and cremini mushrooms. Sauté until soft. Add the garlic, epazote, if using, reserved guajillo powder, and salt and sauté another 2 minutes. Remove the pan from the heat.

3. In a blender or food processor puree the roasted habanero, if using, with the crema and transfer to a bowl. Warm the tortillas. Fill each taco with the mushrooms, then top with the crema, and finish them off with a sprinkle of vegan queso fresco.

Enchilada-Style Tacos

Tacos Potosinos

These tacos remind me of how my mom taught me to make enchiladas, first by passing the tortilla through a sauce and then into the frying pan. It makes the tortilla soft and flavorful. They don't fry long enough to get crispy, just long enough to tighten up the tortilla and sauce. Because the tortillas are fried, these are best eaten moments after they are made, or they can become gummy. Skip the frying process if you want to minimize your fat intake. These tacos are famous throughout Mexico, especially in the state of San Luis Potosí, where they were invented and are served in batches of three. I provide two filling options: mushroom and seitan. **Note:** If you don't have trumpet mushrooms, use 4 cups chopped oyster mushroom or 3 cups sliced cremini mushrooms. The cooking technique is the same.

REGION: SAN LUIS POTOSÍ | HEAT LEVEL: 2 | MAKES 12 TACOS

The Sauce
1 ancho chile, rehydrated
4 plum tomatoes, pan roasted
1/2 medium white onion
3 cloves garlic
1/2 teaspoon dried oregano
1/2 teaspoon dried thyme
3/4 teaspoon salt

The Filling (choose either the mushrooms or seitan)
1 tablespoon olive oil
8 trumpet mushrooms (or other type of mushroom, see Note), cut into 2-inch x
    1/2-inch strips or 2 1/2 cups shredded seitan
1/4 teaspoon salt

The Tortillas
12 (6-inch) thin corn tortillas (storebought tortillas work well in this recipe)
Olive oil, for frying

The Toppings
8 to 10 green beans, cut into 3 inch long pieces
1 large carrot, cut into 3-inch x 1/4 inch sticks
2 medium Yukon gold potatoes, sliced into 3-inch x 1/4-inch sticks
2 cups shredded lettuce
Pickled serrano or jalapeño slices

1. Make the Sauce: Simmer the ancho in a small saucepan of water for 10 minutes, until soft. Remove the stem. Roast the tomatoes in a skillet. In a blender or food processor, puree the ancho, tomatoes, onion, garlic, oregano, thyme, and salt. Transfer the puree to the same saucepan used to simmer the anchos. Simmer 7 to 8 minutes, then turn the heat to low to keep the sauce warm while you make the filling.

2. **Make the filling:** If using **mushrooms,** heat the oil in a wide sauté pan over medium-high heat. Add the mushrooms and salt and sauté until the mushrooms start to brown, 5 to 6 minutes. Remove from the heat. If using **seitan,** pulse the seitan in a blender a few times until you have smaller, shredded pieces. Heat the oil in a wide sauté pan to just above a medium heat. Add the seitan and salt and sauté for about 5 minutes. Set aside.

3. **Make the toppings:** Bring 4 cups of water to a simmer in a large saucepan over high heat. Reduce the heat to a simmer, add 1 teaspoon salt, then add the green beans, carrot, and potato sticks. Simmer for 5 minutes, then drain and set aside.

4. **Assemble the tacos:** Add enough oil to a deep skillet to come about 1/4-to 1/2-inch up the sides of the pan and heat to a medium-high heat. Quickly dip a tortilla through the sauce and then immediately into the oil. Fry the tortilla for about 30 seconds, then remove from the oil and transfer to a plate. Fill the tortilla on one side and roll it close. Repeat this until you are out of tortillas or filling. These are typically served three to a plate and topped with the green beans, carrots, potatoes, shredded lettuce, and pickled chiles.

MAKE IT SIMPLE: Instead of pan-roasting the tomatoes and rehydrating the ancho, puree a 14.5 ounce can of crushed fire-roasted tomatoes with the sauce ingredients except for the chile, which you can omit. Transfer the puree to a saucepan, simmer for about 5 minutes, and you have nearly instant Tacos Potosinos sauce. Quickly dunk the tortillas in the sauce and skip the frying part of the recipe. Make the filling, but just chop everything instead of making small cuts and shredding. Cook them the same way. Cut toppings into cubes instead of sticks. It takes about 15 to 20 minutes.

MAKE IT LOW-FAT: Skip the frying part of the recipe. Instead of sautéing the filling in oil, sauté it in a dry pan if you are using mushrooms. The mushrooms will brown on their own. If you are using seitan, en need to sauté it. Just shred it and you are good to go.

Read Before You Cook!
• • • • • • • • • • • • • • • • • •

Arranging the set-up on and around your stove efficiently will save you a lot of heartache. I usually work from right to left. I place my sauce on the right burner and the oil on the left burner so they are close together. On the counter at left, I have a plate to receive the fried tortillas and fill them, and to the left of that, a plate to which I transfer the filled and rolled tortillas. It allows me to work quickly and transfer the fried tortillas to the plate fast enough that they don't fall apart. It also minimizes the cleanup, since I'm not dripping food as I transfer the tortillas from one pan to the next.

Mushroom Chorizo Tacos with Black Beans and Chayote

Tacos de Chorizo de Champiñones, Chayote y Frijoles Picados

These tacos have a beautiful flavor; slightly spicy, slightly sweet, a little tangy, with an earthy undertone. You can easily cheat with these tacos by using a storebought vegan chorizo, but I think taking the extra time to develop your own chorizo using the wild mushrooms is well worth the wait.

Note: Don't worry about being precise when chopping the beans. Your goal is to get bits of cooked black beans.

REGION: CASA DE JASON | HEAT LEVEL: 2 | MAKES 8 TACOS

The Filling
1 large chayote squash or zucchini, cut into 1/2-inch dice
2 teaspoons olive oil
1/4 teaspoon salt
1/4 cup water
1/2 cup cooked black beans, rinsed and chopped (see Note)
4 cups mushroom chorizo (page 66) or your favorite vegan chorizo

The Tortillas
6 (5 to 6-inch) corn tortillas

The Toppings
Pico de Gallo (page 216)
Queso Fresco (page 205) or chopped avocado
Toasted pepitas

1. Heat the oil in a large skillet over high heat. Add the chayote and salt. Sear the chayote until the skin looks partially blackened. Turn the heat down to medium. Add the water to the pan and cook until the water evaporates. Add the chopped black beans and the chorizo to the skillet with the chayote. Stir to combine, then remove the skillet from the heat.

2. Warm the tortillas. Fill the tortillas with the chorizo mixture, then top with the Pico de Gallo, followed by the vegan queso fresco, and finally, a sprinkling of toasted pepitas.

MAKE IT LOW-FAT: You can skip the oil in both parts of the recipe. Sear the chayote in a dry pan over a medium high heat instead of a high heat until it is partially blackened and then add in 1/2 cup of water instead of 1/4 cup.

Baja-Style Tacos with Lobster Mushrooms

Tacos de Oreja de Puerco Estilo Baja

These tacos are colorful morsels that showcase a strong California influence, owing to the vegan chipotle mayo and the option of using either corn or flour tortillas. It's a succulent contrast between the depth of the black beans, the hearty, almost oceanic flavor of the lobster mushrooms, and the brightness from the lime. On top of that, you have creaminess and heat from the vegan mayo and crunch from the cabbage. It's a complex flavored taco that is incredibly easy to make. Lobster mushrooms are expensive, but you can substitute tempeh, trumpet mushrooms, or a pound of oyster mushrooms.

REGION: BAJA | HEAT LEVEL: 3 | MAKES 8 TACOS

The Filling
8 ounces fresh lobster mushrooms, chopped or 1 cup dried lobster mushrooms
1 tablespoon olive oil
2 cloves garlic, minced
1/3 teaspoon salt
1 tablespoon fresh lime juice
1/2 cup refried black beans

The Tortillas
8 (5 to 6-inch) corn or flour tortillas

The Toppings
1 cup vegan mayonnaise
2 chipotles in adobo
1 cup shredded fresh purple cabbage

1. If using fresh lobster mushrooms: Chop the lobster mushrooms into bite-size pieces.

2. If using dried lobster mushrooms: Place the dried lobster mushroom pieces in a bowl and pour steaming water over them. Let them sit in the water for about 10 minutes. Remove them from the water and pat them dry.

3. Heat the oil in a large skillet to just above a medium heat. Add the lobster mushrooms and give them a quick stir. Sauté until they begin to brown, about 5 minutes. Add the garlic and salt and sauté these for another 2 minutes. Remove the mushrooms from the heat and immediately pour the lime juice over them. Give them a quick stir and set them aside. In a separate pan, warm the beans.

4. Puree the vegan mayo and chipotles in a blender or food processor. Transfer the chipotle mayo to a small bowl. Warm the tortillas. Spread a very thin layer of beans over the tortillas, leaving a 1/2 inch edge around the tortillas. Add the sautéed lobster mushrooms, then the vegan chipotle mayo, and finish the tacos off with a sprinkle of cabbage.

Tacos with Purple Potatoes and Roasted Poblanos

Tacos de Papas Moradas y Rajas

This is a simple taco of potatoes and roasted chiles. It's super easy to make and only has a few ingredients. I used purple potatoes in the recipe, not because they really taste different than any other waxy potato, but because they look cool.

REGION: MEXICO CITY | HEAT LEVEL: 3 | MAKES 12 TACOS

The Filling
4 poblano chiles or jalapeños, pan roasted, stem and seeds removed
1 tablespoon olive oil or Mojo de Ajo (page 60)
6 small purple potatoes, cut into 3/4-inch cubes (about 3 cups)
3/4 teaspoon salt
1/3 cup water
1 tablespoon diced epazote, optional, but recommended

The Tortillas
8 (5 to 6-inch) corn tortillas

The Toppings
Salsa Verde (page 218)
Queso Fresco (page 205) or chopped avocado

1. Cut the roasted chiles into thin strips about 3-inches long. Heat the oil in a large skillet over a medium heat. Add the potatoes and salt and sauté until lightly browned, about 5 minutes. You will need to slowly stir the potatoes so they don't stick to the pan. Once they are browned, add the water and epazote, if using. Cook out all the water and then remove the potatoes from the heat. The potatoes should be browned on the outside and al dente on the inside. If they are still crunchy, add another half cup of water and cook until it evaporates.

2. As soon as the potatoes are off the heat, warm your tortillas one at a time by placing them on top of the potatoes for about 10 seconds each. Fill the tortillas with potatoes, poblanos, salsa, and then vegan queso fresco.

MAKE IT ON THE GRILL: Toss the chopped potatoes in the oil and salt and transfer them to a grill pan. Make sure the bottom of your grill pan is well oiled or else the potatoes will stick to it. Grill the potatoes until they are crispy on the outside and soft on the inside. Also, go ahead and roast the poblanos on the grill since you've already got it going.

Cactus Tacos

Tacos de Nopales

Nopales are prickly pear cactus pads. They take some care to work with properly, but when you do, they are amazing. They have just a little tang and a nice bright flavor. I usually find the fresh ones at a Mexican market. You can make these either in a pan or on the grill.

Note: If you are using jarred nopales, make sure you rinse them thoroughly before adding them to the pan and sear away any of the liquid that comes out of them. If you don't, they'll taste briny and have a slimy texture.

REGION: EVERYWHERE | HEAT LEVEL: 0 TO 5 | MAKES 12 TACOS

The Filling
2 cactus paddles or 3 cups sliced jarred nopales (see Note)
1 tablespoon olive oil
1/4 teaspoon salt

The Tortillas
12 (5 to 6-inch) corn tortillas

The Toppings
Pickled Jalapeños (page 203)
Rough Salted Chile Powder (page 199)
Queso Fresco (page 205) or pepitas
Green Salsa with Avocado (page 214)
Chopped fresh cilantro

1. If you are using fresh nopales, hold the cactus paddle with tongs so you don't get thorns in your hands. Over the sink, scrape the cactus paddle with the back of a knife until all the spines are removed. If you have any doubt as to whether the tiny spines have been removed, you can cut away the nodes from which the spines protrude. Once all the spines are removed, trim away the outer rim of the cactus paddle, including the spot where the paddle was cut from the plant. Cut the paddle into strips about 1/2-inch wide and 3-inches long.

2. Heat the oil in a sauté pan over high heat. Add the cactus strips and sauté these until they are partially blackened. Remove them from the heat and immediately sprinkle them with salt.

3. Warm the tortillas. Fill the tortillas with nopales and any of the toppings.

MAKE IT ON THE GRILL: You can toss the cactus paddles in oil and salt once you have removed the spines and tough outer rim, then grill the whole cactus paddles until they are blistered on both sides. Once they are grilled, slice them up and serve them in your tacos.

Working with Nopales

• • • • • • • • • • • • • •

Nopales are the cactus paddles from the prickly pear cactus. You can usually find them in Mexican markets sold whole or already sliced. If you buy the whole pad, check to see if the spines have been removed. If they haven't, you can scrape them away with the back of a knife. Hold the paddle with tongs and wear gloves. I usually buy the sliced fresh ones because the market has already done that work for me.

Sonoran Tacos

Tacos Estilo Sonora

Sonoran cuisine has a strong affinity to the Southwestern U.S. and this taco is no exception. It uses a flour tortilla instead of the more typical corn tortilla. The preparation is very simple and straightforward, creating a taco with a few strong elements that create several layers of flavor in each bite. I've provided three variations, because I can't decide which one is my favorite! If I have some extra time, I turn these into tacos de asador and grill the filling instead of sautéing it.

REGION: SONORA | HEAT LEVEL: 5 | MAKES 8 TACOS

The Filling (choose either the beans, portobello, or seitan)

1 tablespoon olive oil

1 medium onion, cut into 1/4-inch strips

2 cups cooked pinto beans, rinsed, or 2 large portobello mushrooms, chopped into bite-size pieces, or 2 cups cubed seitan

2 cloves garlic, minced

3/4 teaspoon salt

3/4 teaspoon freshly ground pepper

4 Anaheim chiles or any long green chile, pan- roasted and cut into strips (pan-roast the chiles while you caramelize the onion)

The Tortillas

8 (6-inch) flour tortillas

The Toppings

Chiles de Árbol Salsa (page 220)

Queso Fresco (page 205) or chopped avocado

1. Heat the oil in a large skillet over medium-high heat. Add the onion and sauté until well caramelized, 8 to 10 minutes. Remove the onions from the skillet and return the skillet to the heat. Add the filling of your choice (either the beans, mushrooms, or seitan).

2. Pintos: Lower the heat to medium. Add the beans and garlic to the pan and sauté for about 2 minutes. Season them with the salt and pepper, and then remove them from the heat.

3. Portobellos: Keep the heat at medium-high. Add the portobellos to the pan and sauté for 4 to 5 minutes. Add the garlic about 1 minute before you are done cooking the mushrooms. Season with salt and pepper and remove from the heat.

4. Seitan: Keep the heat at medium-high. Add 1 more teaspoon of oil to the pan. Add the seitan and sauté it for about 5 minutes, until it is well browned. Add the garlic and sauté this for 1 more minute. Season the seitan with salt and pepper and remove it from the heat.

5. Warm your tortillas. Add the filling, followed by the sliced roasted chiles, then the salsa, and a sprinkling of vegan queso fresco.

MAKE IT SIMPLE: Instead of pan-roasting the chiles, just remove the stems and seeds and cut them into strips. Add the chiles, onion, the garlic, the filling, salt, pepper, and oil to the pan all at the same time. Turn the pan to a medium heat and cook this until the onion is lightly browned. It will take you about 10 to 15 minutes to get everything done, but you don't have a bunch of different steps to take and you only need to stir the food every couple of minutes.

MAKE IT LOW-FAT: You can cook the onions without adding any oil to the pan. Just sauté them over a medium high heat in a dry pan, stirring them every minute or so. Once they are browned, add 1/4 cup of water to the pan, give everything a quick stir, and then add your filling of choice, along with the garlic, salt, and pepper. Reduce the heat to medium and cook this until your filling is done, about 2 minutes for the beans, 3 minutes for the mushrooms, and 3 minutes for the seitan.

Tacos with Huitlacoche and Fresh Corn

Tacos de Huitlacoche y Maize Fresco

I love the contrast between fresh and cooked in this recipe. The huitlacoche *(wheat-lah-CO-chay)* has a nice deep flavor, while the fresh corn kernels pop with sweetness. Also known as "corn smut," huitlacoche is a fungus that is a delicacy throughout Mexico. It has a mild earthy flavor that intensifies when lightly cooked. Fresh huitlacoche is difficult to find, but most Mexican markets sell it canned. Just pop the can open, give it a rinse, chop it, and it is ready to cook. It doesn't have the greatest appearance or description, for that matter, but it tastes wonderful once it is cooked, and provides a solid, hearty backdrop for the taco. Top that with some chipotle crema and spicy salsa, and you've got a taco that bursts with flavor.

REGION: CASA DE JASON | HEAT LEVEL: 6 (BASED ON SALSA AMOUNT) | MAKES 6 TACOS

The Filling
1/2 small white onion, cut into 1/4 inch dice (about 1/3 cup)
2 tablespoons chopped fresh epazote, optional but recommended
1 pound huitlacoche, chopped into bite-size pieces
2 tablespoons olive oil
1/2 teaspoon salt
1 ear corn (if you don't have fresh corn, use 1 1/4 cups frozen corn kernels)

The Tortillas
6 (5 to 6-inch) corn tortillas (Salted Lime Tortillas on page 52 are great here)

The Toppings
1 cup Crema (page 204)
2 chipotles in adobo
2 tablespoons cilantro stems
Chiles de Árbol Salsa (page 220)

1. Heat the oil in a sauté pan over a medium heat. Add the onion and epazote, if using. and sauté until the onion is soft, but not quite browned, about 5 minutes. Add the huitlacoche and salt and cook this until all the liquid has cooked out of the pan. Remove the pan from the heat. Cut the corn kernels off the cob, if using fresh corn. Add the kernels to the pan with the huitlacoche and give them a stir.

2. In a blender or food processor, puree the crema with the chipotles in adobo and cilantro stems in a blender or small food processor and then transfer the puree to a small bowl.

3. Warm the tortillas. Fill them with the huitlacoche and fresh corn mixture, then top with the chipotle cilantro crema and chiles de árbol salsa.

Ten-Minute Seitan Carnitas

These are my quick go-to carnitas and are a completely different style of carnitas than Carnitas Micho-acánas. They only take a few minutes to make, and the technique I use makes for a nice crispy and soft contrast, exactly what you are looking for with carnitas. If I am looking for something quick like this, I usually just use a nice storebought tortilla instead of making my own.

Note: You can also use this technique with vegetables such as slightly dried out portobellos, zucchini, chayote, or even sweet potato strips. The key is to brown the outside and then use a little water to soften the inside.

REGION: CASA DE JASON | HEAT LEVEL: 2 | MAKES 4 TACOS

The Filling
1 tablespoon olive oil

2 cups seitan strips (or vegetables—see Note)

2 teaspoons ancho powder or chili powder

A pinch of chipotle powder, optional

1/2 teaspoon dried oregano

1/2 teaspoon ground cumin

1/2 teaspoon salt

1/4 cup water

The Tortillas
4 (6-inch) storebought corn tortillas

The Toppings
Salsa or hot sauce of your choice (try the Roasted Garlic Pequin Chile Sauce on page 228)

1 ripe avocado, diced

1. Heat the oil in a wide sauté pan over medium-high heat. Add the seitan and give it a quick stir. You only need to stir the seitan once every minute or so. Over-stirring it will only prolong the cook time. Once the seitan has developed crispy brown bits, about 7 to 8 minutes in, add the ancho powder, chipotle powder, if using, oregano, cumin, and salt. Give this a quick stir. Immediately add the water to the pan and stir until the water cooks out. This should happen within a minute at most. Remove the pan from the heat.

2. Place the tortillas one at a time on top of the seitan in the pan for about 10 seconds in succession. This will quickly steam them with the residual moisture and heat from the pan. Fill the tortillas with the seitan and top with salsa and then avocado.

Tacos Americanos

These are the classic hard shell tacos served for years in homes and restaurants throughout the U.S. In fact, this is still what most people consider a taco to be. I didn't want to just repeat this style of taco by simply replacing the standard ground meat and cheese with vegan versions, so I added a little extra care to make it more interesting by using beer, ancho powder, and arugula.

Note: If you are soft tortillas, warm them in the oven for 2 minutes at 350°F before filling them.

REGION: USA | HEAT LEVEL: 1 | MAKES 6 TACOS

The Filling
1 small white onion, diced
1 tablespoon olive oil or 2 tablespoons Mojo de Ajo (page 60)
1 1/2 cups ground seitan or cooked brown lentils for a gluten-free option
1/2 cup dark beer or water
1 tablespoon ancho powder or 1 tablespoon chili powder
1/4 teaspoon salt
1/2 teaspoon dried Mexican oregano

The Tortillas
6 hard taco shells, warmed (see Note)

The Toppings
Shredded vegan cheese or chopped avocado
Cholula hot sauce
Baby arugula (use shredded lettuce if you don't have baby arugula available)
Diced tomato

1. Heat the oil in a sauté pan over a medium-high heat. Add the onion and sauté it until it lightly brown, about 4 to 5 minutes. Add the seitan and sauté 3 more minutes. Reduce the heat to medium. Stir in the beer, ancho powder, salt, and oregano. Cook until the beer evaporates. Immediately remove the pan from the heat.

2. Fill the warmed taco shells with the seitan, then the vegan cheese, followed by the hot sauce, then the arugula, and finally the tomato.

Taco Hack!
· · · · · · · ·

You can turn these into tostadas by using tostada shells instead of taco shells and spreading a thin layer of *frijoles refritos* (that's refried beans, gringo) over the tostada before piling on all the other goodies.

Bricklayer Tacos

Tacos de Albañil

This particular style of bricklayers' taco became popular as an afternoon lunch among construction crews in Mexico, hence the name "bricklayers' tacos." Instead of meat and bacon, I use portobello mushrooms in mine and my maple and salt hack for the bacon flavor that is in the traditional taco. If you prefer to use your favorite seitan or other similar ingredient in this recipe, feel free to do so! Theses tacos are very simple and quick to make, but don't compromise on flavor—always a plus in my book.

REGION: MEXICO CITY | HEAT LEVEL: 4 | MAKES 8 TACOS

The Filling (choose either the mushrooms or seitan)

4 large plum tomatoes

1 tablespoon oil

1 medium white onion, cut into 1/2-inch dice (about 1 cup)

2 large portobello mushrooms, cut into 1 1/2-inch dice (use the stems, too) or 3 cups diced seitan

3/4 teaspoon ground black pepper

3/4 teaspoon salt

2 cloves garlic, minced

2 jalapeños, sliced into 1/8 inch thin disks

The Tortillas

8 (5 to 6-inch) corn tortillas

The Toppings

Chopped Guacamole (page 234) (prep this just before you start sautéing your ingredients in the skillet)

Crushed Red Salsa (page 212)

1. Pan-roast the tomatoes. Once they are done, give them a few rough chops. Make sure you keep any of the juice that spills out. Set aside.

2. Heat the oil in a large skillet over medium-high heat. Add the onion and sauté it until it barely starts to brown, 4 to 5 minutes. Add the portobello or seitan, the pepper, and the salt. If you are using the portobellos, sauté until they soften, but not to the point where they release a lot of liquid. If you are using seitan, sauté it until it browns. Add the garlic and jalapeño and sauté 1 more minute. Add the tomatoes and sauté another 2 to 3 minutes, then remove the pan from the heat.

3. Warm the tortillas by placing them one at a time on top of the filling for about 10 seconds each. Fill the tortillas with the filling, then top with guacamole and salsa, fold them closed, and eat!

MAKE IT SIMPLE: Instead of pan roasting the tomatoes, just chop them up. Add all the ingredients from the filling section to the pan at once and turn the pan to a medium heat. Cook this until the onions have completely softened. By the time they are soft, all the other ingredients will have also cooked.

MAKE IT LOW-FAT: You can cook the ingredients the exact same way without oil by sautéing everything in a dry pan. Do not add liquid to replace the oil, or else the ingredients will not cook properly.

Tacos Rápidos with Quick and Easy Pintos Borrachos

This is my fast and simple taco that I make when it's late at night and I don't want to make anything too involved. It's basically a fast cheat on pintos borrachos, jarred salsa, and whatever condiments I have sitting around. I still make the tortillas from scratch for this recipe because I am spoiled now when it comes to tortillas, but even then, it's a very easy recipe.

REGION: CASA DE JASON | HEAT LEVEL: 1 | MAKES 4 TACOS

The Pintos Borrachos
1/2 cup chopped onion
3 cloves garlic, minced
1 (15-ounce) can pinto beans, drained
1/4 cup beer
2 tablespoons chili powder
1 teaspoon cumin
1/4 teaspoon salt

The Tortillas
4 (5 to 6-inch) corn tortillas

The Toppings
Your favorite vegan cheese (I use shredded Daiya brand)
Whatever salsa you have on hand (my favorite is a chipotle salsa for this taco)
Rajas (page 197) or 1 (4-ounce) can diced green chiles

1. In a saucepan, combine the onion, garlic, pinto beans, beer, chili powder, cumin, and salt. Stir them together, then bring to a simmer over medium heat. Simmer for 7 to 8 minutes, stirring every few minutes.

2. To serve, spread about 1/4 cup of the bean mixture onto each tortilla, then top them with the cheese, salsa, and rajas.

CHAPTER

Tacos Dorados

*"Rolled tacos,
fried golden and crisp."*

You may recognize tacos dorados under other aliases, such as *taquitos* and *flautas*. Tacos dorados are rolled closed and fried until crisp. Not the healthiest tacos in the world, but certainly one of the tastiest! Tacos dorados are advanced tacos, so there are no simple versions. However, you can take just about any taco filling, roll it into a tortilla, and fry it to make your own customized tacos dorados. The best ones are made with thin, long, oblong tortillas. Since you only need to roll them closed enough to seal, this shape of tortilla stretches out lengthways so you can line more filling into it. It does, however, take a little practice to press out that shape of tortilla. These work better when I use thin storebought tortillas or day-old handmade tortillas.

• • • • •

When I was very young, my mom made tacos from flour tortillas and roasted veggies. I always looked forward to those. As I got older, I discovered Taco Bell and Jack in the Box, and like most teenagers, I was particularly addicted to the Jack in the Box tacos, which contained fat and salt and were served in a lightly fried tortilla. Essentially, they were a fast-food version of tacos dorados. Looking back, I can't believe I used to eat that way. My health got worse and worse eating such fast food. I feel fortunate now, because my vegan dietary choices made me incredibly healthy. My passion for great vegan food led me to great tacos. I have never looked back.

Though I normally preach making your own tortillas, this should be an exception. Storebought tortillas are drier than homemade, and that makes them crispier. If you do want to press out an oblong tortilla, form your masa ball into a 3-inch long by 1-inch wide oval. You will need a tortilla press that can handle the extra length. Press out the tortilla into a long oval shape wide enough for you to fill it and barely roll it closed. Cook the tortilla as you would a normally shaped tortilla and then fill it and roll it closed. To properly make tacos dorados, you'll need a couple of important techniques, described below.

How to Roll the Tacos: Place the filling along one side of the tortilla and roll it closed starting at that end. Roll it tight, but not so tight that the filling spills out the side. Now here's the important trick. Stick a toothpick through the side of the taco so that it pins the outer flap of the roll to the rest of the rolled taco. This will keep the taco together as you fry it until it crisps enough to hold together on its own.

How to Fry the Tacos: Add enough oil to a pan to come up either 1/2 inch in the pan or enough to cover the rolled taco. The first way conserves oil and the second way is easier. Bring the oil to just above a medium-high heat, about 385°F. Fry the tacos for 2 minutes. If you only added the 1/2 inch of oil, you will need to fry each "side" for 2 minutes. If you added enough to submerge the tacos, 2 minutes will take care of it all. When you serve the tacos, remove the toothpicks.

Tacos Dorados with Plantains, Black Beans, and Roasted Garlic

Tacos Dorados de Plátanos, Frijoles Negros y Ajo Asado

I love how the first taste of this taco is a crisp light corn tortilla, but then it's followed right after by this mix of soft sweetness and dark flavors. Inspired by tropical recipes from the south of Mexico, it features plantains and black beans accented with two different types of chiles and a squeeze of lime to pull everything together. They are highly caloric, but they are so good, I usually eat three or four at a sitting!

REGION: CASA DE JASON | HEAT LEVEL: 1 OR 4 WITH THE SERRANO | MAKES 12 TACOS

The Filling
20 to 25 cloves pan-roasted garlic

2 medium, ripe plantains (the skin should be partially blackened, but not completely blackened and soft)

1 cup cooked black beans, rinsed

1 tablespoon ancho powder

1/4 teaspoon salt

The Tortillas
12 (6-inch) thin corn tortillas

Corn oil, for frying

The Toppings
Crema (page 204)

Pickled Onions (page 203) (prep this well ahead of time)

Serrano chiles, minced

Lime wedges

1. Smash the roasted garlic into a rough paste. Peel and chop the plantains into bite-size pieces. In a bowl, combine the garlic paste, plantains, beans, ancho powder, and salt.

2. Fill each tortilla with about 3 to 4 tablespoons of filling and roll them closed. This works best if you place the filling to one side of the tortilla and roll it closed starting at that side. Place a toothpick through each tortilla to hold the rolled taco closed. Fry the tacos. Top with crema and serve with pickled onions and minced serrano chiles and lime wedges on the side.

MAKE IT SIMPLE: Instead of using the toothpicks, you can fold the tortilla in half instead of rolling it closed. Once the bottom side is fried, quickly flip the taco with a wide spatula and fry the other side.

Tacos Dorados
with Squash Blossoms and Potato
Tacos Dorados de Flores de Calabazas y Papas

Squash blossoms create a nice delicate contrast with the crispy fried tortilla, while lightly salted potato provides substance to the taco. When I make these, I like getting down low towards the pan and watching the squash blossoms cook inside the tortilla. It's the little things like that that make cooking so interesting and fun for me.

REGION: CASA DE JASON | HEAT LEVEL: 3 | MAKES 12 TACOS

The Filling
12 squash blossoms
Salt
4 medium red potatoes, cut into 1/2-inch dice (about 2 cups diced)
3 tablespoons minced epazote, optional but recommended
Chipotle flakes

The Tortillas
12 (6-inch) thin corn tortillas
Corn oil

The Toppings
Salsa Verde (page 218)
Queso Fresco (page 205) or toasted pine nuts

1. If your squash blossoms are longer than your tortillas, chop them in half. Otherwise, leave them whole. Bring 4 cups of water to a boil in a large saucepan. Add about 2 teaspoons of salt. Add the diced potatoes. Boil the potatoes for 6 to 7 minutes, just long enough to make them soft. Drain well and set aside.

2. Fill each tortilla with a squash blossom, about 2 tablespoons of potato, a sprinkle of minced epazote, if using, and a sprinkle of chipotle flakes. Roll the tortilla closed. This works best if you place the filling on one side of the tortilla and start rolling it closed from that end. Pierce the tacos with toothpicks to keep them from unrolling. Fry the tacos. Top with salsa verde and then vegan queso fresco.

Guacamole Tacos (page 143), Carrots Escabeche (page 200), and Pickled Red Onions (page 203)

Los Otros Tacos

*"Other tacos in a
class by themselves."*

What about the other tacos?—those tacos that don't quite fit in any of our categories. That's what this section is all about.

Some of these tacos create categories of their own, such as *tacos de carnitas* and *tacos de mixiote*, but since we only have one version of them, they find their home here.

They also happen to be some of my favorite tacos, simply because they are so unique. They inspire my creativity and my passion for food.

Tacos with Black Beans and Chile Peanuts and the Guacamole Tacos are two of the easiest, quickest tacos to make in this entire book.

Guacamole Tacos

Tacos de Guacamole

Guacamole tacos are incredibly popular in Mexico and in my home. They are easy to make and highly addictive. I think it's the very warm, satisfying feeling of the fresh tortilla coupled with creamy avocado. Even without the toppings, they are delicious. With them, these tacos become lively with lots of heat from the salsa and lots of zing from the pickled onions. When you are traveling, guacamole tacos are a fairly safe bet to be vegan at a taquería. (See photo on page 140.)

REGION: EVERYWHERE | HEAT LEVEL: 6 | MAKES 4 TACOS

The Filling
1 cup Wilted Chard in Mojo de Ajo (page 199), optional but recommended,
    (prep this before making the guacamole)
1 cup any guacamole (page 234)

The Tortillas
4 (5- to 6-inch) corn tortillas

The Toppings
Pickled Red Onions (page 203) (prep this well ahead of time)
Taquería-Style Carrots Escabeche (page 200) or the quick variation below
Dog Nose Salsa (page 223)

Prepare the chard, if using. Make the guacamole and set it aside. Warm the tortillas, top with the guacamole, and then the onions, carrot, and salsa.

Quick Carrots Escabeche

If you don't have time to make the recipe on page 200, try this quickie version.

    1 teaspoon olive oil
    1 carrot, cut diagonally into 1/8-inch thick slices
    1/4 teaspoon Mexican oregano
    Pinch of salt

Heat the oil in a small skillet over a medium heat. Add the carrot, oregano, and salt and sauté for about 1 minute. The slices should still be firm, but not crunchy.

Michoacan-Style Carnitas

Carnitas Michoacánas

Carnitas are one of the most popular types of taco served throughout Mexico and the United States. This particular version comes from the state of Michoacán and is considered one of the best, if not the best, variation of carnitas, but be forewarned: Michoacános use some pretty crazy ingredients in their carnitas, like Coca-Cola and a lot, and I mean a lot, of fat. They also use some cool ingredients like lots of herbs and sliced sour oranges. I have created several variations of this recipe, so you can choose whether or not you want to go full out Michoacán style or tone it down and have healthier tacos carnitas.

REGION: MICHOACÁN | HEAT LEVEL: 0 TO 3, DEPENDS ON TOPPINGS | MAKES 12 TACOS

The Simmering Sauce

2 bay leaves

1 teaspoon dried thyme

1 teaspoon dried marjoram

1/2 teaspoon ground black pepper

1 teaspoon salt

1 sour orange, sliced into 4 or 5 disks (use a navel orange)

1 tablespoon brown sugar (omit this if you use the cola)

1 tablespoon vegan Better than Beef Bouillon, optional (for a deeper taste)

1 (12-ounce) can or bottle organic cola, like Blue Sky, optional or 1 (12-ounce)
   bottle dark beer, optional (use one or the other, not both)

3/4 cup vegan shortening, optional

The Filling (choose either seitan or jackfruit or do a mix of half and half)

4 cups seitan strips or 4 cups jackfruit pieces

2 tablespoons olive oil

The Tortillas

12 thick (6-inch) corn tortillas

The Toppings

Chiles de Árbol Salsa (page 220) or Green Salsa with Avocado (page 214)

1. In a large saucepan, combine the bay leaves, thyme, marjoram, pepper, salt, sliced orange, brown sugar, any of the optional ingredients, and the seitan or jackfruit. Add enough water to cover the ingredients and bring to a low simmer. Simmer until the liquid completely cooks out, 30 to 45 minutes. Add 2 tablespoons of oil to the pot and turn the heat up to medium-high. Continue cooking until you have some crispy bits. Remove the bay leaves.

2. Warm your tortillas. Fill the tortillas, fold them, and top with the salsa of your choice.

The Jackfruit vs. Seitan Throwdown
• •

Jackfruit is a popular substitute for pulled or shredded meat because of its unique texture. I made several versions of this recipe to do a texture and taste test, and here is what I found. Jackfruit is a good choice if you are adding the shortening to the recipe. The fat carries a lot of the flavor from the sauce, and it completely coats the jackfruit, making a great texture and flavor combination. Canned jackfruit tends to have a briny taste that diminishes the flavor of the carnitas. Also, without the shortening, the jackfruit can taste a little dull. Seitan will absorb the flavors better, and some of it will fall apart into smaller bits as it simmers, creating a pulled texture. Seitan looks like the clear winner, but if you want to avoid gluten, jackfruit is your choice. My favorite taste-test winner was a half-and-half combination of the two because I got large bits from the seitan and a better pulled texture from the jackfruit.

Mixiote Tacos with Mushrooms and Squash

Tacos de Mixiote de Hongos y Calabacin

These lesser-known tacos are a real treasure. They are made with mushrooms, squash, nopales, and onions slathered with an aromatic chile guajillo sauce and steamed until all the flavors meld together. Traditionally, they are made from parchment derived from the film of maguey leaves. (Mixiote is the Nahuatl word for maguey film.) However, removing the film from maguey leaves often harms the plant, so mixiote is heavily regulated. So many preparations of mixiote now use parchment paper or plastic baggies instead of real mixiote, unless you are in Mexico. While using parchment does impact the flavor, it is still an absolutely delicious meal.

REGION: CENTRAL MEXICO | HEAT LEVEL: 3 | MAKES 12 TACOS

The Filling
12 to 15 cremini mushrooms, quartered

2 zucchini, cut into 1/2-inch dice

1 small white onion, cut into 1/4-inch dice

1/2 cup fresh or jarred nopales strips

2 tablespoons chopped fresh epazote or 1 teaspoon dried, optional

1/4 cup roasted, salted pepitas

2 to 3 avocado leaves, optional

The Adobo for Mixiote
3 chiles guajillo, toasted

1/2 medium white onion, roughly chopped

3 cloves garlic

1 teaspoon dried oregano

1/2 teaspoon coarse ground black pepper

Pinch cloves

1/2 teaspoon salt

1 tablespoon achiote paste

1 cup fresh orange juice

The Tortillas
12 (6-inch) thick corn tortillas or 24 (4 to 5-inch) thin corn tortillas, served doubled

The Toppings
Whole roasted jalapeños

4 to 6 squash blossoms sautéed with olive oil and salt, optional

1. In a large bowl, combine the mushrooms (stems included), zucchini, onion, nopales, and epazote, if using, along with the pepitas and avocado leaves, if using. Set aside.

2. Remove the stems from the toasted chiles. Some people remove the seeds and veins from the chiles, as well, but I prefer to keep them. In a blender or food processor, puree the chiles, onion, garlic, oregano, pepper, cloves, salt, achiote, and orange juice.

3. Set up a steaming basket and spread enough parchment paper in it to run up the sides. This will hold the adobo liquid in the basket. Add the filling and then pour the abobo over it. If you do not have a large steaming basket, you may need to divide this between the layers of your basket, so make sure to divide everything evenly. As soon as you pour the adobo over the filling, clean your blender. The achiote in the adobo stains quickly. Also, if it gets on your steamer instead of staying on the parchment, it will stain your steamer. I have a conical basket that I use to create a bowl with the paper so the filing and adobo doesn't get everywh ere. Cover the steaming basket and steam for 30 minutes.

4. If you have mixiote film available, you can wrap the filling in the mixiote and gently tie it closed with thick twine. Be gentle when you transfer the mixiote-wrapped filling to the steaming basket so the mixiote film doesn't break.

5. While the mixiote is steaming, roast the jalapeños. If you are using squash blossoms, sauté them in a skillet with 2 teaspoons of olive oil and a little salt over a medium heat until they are slightly browned.

6. Warm the tortillas, then fill them with the mixiote, and top with the roasted jalapeños and squash blossoms, if using.

Tacos with Black Beans and Chile Peanuts

Tacos de Frijoles Negros y Cacahuates con Chile

This is one of my fast, "I want tacos now!" recipes. I make fresh tortillas for these, and then raid my pantry for a can of refried black beans, chile peanuts, and salsa. Sometimes simple recipes are the best ones. The tacos look small, but they are deceptively filling. I usually eat four, though I am easily full after three! **Note:** If you decide to make the poblano strips, pan-roast them before you make the tortillas.

REGION: CASA DE JASON | HEAT LEVEL: 3 | MAKES 4 TACOS

The Tortillas
4 (5- to 6-inch) corn tortillas

The Filling
1/2 cup refried black beans, warmed
1 pan-roasted poblano, cut into strips (optional)

The Toppings
8 to 10 Chile-Lime Peanuts (page 198) per taco (about 1/3 cup total)
Your favorite salsa (I use whatever I have on hand)

Make the tortillas or warm some pre-made ones. Spread 2 tablespoons of refried black beans on each tortilla. Add the poblano strips, if using. Sprinkle peanuts down the center and top with salsa.

Tacos de Canasta

*"Classic breakfast 'basket' tacos,
sauced and steamed."*

Tacos de canasta are traditional Mexican breakfast tacos, although they are sold through late afternoon. The name means "basket tacos," and they are also called *tacos sudados,* or "sweated tacos." These are the "sliders" of Mexican food. Imagine a handmade corn tortilla, quickly dipped in a light chile sauce and griddled just enough to toast the corn and make the tortilla soft enough to absorb all that wonderful chile flavor. Now, imagine a basket of tacos where the tacos have been smothered in onions and wrapped in cloth so they steam from their own heat and moisture for hours, allowing all the succulent juices from the filling to suffuse the tortilla from the inside and from the caramelized onion on the outside. As the moisture permeates the tacos, and the weight of layers and layers of tacos and onions presses down upon them, the tacos condense into tight bites of perfection. Served straight from the basket by street vendors, and in Mexico City from the backs of bicycles, they are soft and melty and the essence of good street food. No wonder they are ordered by the threes and fours.

• • • • •

¡Muy Importante!: Read through the entire chapter before making tacos de canasta. This is definitely a chapter for experienced taqueros.

The number of tacos you get from these recipes assume you are using smaller sized tortillas. If you are using regular sized tortillas, cut the amount of tacos you will get out of the recipes by one third. Typically, I only make these when I am entertaining large groups of people, because the basket style of serving begs for lots of tacos. When I do that, I find myself making all three types of tacos sudados, doing a layer of one type, and then a layer of another type, and so on. That way, the large basket of tacos is always interesting because the layers keep changing.

Note: You need thick tortillas for tacos de canasta. The thin tortillas you find in most grocery stores will fall apart. Trader Joe's has an excellent handmade white corn tortilla that works well for this recipe, though making your own is even better.

Making Tacos de Canasta: Traditional or Easy

Making Tacos de Canasta can be fairly complex. For best results, please read over the entire beginning section of this chapter. If you just skim it, you may end up with tacos de disaster. Each time you make them, you'll need to have the sauce and onions ready (they can be prepared ahead of time); prep your steaming basket, terra cotta dish, or slow-cooker; and assemble your cooking station. These tacos are designed to be served in large batches, so they are best for parties as opposed to small family dinners.

Between the stove and the table, Tacos de Canasta require "sweating" time in a sealed container. Mexican street vendors often use a bicycle-mounted basket or cooler. In the small villages, they use baskets and a lot of cloth wrapped around the taco basket to keep the steam and heat inside. I always use an insulated cooler and a basket (see sidebar on page 155), but you can also make these by sealing them inside a slow-cooker or terra cotta baking dish. (You can instead use a large plastic bag, lining the interior with a double layer of foil and tying it closed once you layer the tacos inside it.)

The four basket tacos in this chapter require some resting time for the tacos to sweat. The tortillas for tacos de canasta are on the small side, around four to five inches. Unless you are making your own or you have a Mexican market available to you, go ahead and use full-size, thick corn tortillas.

An Easy Alternative: If you want to enjoy the great flavor of tacos de canasta but without all the fuss, then you can make the easy version called Tacos al Vapor instead (below).

Easy Canastas: Tacos al Vapor

. . . .

Here's a short-cut variation for basket tacos is Tacos al Vapor, or steamed tacos; a style of taco very similar to Tacos de Canasta.

To make this streamlined version of "basket tacos," skip making the onions and the sauce (page 154), and simply proceed with the recipes using the filling, tortillas, and toppings. Then, just steam the tacos for 10 minutes to turn them into tacos al vapor. This shortcut will allow you to enjoy Tacos de Canasta as they are intended, but with much less time and effort.

Steps to Make Steamed Tacos (Tacos al Vapor):

1. Choose a filling from one of the four Tacos de Canasta recipes.

2. Assemble the tacos with just the tortillas, filling, and sauce, but no onions.

3. Steam the tacos in a steamer for 5 minutes.

Instructions for Traditional Tacos de Canasta

1. Prepare a Serving Vessel: Take a very large cloth and fold it into four layers. You need enough parchment paper to separate the taco layers so they don't become one mass of taco stuff. Place your slow cooker near your cooking area and set it on low.

2. Assembling the Tacos: Make one of the fillings from the four recipes below.

3. Cook the Tortillas and Assemble the Tacos: Heat an iron skillet or griddle to medium heat.

Quickly dip as many tortillas as will fit on your griddle into the Sauce for Tacos de Canasta (recipe follows) and slap them on the griddle. They only need about 30 seconds per side. Because they are dipped in the sauce, they will be very soft, so be gentle when you handle them.

Spread whichever filling you're making along half of each tortilla, leaving an edge. Fold them closed and immediately place them in your cooler, slow-cooker, or terra cotta dish.

Once you have one complete layer in your serving vessel, spread some of the caramelized onions (recipe follows) on top of them, then cover that layer with parchment paper. Place the next layer of tacos on top of these, then the Onions, then another layer of parchment paper, until you're out of filling or tortillas.

4. Sweat and Serve: Once you have made all your tacos, close the container tightly. Let them sweat for at least 30 minutes before serving. If you are using a cooler, transfer them to your basket and bring them to the table (or serve them directly from the cooler for a more laid-back serving style.) If you are using the slow cooker or terra cotta dish, bring them directly to the table.

Note: If you're taking the easy way and making Tacos de Vapor instead, you can omit the sauce and onions.

Sauce for Tacos de Canasta

2 guajillo chiles
2 morita chiles (or 2 more guajillos)
3 cups water
2 cloves garlic
3/4 teaspoon salt

Combine the chiles and the water in a saucepan and bring it just to a boil. Reduce the heat to a simmer and cook the chiles for about 15 minutes. Puree the chiles, water, garlic, and salt in a blender or food processor, then set the sauce aside.

Onions for Tacos de Canasta

2 medium white onions, cut into paper-thin slices
2 teaspoons olive oil
1 teaspoon dried Mexican oregano
1/2 teaspoon salt
1/4 cup water

Heat the oil in a large skillet over a medium-high heat. Add the onions and sauté them until very well browned, 12 to 15 minutes. Add the oregano and salt and sauté for 2 to 3 minutes longer. Add 1/4 cup of water, stir the onions, and continue to cook for another minute, until the water evaporates. Remove the skillet from the heat and set aside.

Traditional Canastas: With a Cooler and Basket

- Make the Sauce (See Recipe)
- Make the Onions (See Recipe)
- Make the filling
- Prepare the cooler or basket
- Assemble the tacos
- If the tacos were sweated in a cooler or plastic bag, transfer them to a serving basket

1. **Prepare the Cooler:** Take a very large cloth and fold it into four layers. Take a very large and place it inside the cooler with the cloth coming up and over the sides of the cooler, forming a cloth basket inside your cooler. Have some parchment paper ready to place between the layers of tacos so they don't become one mass.

2. **Place the Cooked Tacos in the Cooler:** Place the cooked tacos in your cooler. When you have one complete layer, spread some of the caramelized onions on top of them and cover that layer with parchment paper. Place the next layer of tacos on top of these, then the onion, then another layer of parchment paper, and so on.

3. **Seal the Cooler for Steaming:** Once you have made all your tacos, fold the remaining cloth over them and tightly close the cooler. Let them sit for at least 30 minutes before serving. A well-insulated cooler will not only trap in the steam from the hot tacos, it will keep the tacos warm. Alternatively, you can line a basket with a double layer of cloth, which in turn is lined with foil, or use a large plastic bag, lining the interior of the bag with a double layer of foil and tying it closed once you layer the tacos into it.

4. **Transfer to the Basket:** Place your basket next to the cooler. Lift the cloth "sack" filled with tacos out of the cooler and place it in the basket, which you can now transfer to the table or wherever you plan on serving the tacos.

Miners Tacos

Tacos Mineros

Tacos Mineros, which means miners tacos, were originally a taco commonly eaten by silver miners in the eighteenth century. Over time, tacos mineros became incredibly popular and started being sold in baskets throughout Mexico (later morphing into tacos de canasta). The tacos steamed while sitting in the basket, causing them to sweat. Now they are the most popular form of *tacos sudados* sold in Mexico City. You can also find these less frequently as tacos dorados. Either way, they are outstanding. Traditionally, they are beans cooked with bacon, potatoes, and shredded meat. I use my vegan bacon flavor hack of liquid smoke or smoked salt and a touch of maple syrup to add that flavor to the beans, while I use shredded seitan or finely sliced seared portobellos in them. (See photo page 158.)

REGION: EVERYWHERE | HEAT LEVEL: 2 | MAKES 12 TACOS

The Filling
Beans:

2 tablespoons chopped fresh epazote, optional but recommended

1/2 cup chopped onion

2 cups cooked pinto beans

1 cup water

1/4 teaspoon salt (I use mesquite smoked salt)

1 teaspoon maple syrup

1/2 teaspoon liquid smoke

Potatoes:

2 Yukon gold or other waxy potatoes, chopped into bite-size pieces

Seitan or Portobellos:

2 large plum tomatoes, roughly chopped

1/2 cup chopped onion

4 cloves garlic, minced

1 güero or jalapeño chile, diced

2 cups shredded seitan *or* 4 portobello mushrooms, cut into 1/2-inch pieces

1 tablespoon olive oil

2 bay leaves

1/4 teaspoon salt

1/2 teaspoon dried oregano

The Tortillas

12 (4 to 5-inch) corn tortillas

The Toppings

2 cups shredded lettuce

Crema (page 204) drizzled over each taco

1. **Make the Beans:** In a saucepan, combine the epazote (if using), onion, beans, water, salt, maple syrup, and liquid smoke. Bring to a low simmer and simmer for 10 minutes. Once it is done simmering, smash the beans into a rough paste.

2. **Make the Potatoes:** Steam the chopped potatoes for 10 minutes or boil them for 7 to 8 minutes.

3. **Make the Seitan or Portobellos:** If using **seitan**, heat the oil in a skillet over a medium heat. Add the onion and sauté until lightly browned, about 5 minutes. Add the shredded seitan, garlic, and bay leaves and continue sautéing until the seitan browns, about 5 minutes. Add the tomato, chile güero, salt, and oregano, and cook until the tomato softens. Turn off the heat. If using **portobellos,** heat the oil in a skillet over a high heat. Add the portobellos and sauté until they are reduced to about one-third their original size and are well browned. Reduce the heat to medium high. Add the onion and bay leaves and sauté this until the onion is lightly browned, about 5 minutes. Add the tomato, chile güeros, salt, and oregano, and cook until the tomato softens, about 2 minutes longer. Turn off the heat.

4. **Assembling the tacos:** Add the beans and potatoes to the pan with the seitan or portobellos and stir a few times to combine   Fill each tortilla generously with the filling and fold the tortillas. Place the filled tortillas in a basket, lining each layer with parchment paper, until you are ready to serve. I usually let these sit for about 30 minutes (they are so moist, they do not need to sit that long). Alternatively, place the filled tortillas in slow cooker set on low or a large tightly-covered terra cotta baking dish.

Note: These tacos do not use the sauce or onions for Tacos de Canasta. When you serve them, garnish them with vegan crema and shredded lettuce. Alternatively, you can roll them closed, forming a cylinder and fry them over a medium high heat.

TIME-SAVING TIP: When I make these, I have three pans going at the same time. One for the beans, one for the seitan/portobellos, and one for the potatoes. Everything comes together at the same time that way.

MAKE IT SIMPLE: If you don't want to have three separate pans going at once, you can make this a one-pot meal and be done with it in about 25 minutes and a minimal amount of work. Dice both halves of the onion used in the recipe and brown them in a large saucepan over a medium-high heat. Prep the remaining ingredients for all steps of the recipe. Add all the ingredients for the beans, potatoes, and seitan/portobellos to the saucepan at once. Basically, you are going to have one big pot which contains all the ingredients for each of the three filling sections. Bring this to a simmer and simmer it until most of the liquid has cooked out. It should take about 15 minutes. Fill the tortillas, fold them, garnish them, and serve. Simple and fast.

Miners Tacos (page 156)

Basket Tacos with Cascabel Seitan

Tacos de Canasta de Seitan en Salsa de Chiles Cascabel

The cascabel seitan coupled with the super soft tortillas is what makes these tacos exceptional. The cascabels have a rugged red flavor that isn't too spicy, while the garlic provides a pungent base note to the recipe. Rather than cutting through the tortilla, the flavor of the sauce and the texture of the seitan sit in perfect balance with it. These feel decadent without actually being so.

REGION: MEXICO CITY | HEAT LEVEL: 3 | MAKES 12 TACOS

The Filling
12 cascabel chiles or 2 large dried red chiles, rehydrated
1 cup water (use the water you used to rehydrate the cascabels)
8 cloves garlic
2 tablespoon white vinegar (my favorite is white balsamic)
1 teaspoon salt
4 cups shredded seitan
1 tablespoon olive oil

The Tortillas
12 (4- to 5-inch) corn tortillas
Sauce for Tacos de Canasta (page 154)
Onions for Tacos de Canasta (page 154)

1. Combine the cascabels and the water in a saucepan and simmer them for about 10 minutes, or until they are soft. Remove the chiles from the water with a slotted spoon and remove and discard the stems and seeds. In a blender or small food processor, puree the cascabels, 1/2 cup of water, garlic, vinegar, and salt. Set this aside.

2. Heat the oil in a skillet over medium-high heat. Add the seitan and sauté it until the seitan is partially browned, 7 to 8 minutes. Reduce the heat to medium and stir in the cascabel sauce. Cook this until the sauce has condensed around the seitan and mostly cooked out. Remove the seitan from the heat.

3. Quickly dip the tortillas in the Sauce for Tacos de Canasta. Warm the tortillas in an iron skillet for about 30 seconds per side. Spread the cascabel seitan on one half of each tortilla, leaving an edge. Fold the tortillas. Place them in a cooler, a slow cooker set on Low, or a terra-cotta baking dish, topping each layer of tacos with a layer of Onions de Canasta, with a sheet of parchment paper in between. Cover and let them sit for 30 minutes before serving.

NON-SEITAN OPTION: Use 3 cups of dried mushrooms and 1 cup of cooked, rinsed black beans. Sauté the dried mushrooms and beans just like you would the seitan, then add the sauce to the pan. The sauce will quickly reduce as the mushrooms absorb it.

Basket Tacos with Potatoes and Chorizo

Tacos de Canasta de Papas y Chorizo

Potatoes and chorizo is a popular filling for many different types of tacos, but I like them best in tacos de canasta. The light steam keeps the potatoes extra moist. They fall apart when you bite into the tacos and the chorizo gives the taco a spicy robust flavor. This particular filling also makes it a very hearty taco, despite its small size.

REGION: MEXICO CITY | HEAT LEVEL: 4 | MAKES 20 TACOS

The Filling
6 Yukon gold potatoes, cut into 1/2-inch dice
2 tablespoons olive oil
1 large white onion, cut into 1/2-inch dice (about 1 1/2 cups)
1 large poblano chile, roasted, deseeded, and chopped
1/2 teaspoon salt
2 cups vegan chorizo, storebought or homemade (page 66)

The Tortillas
12 (4 to 5-inch) corn tortillas
Sauce for Tacos de Canasta (page 154)
Onions for Tacos de Canasta (page 154)

1. Steam the potatoes for about 10 minutes or boil them for 5 minutes, then drain them.

2. Heat the oil to just above a medium heat in a 14-inch sauté pan. Add the partially cooked potatoes and fry them until they just start to turn golden brown, 7 to 8 minutes. Add the onion and cook 2 to 3 minutes, then add the diced poblano, salt, and chorizo and cook 2 to 3 minutes longer.

3. Dip each tortilla quickly in the sauce for Tacos de Canasta. Warm them in an iron skillet for about 30 seconds per side, then fill them. Spread the filling on one half of each tortilla, leaving a little edge. Fold the tortilla over. Place them in a cooler, slow cooker set on Low, or terra-cotta baking dish. Top each layer of tacos with the Onions for Tacos de Canasta. Cover and let the tacos sit for 30 minutes before serving.

Enjoy "Breakfast" Tacos Anytime
• • • • • • • • • • • • • • • • • • •

While Tacos de Canasta are typically eaten for breakfast, they take a while to make, and I am not one to get out of bed early just to make breakfast! When I buy them from a street vendor, they make a great morning snack. If I make them for myself, they become an afternoon treat.

Basket Tacos with Chipotle Coconut Beans

Tacos de Canasta de Chiles Chipotle y Frijoles
en Leche de Coco

The chipotle coconut beans are perfect for tacos de canasta. The light steam keeps the beans nice and moist and the coconut chipotle sauce melts into the tortilla. It creates a melt-in-your-mouth taco. I dare you to eat just one!

REGION: CASA DE JASON | HEAT LEVEL: 5 | MAKES 12 TACOS

The Filling
4 cups cooked black beans, rinsed
4 chipotles adobo, minced
1 1/2 cups unsweetened coconut milk
2 tablespoon Mojo de Ajo (page 60)
1 teaspoon salt
1 teaspoon ground cumin
Optional: 8-ounces vegan chorizo, storebought or homemade (page 66)
1 1/2 cups Queso Fresco (page 205) or pepitas

The Tortillas
12 (4- to 5-inch) corn tortillas
Sauce for Tacos de Canasta (page 154)
Onions for Tacos de Canasta (page 154)

Toppings (served on the side)
Salsa Verde (page 218)
Pickled jalapeños (see Pickled Chiles, page 203)

1. Combine the beans, chipotles, coconut milk, mojo de ajo, salt, and cumin in a small pot. Bring it to a low simmer and simmer this for 7 to 8 minutes. The beans should be barely saucy by the time they are done simmering.

2. Dip each tortilla quickly in the Sauce for Tacos de Canasta. Warm them in an iron skillet for about 30 seconds per side, then fill them. Spread the beans on one half of each tortilla, leaving a little edge. Sprinkle queso fresco on top of the beans. Fold the tortilla over. Place them in a cooler, slow cooker set on Low, or a terra-cotta baking dish. Top each layer of tacos with the Onions for Tacos de Canasta. Cover and let the tacos sweat for 30 minutes and serve with salsa verde and pickled jalapeños.

Tacos Mañaneros

*"Breakfast tacos from
both sides of the border."*

While tacos de canasta are the mainstay breakfast taco in Mexico, they aren't the only ones. Last night's guisado is often served with scrambled eggs or a hard-boiled egg (we serve them with a tofu scramble). Battered and fried vegetables and *quelites* (edible greens) also round out the breakfast taco experience.

In Texas, breakfast tacos are a way of life. When I lived in Fort Worth, I could find them at just about any restaurant that served Tex Mex. Tacos Mañaneros tend to be steamed or stewed tacos, as opposed to tacos de asador or tacos de comal, but really, there are no hard-and-fast rules.

The easiest breakfast taco to make is the one with poblano strips, mojo scramble, and pinto peans, especially if you use the time-savers in the recipe. If you want to make your own tacos mañaneros creations, you can take just about any leftover you have, add the Mojo Scramble to it, and you have near-instant tacos.

Chiles Rellenos Tacos

Tacos de Chiles Rellenos

Typically served as a lunch or dinner item in the U.S., chiles rellenos are used as a breakfast taco filling in Mexico. Sometimes the chiles are battered and fried; other times, they're simply roasted and stuffed. The poblano chile is the staple chile used to make chiles rellenos, but any large green chile will do. Instead of stuffing mine with a vegan cheese, I used a roasted garlic *pipián verde* (made with pumpkin seeds), and liked it better. It tastes more lush and cleaner at the same time, and the roasted garlic *pipián* adds a depth of flavor you just can't get using cheese.

REGION: MEXICO CITY | LEVEL: 2 | MAKES 4 TACOS

The Filling
4 poblano chiles or other large green chiles, pan-roasted

3 tomatillos, pan-roasted

20 cloves garlic, pan-roasted

1 cup toasted, salted pepitas (pumpkin seeds)

1 tablespoon white vinegar

1/2 teaspoon salt

The Tortillas
4 (6- to 7-inch) corn tortillas large enough to hold a chile poblano

The Topping
Lime wedges

Crushed Red Salsa (page 212) or whatever salsa you have on hand

1. Rub the charred skin off the chiles and cut off the tops of the chiles so that the seed packet comes out and you have a chile ready to be stuffed. Set aside.

2. In a blender or food processor, puree the tomatillos, garlic, pepitas, vinegar, and salt. Transfer to a small bowl. To serve, stuff the tomatillo mixture into the chiles poblano. Place the stuffed chiles in the tortillas and serve with salsa and lime wedges.

VARIATION: If you want to batter and fry the chiles, you will need 2 cups of tempura batter from the Tempura Tacos (page 182). Pour enough oil into a pot to cover a stuffed chile. Heat the oil over a medium-high heat. When you stuff the chiles, don't stuff them all the way to the top. Leave about an inch and a half free. Otherwise, the filling will ooze out the top of the chile. Make 2 cups of the tempura batter and, holding the tops closed, dredge the stuffed chiles through the tempura batter. Add the battered chiles to the hot oil and fry them for 2 to 3 minutes each.

Breakfast Tacos with Poblano Strips, Mojo Scramble, and Pinto Beans

I've never been a fan of breakfast, so I created these as a challenge to myself to find something for breakfast that I was both willing to make and willing to eat for breakfast. That's how my breakfast tacos were created. I had roasted poblanos and black beans sitting around and some tofu and avocado that I needed to use. Add in Hatch and ancho chile powder, olives, mojo de ajo, and good quality corn tortillas, and I could not resist.

REGION: TEXAS/CASA DE JASON | HEAT LEVEL: 4 | MAKES 6 TACOS

The Filling
16 ounces firm tofu
1 teaspoon turmeric
1/2 teaspoon salt or Indian black salt (kala namak) for the most egg-like flavor
2 teaspoon ancho chile powder or other chile powder
2 teaspoon Hatch chile powder or other chile powder
1 to 2 tablespoons Mojo de Ajo (page 60) or garlic-flavored olive oil
1 1/2 cups cooked black beans, rinsed

The Tortillas
6 (5- to 6-inch) corn tortillas

The Toppings
1 roasted poblano, stemmed, seeded, and chopped into 1/2-inch pieces
5 green olives, pitted and sliced
1 firm plum tomato, chopped
1 avocado, chopped (prep after you finish making the filling)
Salsa Verde (page 218)

1. Start pan-roasting the poblano just before you make the filling. Use your hands to break up the tofu until it crumbles. Transfer the crumbled tofu to a cazuela or large skillet. Stir in the turmeric, salt, ancho chile powder, Hatch chile powder, mojo de ajo, and black beans. Warm this over a medium heat (remember to slowly heat up your cazuela instead of going straight to medium) and warm it for about 7 to 8 minutes. Stir it a few times during this process, but for the most part, you can leave it alone.

2. Warm the tortillas. Add the filling, then the toppings, and finish it off with salsa verde.

MAKE IT LOW-FAT: Omit the mojo de ajo.

"Food is revelatory for me. There are moments in my culinary journey when my experience of the world shifts sideways, and the moment becomes transformative. Eating my first homemade tortilla with a simple spread of beans and salsa was one of these moments of revelation. As soon as I took my first bite, I understood food, at least this part of it, in a completely new way, and I was instantly captivated. The taco went from being just another Mexican treat to being magical."

Hash Brown and Black Bean Tacos with Tomatillo Avocado Salsa

When you first bite into these tacos, they have that warm, soft feel from the corn tortilla, and then you immediately get the crunch from the hash browns. Spike that with some lively green salsa, and you've got a fun twist on a pretty classic breakfast, all put together in taco form.

REGION: CASA DE JASON | HEAT LEVEL: 3 | MAKES 4 TACOS

The Filling
2 medium russet potatoes, shredded
1/4 cup olive oil or Mojo de Ajo (page 60)
6 cloves garlic, minced
1/2 teaspoon chipotle powder
3/4 teaspoon salt
3/4 cup cooked black beans, rinsed

The Tortillas
4 (5- to 6-inch) corn tortillas

The Toppings
Green Salsa with Avocado (page 214)

1. Pat the shredded potatoes dry as best you can. Heat the oil in a large skillet over medium-high heat. Add the potato shreds, slowly stirring and flipping as they fry to crisp. This will take 5 to 10 minutes depending on how wide your pan is. The more you can spread the shreds out in the pan, the faster they crisp. Once about half the shreds are crisped, add the garlic and cook 1 more minute. Remove the pan from the heat and immediately add the chipotle powder, salt, and beans and give everything a quick stir.

2. Warm your tortillas. Fill them with a generous portion of the hash brown black bean filling, then top them with Tomatillo Avocado Salsa.

Tacos with Crispy Greens

Tacos de Quelites Fritos

Quelites are any of a variety of edible field greens, such as chard, purslane, and kale. The Nahuatl word for them is *itzmiquilitl* (purslane), which then became the word *quelite* and took on the broader meaning. These are often battered and fried and served as breakfast tacos. They are a very simple, delicious dish, and, because the greens are delicate and the batter is fried, they need to be served as soon as they come out of the frying pan or they lose their luster. I usually serve mine with a side of beans to round out the breakfast experience.

REGION: EVERYWHERE | HEAT LEVEL: 5 OR 0 IF YOU SKIP THE SALSA | MAKES 8 TACOS

The Filling
Olive oil, to fry
4 cups torn chard leaves (torn into large pieces that will fit within a tortilla)
2 cups tempura batter from Tacos Tempura (page 182)

The Tortillas
8 (5- to 6-inch) corn tortillas

The Toppings
Salsa de Chiles de Árbol (page 220) or whatever salsa you have on hand
Lime wedges

Fill a pot or pan with oil at least 3/4-inch deep and bring it to a medium-high heat. Dredge the leaves in the tempura batter and fry them in the oil for about 2 minutes, working in batches. Fill the tortillas immediately with the tempura leaves and serve with salsa and lime wedges.

Tacos para la Mañana, Tacos para la Noche
• •

Many people who visit Mexico think that tacos are available all day. While it's true that there is most likely a taco stand open somewhere nearby, the majority of the daytime taquerías close up by mid-afternoon since that is when the largest meal of the day is eaten. Once night rolls around, a different set of taquerías open. The nighttime establishments tend to focus more on *tacos de asador* and *tacos de comal* while *tacos de canasta* are more prevalent during the morning and *tacos de guisado* are served all day. At home, I don't make any distinction, but you may want to be aware of taco timing when you travel.

Top: Sweet Crispy Tacos with Ancho Vanilla Bean Ice Cream, Shaved Mexican Chocolate, and Salted Peanuts (page 176). Bottom: Spicy Cinnamon Tacos with Salted Coconut Cajeta Apples and Agave Crema (page 174). At sides, cinnamon sticks (right) and piloncillos.

CHAPTER

12

Tacos Dulces

"Sweet and decadent dessert tacos."

Tacos can be enjoyed beyond a main meal or snack. You can also eat them for dessert! I love these particular recipes, because they are so much fun, and I have an admitted sweet tooth.

Actually, it's more like sweet teeth. I'll eat two or three of these in one sitting, which is why I make them a bit smaller than the standard taco. That way I can justify having two. The key to getting a good dessert taco is in how you work the tortilla. First, you want a thin tortilla. A thick one won't have the right texture to support all the sweet goodness of your dessert. Also, be sure to sweeten the tortilla or heavily scent it with an aromatic spice like cinnamon, or the taco won't have the desired dessertiness. And that's the truthiness of the matter.

The Pineapple and Banana Dessert Taco recipe is one of the easiest recipes in the book. You can take that recipe and add any sweet fruit or other sweet element to it to create simple, delicious tacos dulces. The Sweet Crispy Tacos with Ancho-Vanilla Ice Cream can be made a bit easier if you purchase a vegan ice cream instead of making it from scratch.

Make All the Dessert Tacos Easy!

You can make all the dessert tacos using the sweet tortillas found in the Pineapple and Banana Dessert Tacos instead of making your own tortillas. It will turn the Sweet Crispy Tacos into Sweet Soft Tacos, but it also saves a lot of work.

Pineapple and Banana Dessert Tacos

I created this dessert taco in part because the others are fairly complex creations, and this one is simply designed to be easy and fun. You can take any sweet fruit or other ingredient and replace the pineapple and banana with it. The real key for this taco is to lightly soak the tortilla in the sweetened sauce. It's very much like dredging a tortilla through chile sauce to make some of the other savory tacos. Have fun with this one. It's one of the key ingredients!

Note: The tortilla will be sticky, so keep wet napkins nearby.

REGION: CASA DE JASON | HEAT LEVEL: 0 | MAKES 4 TACOS

The Filling
1/2 cup water
1/2 cup agave nectar or vegan cajeta (use the filling recipe on page 174 and omit the apples)
1 medium banana, peeled and chopped into bite-size pieces
1 cup diced pineapple

The Torillas
4 thin (4 to 5-inch) corn tortillas

1. Warm the water and agave or cajeta in a small skillet over a medium heat, stirring until it all melts together. Keep this warm over a low heat.

2. In a bowl, combine the banana and pineapple.

3. Dredge each tortilla in the warm water for about 5 seconds per side. Fill the tortillas immediately with the fruit and eat.

Spicy Cinnamon Tacos with Salted Coconut Cajeta Apples and Agave Crema

Cajeta is a Mexican style of caramel sauce. It's rich and smooth, with a complex flavor you don't get with other caramel. This dessert is like a caramel apple pie, but in taco form and kicked up with some candied chiles de árbol. There are so many flavors going on with this dessert, I always want to come back for more. I think it's the rich cajeta in counterpoint to the sweet and spicy chiles. This recipe takes a little advance planning to make the cajeta and *agave crema,* but you can also make these in larger quantities than the recipe calls for and simply refrigerate. The crema will last several days and the cajeta will last for over a month. Just keep them both sealed.

REGION: CASA DE JASON | HEAT LEVEL: 4 | MAKES 6 TACOS

The Filling (apples in cajeta)
1 (13-ounce) can unsweetened coconut milk
1 (2-inch) piece cinnamon or 1/4 teaspoon ground cinnamon
2 1/2 tablespoons rum, optional
2/3 cup brown sugar
1 teaspoon salt
2 tart green apples, cored and sliced into 16 wedges each (prep towards the end of making the filling)

The Tortillas
1 cup fresh masa (store-bought or homemade)
1 teaspoon ground cinnamon mixed with 1/4 cup of sugar (I like using a fine turbinado sugar for this)

The Toppings
3/4 cup Crema (page 204)
3 tablespoons agave nectar
1/2 cup chopped pecan pieces, toasted
12 fried chiles de árbol (page 201)
1/2 cup water
1/2 cup sugar

1. Bring the coconut milk to a simmer in a saucepan at just below a medium heat. Add the cinnamon stick and rum, if using. Dissolve the sugar and salt in the coconut milk and cook this sauce, stirring every 2 to 3 minutes for 1 hour. Towards the end of that hour, core and slice your apples.

2. The next 15 to 20 minutes is where most of the action happens. Once the sauce has cooked for an hour or so, it should have thickened so it drips, but not pours, off your stirring spoon. You need to continuously and slowly stir the sauce until it oozes off your spoon and leaves a clear trail on the bottom of your pan that when you scrape the sauce, slowly fills in. There is no predetermined time here. You need to judge the readiness of the cajeta by its appearance. It should have a thick, caramel sauce consistency. Add the apples at the beginning of that final 15 to 20 minutes where you need to continuously stir. This will give the apples time to soften and flavor the cajeta.

3. While the cajeta is simmering, make the toppings. In a bowl, combine the crema with the agave and set it aside.

4. Over a medium heat, toast the pecan pieces in a skillet, slowly stirring them for about 2 minutes. When you can smell them toasting in the pan, they are done. Remove the pecans from the pan immediately to keep them from further toasting.

5. After you've fried the chiles, remove the stems. In a saucepan over medium-low heat, combine the water and sugar, stirring to dissolve the sugar. Add the fried chiles to the sugar water and simmer until the sugar has turned into a thick syrup. Remove the chiles from the pot and transfer them to a plate to cool. Immediately soak the pot in hot water or you will have sugar stuck at the bottom!

6. Once the entire cajeta apple portion of the recipe is done, make the tortillas. Combine the cinnamon and sugar. Press out your tortillas. Before they go on the griddle, sprinkle one side with about half a teaspoon of cinnamon sugar per tortilla and give them a very gentle press with your palm to embed the cinnamon sugar in the tortilla. Cook the tortillas as normal.

7. Fill each tortilla with cajeta apples, topped with the vegan crema. Finish it off with a couple candied chiles de árbol and about 1 1/2 tablespoons of the toasted pecans.

MAKE IT SIMPLE (SORT OF): Make the cajeta apples a day ahead. If you really like the cajeta, you can make a large batch of it without the apples. Keep it jarred and refrigerated and it will last at least a month. I also suggest making the candied fried chiles de árbol a day ahead. That way, when you want to serve the tacos, all you have to do is make a few tortillas, toast some pecans, and warm the cajeta apples. To do that, just warm them over a medium heat until the sauce feels warm, bordering on hot, to the touch. You can save even more time with this recipe if you prepare the tortillas the same way you do with the Pineapple and Banana Dessert Tacos (page 173) instead of making your own tortillas.

No Need for Baking Soda
• • • • • • • • • • • • • • • • •

Traditional cajeta is made with goat's milk. Baking soda is added to lower the pH level of the sauce so the goat's milk does not coagulate while it cooks. We don't have to worry about that with coconut milk, so this recipe forgoes the use of baking soda.

Sweet Crispy Tacos with Ancho-Vanilla Ice Cream, Mexican Chocolate, and Salted Peanuts

This is my taco version of an ice cream sandwich. That is, if an ice cream sandwich were made with ancho-flavored ice cream. From the first bite, you get crunchy and sweet from the fried tortilla, followed by the exotic flavor of chile-enhanced ice cream and hints of Mexican chocolate. The peanuts give it a second crunch and saltiness to balance out all the sweet. It's a beautiful looking taco. (See photo on page 170.)

REGION: CASA DE JASON | HEAT LEVEL: 1 | MAKES 6 TACOS

The Ice Cream Filling
1 cup almond milk
1 piloncillo (4.5 ounces), smashed into small pieces or 1/3 cup of brown sugar
1 (13-ounce) can full-fat coconut milk
2 ancho chiles, crushed into flakes (about 1/3 cup)
1 vanilla bean, split open
2 teaspoons Mexican vanilla extract or plain vanilla extract

The Crispy Tortillas
6 (5-inch) cooked handmade corn tortillas
Corn oil, for frying
1/2 cup granulated sugar

The Toppings
2 (1/2 ounce) Mexican chocolate wedges (not the full disks, just two of the small triangular wedges)
1/2 cup roasted and salted peanuts

1. Warm the almond milk over a medium-low heat. Add the piloncillo or brown sugar and melt it. Turn the heat to just below medium. Stir in the coconut milk, ancho flakes, and vanilla bean. Bring this to a simmer and simmer it for 10 minutes, stirring it every minute or so. Remove from the heat and stir in the vanilla. Place this in a container, cover it, and refrigerate it for 2 hours. Place the ice cream mixture in an ice cream machine and follow the directions for the machine. Once it has reached soft-serve consistency, return the ice cream to the container and place it in the freezer for 2 to 3 hours.

2. Press out and cook the tortillas as though you were making them for regular tacos. While you are doing this, heat the oil to 375°F. Using a taco form for frying, fold the tortillas in the form and fry them for 1 1/2 to 2 minutes, until they are golden brown. As soon as they come out of the fryer, slide them onto a plate covered with a paper towel and immediately and liberally sprinkle sugar on them, about 1 1/2 tablespoons per taco. Set them aside and allow the tortillas to cool.

Serve Your Sweet Crispy Tacos in Two Ways

There are two ways I serve these tacos:

1. Serve warm just a few minutes after the tortillas come out of the fryer. You'll need to serve this taco as soon as you fill it with ice cream so the ice cream doesn't entirely melt out of the taco, but if you do this version, you'll have the interplay of warm followed by cool and creamy.

2. Make the tortilla and chill it. Once it's cold, you can fill it so the ice cream doesn't melt. In fact, you can store these on a taco rack in your freezer to serve later. It's a great way to make these ahead and have them ready for guests.

3. Shave the chocolate into a small bowl until you have about 2 tablespoons shaved chocolate. Fill the tortillas with 2 to 3 small scoops of ice cream (however many will fit). Top them with the peanuts. Immediately spoon the chocolate onto the tacos, sprinkling it on top as best you can. Make sure to use a spoon and not your fingers so that you don't melt the chocolate shavings. Either serve them now or place them on a taco rack and let them chill in your freezer until needed.

MAKE IT SIMPLE: In a bowl, combine softened store-bought ice cream with the ancho powder. Stir to incorporate the ancho into the ice cream. Cover and return the ice cream to the freezer to firm up.

VARIATION: Instead of making the tortillas into taco shells, you can make them into tortilla chips. Cut the pressed out masa into eighths and then fry them at 350°F for 2 minutes. Plate these and scoop the ice cream on top, followed by the peanuts and chocolate (you'll probably want a little extra chocolate). Now you have dessert nachos.

Kimchi Tacos (page 181)

CHAPTER

Fusion Tacos

*"Flavors from cuisines
around the world."*

Vegan tacos are the ultimate in fusion cuisine. The Mexican palate has so much of the world integrated into it, not only a Spanish influence, which itself borrows heavily from Middle Eastern cuisine, but also from places like France and even Japan.

In fact, you can see the Japanese influence directly in Tacos Tempura, a recipe from Baja, Mexico, a region that has plenty of Japanese visitors and immigrants. But it's more than that. It's a fusion of authentic world cuisine with a sense of compassion. To me, that's what makes vegan tacos the height of fusion. They are travel, culture, anthropology, and philosophy, all in one superbly delicious meal.

With the rise to prominence of Mexican cuisine around the world in the last few decades, it's no surprise that tacos have been adapted to regional tastes. Mexican cuisine influences the cultures it touches, but in turn is appropriated and integrated into those cultures. Even in Norway, the taco reigns supreme, so much so that I have heard Norwegian friends refer to tacos as a taste of home. In Okinawa, tacos are made with rice tortillas and filled with Tacos Americanos ingredients.

• • • • •

You can find tacos in just about every part of the world. Of course, the mighty reach of tacos is even more prevalent here at home in the American Southwest. Taco trucks are all over Southern California while L.A. is the birthplace of a plethora of taco innovations like the Kimchi Taco. In Texas, tacos are part of the state identity, and you can find tacos filled with quintessential Texas dishes like BBQ. In Arizona, authentic taquerías run by immigrants and second-generation Mexican-Americans sell their street creations alongside upscale taco bars that sell fancy versions. The diversity of these tacos would impress even Charles Darwin!

Because anything can be stuffed and folded into a tortilla, a taco is an empty canvas for home cooks and chefs alike. That means fusion tacos can be just about whatever you want, as long as a major component, either an ingredient or flavor combination, of the taco is decidedly not Mexican. If it was straight-up Mexican, it wouldn't be a fusion taco. Have fun with these. Take some of your own regional dishes and fold them up in a tortilla to create your own fusion tacos. Play around with the tortillas—you're not limited to corn. Playing around with salsa is how soy sauce came to be used at some taquerías in Baja. There is an entire world cuisine waiting to be stuffed into a tortilla. The BBQ Tacos and Kimchi Tacos will be the easiest to make in this section.

Kimchi Tacos

Kimchi tacos are popular all over Southern California, particularly in Los Angeles, where they were invented by Chef Roy Choi and sold from his fleet of Korean taco trucks. The filling is marinated in a sweet and salty pear juice sauce, then quickly seared and topped with kimchi and fresh cabbage. You can think of this taco as cabbage two ways, but I like to just think of it as good eats. (See photo on page 178.)

REGION: KOREA/CALIFORNIA MEXICAN | HEAT LEVEL: 5 | MAKES 8 TACOS

The Filling (choose either the shiitakes or the seitan or half of each)

1 cup pear juice

3 tablespoons soy sauce

3 tablespoons sake

2 teaspoons agave nectar

4 cloves garlic, minced

1 tablespoon grated fresh ginger

8 dried shiitake caps or 1 1/2 cups sliced, flattened seitan (see page 60) or chopped seitan strips

1 tablespoon sesame oil

2 teaspoons sesame seeds

3/4 teaspoon freshly ground black pepper

2 cups shredded cabbage

1 1/2 cups kimchi

The Tortillas

8 (5 to 6-inch) corn or flour tortillas

The Toppings

Sliced cucumber

1. Combine the pear juice, soy sauce, sake, agave, garlic, and ginger in a bowl. Add the dried shiitakes or the seitan. If using shiitakes, they will be ready to cook in about 20 minutes. If using seitan, wait a full hour before working with it. If you are using both shiitakes and seitan, you can leave the shiitakes in the marinade along with the seitan for the full hour without any adverse effect.

2. Remove the shiitakes and/or seitan from the marinade and cut into 1/4-inch wide strips. Heat the sesame oil in a sauté pan over high heat. Add the shiitakes or seitan and sauté for about 3 minutes. Toss in sesame seeds and black pepper, give this a quick stir, and get the pan off the heat right away.

3. Warm the tortillas. Fill them with about 3 tablespoons of the fresh cabbage, then 3 tablespoons of the kimchi, and finally the seared shiitakes or seitan. Top with thinly sliced cucumber.

MAKE IT LOW-FAT: Once you marinate the shiitakes or seitan, add them to a pan over medium heat and warm them for about 5 minutes. No liquid should be added to the pan.

Tempura Tacos

The Japanese influence in Baja, Mexico is very pronounced, so much so that soy sauce is on the table of many taquerías in the area. Of course, tourism and migration to and from California also play a huge role in the flavor of these tacos. Traditionally, these are fish tacos, but I use oyster mushrooms, not only because it's the compassionate choice, but also because they have a flaky texture and taste great. Make sure you serve these right away. Otherwise, the tempura becomes limp and soggy, resulting in a very sad taco.

REGION: BAJA, MEXICO | HEAT LEVEL: 0 OR 5 WITH SALSA | MAKES 8 TACOS

The Tempura
1 pound oyster mushrooms (or other vegetables, see Note), cut into large pieces
1 sheet nori
3 cloves garlic
1 cup unbleached all-purpose flour
1 teaspoon dried oregano
1/2 teaspoon baking powder
1 teaspoon coarse salt
1 cup cold beer
1 tablespoon prepared yellow mustard
Corn oil, for frying

The Tortillas
8 (5 to 6-inch) corn or flour tortillas

The Toppings
3/4 cup vegan mayonnaise
1/2 cup Crema (page 204) or vegan sour cream
1 cup shredded purple cabbage
Lemon and lime wedges
Chile de Árbol Salsa (page 220)

1. Cut the oyster mushrooms into very large pieces (bigger than bite-size) until you have about 4 cups. Tear a sheet of nori into a few large pieces, transfer to a blender or small food processor, and pulse it until it is coarsely ground. Set these aside. Smash the garlic into a paste. This works best in a molcajete or mortar and pestle, but you can also smash it by rocking the flat side of your knife over the garlic. Be careful, though, if you do this. If you are not comfortable doing this, just mince the garlic.

2. In a bowl, combine the flour, oregano, baking powder, salt, nori, and garlic. Add the beer and yellow mustard to the mix and stir until everything is evenly combined.

3. In a deep skillet, wok, or Dutch oven, add enough oil to come about 2 inches up the sides Heat this to 375°F. Place a plate covered with a paper towel next to the skillet. Dredge the oyster mushrooms in the batter. Working in batches, add a few battered mushrooms to the hot oil and fry for 3 to 4 minutes. They should be a dark golden color. Scoop out the tempura mushrooms with a frying basket or slotted spoon and transfer them to the plate. This works best if you batter and fry about one cup of oyster mushrooms at a time.

4. In a small bowl, combine the mayo and crema or sour cream, stirring to blend.

5. Warm the tortillas. Spread 2 to 3 tablespoons of the mayo/crema mix over the tortilla. Add the oyster mushrooms tempura and then the cabbage. Serve with lemon and lime wedges and Chile de Árbol Salsa on the side.

NOTE: Instead of oyster mushrooms, you can also use thinly sliced zucchini, onion, whole cloves of garlic, asparagus, or other vegetables.

BBQ Sweet Potato and Chile Peanut Tacos

I lived in Fort Worth, Texas for eleven years, and while I lived there, I had some of the best BBQ I've ever eaten. This taco is an ode to my second home. It's basically a BBQ sandwich served inside a flour tortilla. It's messy, a bit decadent, but oh-so-tasty. If you want to up the heat level, add some minced serrano chiles to the top.

REGION: TEXAS/CASA DE JASON | HEAT LEVEL: 4 | MAKES 12 TACOS

The Filling
1 medium yellow onion, cut into 1/4 inch strips
2 small sweet potatoes, cut into 2 x 1/2-inch strips
1 tablespoon olive oil
Water
1/2 teaspoon salt
2 cups Texas-style BBQ sauce
2 tablespoons peanut butter

The Slaw
1 cup vegan mayonnaise
4 cloves garlic
Juice of 2 limes
1/2 teaspoon salt
2 cups shredded cabbage

The Chile Peanuts
1 tablespoon olive oil
1/2 cup chopped, roasted salted peanuts
1/2 teaspoon chipotle powder
1 teaspoon ancho powder or chili powder

The Tortillas
12 (6-inch) flour tortillas

1. Heat the oil in a skillet over a medium-high heat. Add the onion and sauté until well browned, about 10 minutes. Add the sweet potatoes and enough water to come up about 1/2 inch up the pan. Cook the sweet potatoes until they are soft, about 8 minutes. You will need to replenish the water as it cooks down. Season with the salt and lower the heat to medium.

2. In a bowl, stir together the BBQ sauce and peanut butter, then stir the sauce mixture into the pan with the sweet potatoes and bring to a simmer. Cook for 5 minutes, then set it aside.

3. In a bowl, combine the vegan mayo, garlic, lime juice, and salt. Toss the cabbage with this mix and set it aside.

4. In a small skillet, heat 1 tablespoon of oil over medium heat. Add the peanuts and sauté for about 2 minutes, slowly stirring them. Remove the pan from the heat and immediately season the peanuts with the chipotle and ancho powder.

5. Warm the tortillas. Fill them with the BBQ sweet potatoes and onions, then the slaw, and top with chile peanuts.

Jerk Tempeh Tacos

This is basically a Jamaican jerk served right into a tortilla. It's filled with aromatic spices, plenty of heat from Scotch Bonnet chiles, and finished off on the grill for a little smoky touch. I am infatuated with bold flavors, and this has ended up being one of my favorite tacos. Although these are filling enough that I can get full on one taco, there is no way I am eating just one. These tacos are also great made with seitan instead of tempeh.

REGION: JAMAICA/CASA DE JASON | HEAT LEVEL: 8 | MAKES 8 TACOS

The Rub
2 Scotch Bonnet or habanero chiles (wear gloves when you work with these and don't rub your eyes!)
1/2 cup coarsely chopped white onion
4 cloves garlic
1/4 cup sliced green onions
1 teaspoon fresh thyme
1/2 teaspoon coarse sea salt
1/2 teaspoon ground allspice
1/4 teaspoon ground nutmeg
1/4 teaspoon ground cinnamon
1/2 teaspoon freshly ground black pepper
1 teaspoon finely ground turbinado sugar
2 tablespoons olive oil

The Tempeh
2 1/2 cups tempeh strips

The Tortillas
8 (5 to 6-inch) corn or flour tortillas

The Toppings
1 cup shredded purple cabbage
1/2 cup Salsa Verde (page 218)
1 cup pineapple, cut into 1/2-inch dice (prep this just before serving)

1. Remove the stems and seeds from the chiles and gently slice away the veins inside the chiles. In a food processor or blender, puree the chiles, onion, garlic, green onions, thyme, salt, allspice, nutmeg, cinnamon, pepper, sugar, and olive oil. In a shallow bowl, toss the tempeh with the rub. Set this aside for 1 hour to allow the flavor of the rub to seep into the tempeh.

2. Preheat the grill. If using a wood-fire grill (my preferred method for this recipe), light it. Shove the coals to one side once they turn white and you don't see large flames coming from them. If you are using a gas grill, light one side of the grill and use wood chips.

3. Wrap the rubbed tempeh in foil and liberally pierce it with a fork so you have lots of holes. The holes will let the smoke into the packet while the foil will keep the tempeh moist. Place this on the side of the grill that does not have the coals directly under it. Let this smoke for about 2 hours.

4. Warm your tortillas. Unwrap the tempeh. Fill the tortillas with the tempeh, then the cabbage, then the salsa, and finish it off with three or four pieces of diced pineapple.

MAKE IT LOW-FAT: You can skip the oil in the recipe. Add 2 tablespoons of water to the marinade instead. Every 20 minutes or so, peel back the top of the foil while the tempeh is on the grill and spritz it with water. The oil in the main recipe keeps the tempeh moist, so spritzing it is necessary to achieve the same result.

MAKE IT FAST: I will admit, I sometimes do not have the patience to wait for the seitan to marinade or for it to smoke. In those cases, I put the tempeh in a grill pan, toss it in an extra tablespoon of oil, and grill it over a high heat. Slowly stir it while it is in the grill pan and grill it until you see blackened bits appear on the tempeh. This should happen within just a couple of minutes. You don't get a smoky taco, but you get an excellent taco de asador.

MAKE IT ON THE STOVETOP: Don't wait for the tempeh to marinate. There is a trick to getting the flavor into the seitan quickly when you are working on the stovetop. Once you have the rub on it, bring the pan to a medium high heat. Add the tempeh and slowly stir it for about 5 to 6 minutes, until you see a little blackening on it. Add 1/4 cup of water to the pan at this point, give it a quick stir, and let the water cook out. What happens is that the rub infuses the water and the tempeh absorbs much of the water while it cooks, transferring the flavor of the rub to the interior of the tempeh. Be warned, though, that the chiles will release a lot of capsaicin into the air using this method. Keep your windows open!

That Is Frackin' Hot!
· · · · · · · · · · · · · ·

Why, yes it is. It's a pretty traditional Jamaican jerk, and it is not for the weak. If you want some heat, but not a killer level of heat, you can substitute serrano chiles or even a ripe, red jalapeño. Those also make great substitutes, if you don't have Scotch Bonnets or habaneros. Finally, if you want the jerk flavor without the heat, just omit the chiles, and you'll be fine.

Dosa Tacos with Chipotle Tomato Chutney

A dosa is a giant, thin rice-and-lentil cone or scroll popular in the south of India. They are filled with myriad ingredients and served with various chutneys, and are perfectly formed to eat with your hands. Kind of sounds like a taco, doesn't it? I thought it did, so I created this fusion taco filled with curried lemon potatoes and topped with a chipotle tomato chutney. This is one of those tacos that pops with lots of different flavors. It has curry, then bright lemon juice, then a rich tomato chutney. It's spicy and intense, but you can easily tone it down by cutting down the amount of chiles or simply omitting them.

REGION: SOUTH INDIA/CASA DE JASON | HEAT LEVEL: 7 | MAKES 8 TACOS

The Filling
8 small Yukon gold or other waxy potatoes
Water for boiling
1 tablespoon grated fresh ginger
4 cloves garlic, minced
1 tablespoon olive oil
1 1/2 teaspoons whole cumin seeds
2 teaspoons whole coriander seeds
1 teaspoon brown mustard seeds
1 teaspoon salt
1 tablespoon ground turmeric
1 tablespoon paprika
2 tablespoons lemon juice

The Tortillas
8 (5 to 6-inch) thin corn tortillas

The Toppings
Fried Chiles de Árbol (page 201)
Minced fresh cilantro (prep just before serving)
Chipotle Tomato Chutney (recipe follows)

1. Chop the potatoes (this will help them cook faster). Boil them in water for about 10 minutes. Once they are soft, drain them. Mash them and set them aside.

2. Heat the oil in a skillet over a medium heat. Add the ginger, garlic, cumin seeds, coriander seeds, and brown mustard seeds. As soon as the mustard seeds pop, after about 30 to 60 seconds, remove the pan from the heat. If you have a mortar and pestle, crush the mixture into a paste. If you don't have one, don't worry about it. Stir the seasoning mixture to the mashed potatoes, along with the salt, turmeric, paprika, and lemon juice until they are incorporated.

3. Warm the tortillas. Fill them liberally with the mashed potatoes, then top with the chutney, the fried chiles, and the cilantro.

MAKE IT LOW-FAT: When making the mashed potatoes, toast only the seeds, not the ginger and garlic, in a dry pan over a medium heat for about a minute. Get them out of the pan right away. Combine the minced garlic and grated ginger with the lemon juice and let it sit for about 15 minutes. This will mellow out the garlic and ginger and take away their raw bite. Once you've done this, go ahead and mix all of your ingredients into the mashed potatoes. When you make the chutney, toast the spices in a dry pot over a medium heat for about 1 minute, then add the bay leaves. Wait about 15 seconds before adding in the water, then proceed with making the chutney as you see above. Omit the fried chiles and you have a very low-fat, delicious taco.

MAKE IT SIMPLE: This is a bit of a meticulous recipe, but you can use yellow curry powder to take two shortcuts that can save a lot of time and hassle. Here's how. Mince the garlic and grate the ginger just like you would in the standard recipe. Sauté only those in the oil for about 1 minute, then get them out of the pan. Instead of using all the different spices, just add the garlic and ginger, the lemon juice, the salt, and 1 tablespoon of curry powder to the mashed potatoes. You'll be done with that part in just a few minutes. To make the chutney, in a saucepan, combine 1 (14.5) ounce can of crushed tomatoes, add 1 tablespoon of curry powder, 2 chopped chipotles in adobo, the salt, and the tomato paste. Stir everything until it is incorporated and simmer over a medium heat for about 5 minutes. That's all there is to it.

Chipotle Tomato Chutney

1 tablespoon olive oil

1 1/2 teaspoons fennel seeds

3/4 teaspoon brown mustard seeds

2 bay leaves

1/4 cup water

4 plum tomatoes, roughly chopped

2 chipotles in adobo, roughly chopped

1 teaspoon ground turmeric

3/4 teaspoon salt

1 tablespoon tomato paste

1. Heat the oil in a saucepan over medium heat. Add the fennel seeds and brown mustard seeds. As soon as the mustard seeds pop, (after about 30 to 60 seconds), add the bay leaves to the pan. Immediately add the water. The bay leaves only need a couple of seconds to toast, which is why you should get the water in the pan right after adding the bay leaves.

2. Add the tomatoes, chipotles, turmeric, and salt and simmer, stirring to combine. Once the tomatoes have cooked to the point where they are soft, smash them in the saucepan. Add the tomato paste, stir, and cook 1 more minute.

Tacos with Yuca and Chimichurri

One night I was craving Brazilian chimichurri sauce. I had just bought some yuca from my local Mexican market, so I decided to make yuca fries which then inspired me to make these simple tacos. The chimichurri gives them a brilliant, acidic, herbal flavor and the yuca fries provide a nice crunch. For a low-fat version, you can forgo frying the yuca and enjoy them as a soft taco. Use the sauce sparingly because it is potent, not necessarily in heat, but simply in its acidity. A little bit goes a long way.

REGION: BRAZIL/CASA DE JASON | HEAT LEVEL: 3 | MAKES 6 TACOS

The Yuca
2 yuca (about 1 1/2 pounds), peeled and cut into 2- inch x 3/4-inch strips
Water for boiling
Corn oil, for frying
3/4 teaspoon salt
3/4 teaspoon freshly ground black pepper

The Chimichurri
3 cloves garlic
1 cup flat leaf parsley leaves

1/4 cup cilantro leaves

1 tablespoon fresh oregano

1 serrano chile

1/4 teaspoon salt

1/2 teaspoon black pepper

1/4 cup olive oil

3 tablespoons red wine vinegar

The Tortillas

6 (5 to 6-inch) corn or flour tortillas

1. As you cut the yuca into strips, submerge them in a bowl of water. Be sure the bowl contains enough water to cover the yuca. Bring a pot of water to a boil over high heat. Add the yuca. The water should cover the yuca by about 2 inches. Boil the yuca for 15 minutes. Drain the yuca and then pat them dry.

2. To make the chimichurri, puree the garlic, parsley, cilantro, oregano, chile, salt, pepper, olive oil, and vinegar in a blender or food processor. Transfer to a bowl and set aside. Add enough oil to a deep skillet, wok, Dutch oven, or fryer to come up about 2 inches up the pan. Heat the oil to 350°F. Set a plate covered with a couple layers of paper towel next to the skillet. Add 8 to 10 pieces of yuca to the skillet at a time (do not overcrowd the skillet or the yuca will get soggy). Keep flipping the yuca and moving it around as it fries. It will take about 3 minutes. Remove the first batch of yuca and transfer it to the plate. Immediately season it with salt and pepper. Repeat until you have fried all the yuca.

3. Warm the tortillas. Add the yuca and top with chimichurri.

MAKE IT LOW-FAT: You can skip the frying process and still have a great soft taco. Don't pat the yuca dry, though. That's only to make them fry better. Leave them a little wet and dress them with the salt and pepper. The moisture will help those stick to the yuca. When you make the chimichurri, omit the olive oil and replace it with a couple tablespoons of water.

Working with Yuca

• • • • • • • • • • • • •

Yuca, also called cassava and mantioc, is a popular ingredient throughout Latin America. It is fairly hard, so it's best to cut it with a sharp, heavy knife. It reacts with oxygen quickly and will turn dark brown, so after you cut a few pieces, submerge them in water to prevent this. Boiling it before frying it is particularly important, because it is such a hard vegetable. You may see some recipes for fried yuca that call for boiling the entire yuca before peeling and cutting it. However, this will not produce fried yuca that is as crisp or evenly cooked as when you cut and then boiled it. If you don't have access to yuca, you can still make this taco by using potatoes instead. Just boil the potatoes for about 5 minutes and then fry the potatoes twice instead of once.

Toppings
Sides
and Drinks

CHAPTER

Top That Taco!

*"Chile-lime peanuts, crema,
queso fresco, and more."*

Toppings are those little accents that bring pop and extra texture to tacos. They often add heat and acidity, but their two primary jobs are to make your taco more complex and to allow you to customize it.

When you visit a taquería, you'll often see a mix of pickled chiles, sliced fresh veggies, fried chiles, and pickled onions, in addition to salsas, which I'll cover in the next chapter. Imagine taking a simple taco like tacos with pintos borrachos and then adding fried chiles to one, pickled onions to another, and fresh cabbage to yet another. Each of those tacos is a unique experience, all made different by simply switching out the toppings. Making your own taco creations is one of the most fun experiences you can have!

There are, of course, many more, but these are the most common ones, because they can all go with just about any taco in this book. I keep several around in my refrigerator or pantry because they keep for a long time, they are versatile, and let's be honest—the more components I have pre-made for a meal, the more likely I am to use them! Those components include fried chiles de árbol, pickled onions and chiles, chile peanuts, and vegan queso fresco. You can also freeze both the chile peanuts and fried chiles de árbol. Just keep the storage bag completely sealed, press as much air out of the bags as possible, and these will last for months on end.

Two of my favorite crunchy ingredients are fried chiles de árbol and chile peanuts. These two toppings go particularly well with tacos with beans, because it adds a crunchy, complex texture to those tacos, and with tacos de asador, too, because their flavors complement the flavors of the grill. They are also two of the components I always keep around my kitchen.

Grilled Spring Onions

Cebollitas Asadas

These are a popular topping for northern-style tacos de asador, but they go very well with any sort of grilled taco filling. The ones use most commonly in Mexico have large bulbs, about one inch to one and a half inches in diameter, but you can make these with the thin green onions more commonly found in U.S. grocery markets.

MAKES ABOUT 2 CUPS

5 large or 10 small spring onions (scallions)
1 teaspoon olive oil
Salt
A squeeze of lime or lemon juice

1. In a bowl, combine the spring onions, olive oil, and salt to taste. Toss to coat.

2. For large spring onions: Place the onions on the grill away from the hottest part of the grill. Grilling them off center from the hot part of the grill gives them more time to cook without burning the thin green part of the onion. Rotate the onions every 30 seconds or so. Once the big white bulbs are barely soft and show some blackening, remove the onions from the grill.

3. For small spring onions: Place the onions off-center of the hottest part of the grill. They only need about 30 seconds to 1 minute on the grill and then they are done.

4. As soon as the onions are cooked, sprinkle them with a squeeze of lime or lemon juice.

VARIATION: If you want to roast the onion instead of grilling them, place them in a covered baking dish and roast at 400°F for 10 minutes.

Rajas
· · · ·

Rajas are, at their heart, strips of roasted chiles. Typically, they are made with poblanos, but any strip of roasted chile will do. These are a great accent to just about any taco. O.K., maybe not the dessert tacos, but all the other tacos in this book are rajas friendly.

To make rajas, either pan roast or fire-roast the chiles. Once they are roasted, place the chiles in a bowl and cover them for about 20 minutes. Peel the chiles and pull the stem out of them. Most of the time, the seed packet attached to the stem will lift right out of the chile, too. Cut the chiles into strips that are 1/2-inch wide by up to 4-inches long, and you're done.

Chile-Lime Peanuts

Cacahuates con Chile y Limón

These don't just make a great taco topping, they make a great snack, as well. They are easy to make and last a very long time if you keep them well-sealed. The key is to get the peanuts roasted and partially browned to enhance their flavor. However, if you want to cheat, you can purchase roasted peanuts from the store, toss them with the lime juice, and then toss them with the salt and chile powder. That's also how you make the no-oil-added version of these chile peanuts. To make these, you will need: a sauté pan (a wide one works best as the more peanuts you can expose to the pan, the faster they roast); a stirring spoon; and a bowl.

MAKES 2 CUPS

2 tablespoons corn or peanut oil
2 cups Spanish peanuts
Juice of 2 limes
2 teaspoons chile powder (I usually grind about 10 chiles de árbol into powder)
3/4 teaspoon coarse salt

Heat the oil in a large sauté pan over medium heat. Add the peanuts and slowly stir them until they begin to brown, about 4 to 5 minutes. Remove the peanuts from the heat and place them in a mixing bowl. Immediately toss them with the lime juice, and then add the chile powder and salt and toss them again to coat them. Spread out the peanuts on a platter or rimmed baking pan and let them cool. For extra flavor, zest the limes before you juice them and add the lime zest along with the chile powder and salt.

Whole Roasted Jalapeños and Serranos
• •

These are smoky bombs of fiery heat. Like rajas, these go great with just about any taco. You will only need one or two per taco and only use them if you want a backend heat to your taco that will linger for several minutes. To make them, pan roast or fire roast the whole chiles. When you place them on the taco, just tear off the stem, but don't make an effort to get rid of all the seeds. They are part of the whole roasted chile experience.

Wilted Chard in Mojo de Ajo

For me, this recipe isn't just a taco topping, it's a great lunch, a snack, and my favorite way to eat chard. You can even make tacos that are solely comprised of a tortilla and wilted chard in mojo de ajo.

MAKES 1 1/2 CUPS

1 large bunch chard, sliced, stems included
1 tablespoon Mojo de Ajo (page 60)
1/4 teaspoon salt

Slice the chard. It doesn't matter much how well you slice the leaves, but the stems should be sliced about 1/4 inch thick. Bring the mojo de ajo to a medium heat. Add the chard and salt. Cook this, stirring every couple of minutes, until the chard is completely wilted and the stems are soft. It usually takes 5 to 8 minutes.

Rough-Salted Chile Powder

This condiment is a powerful addition to any taco, but goes particularly well sprinkled on tacos de asador. It's got a heavy, spicy flavor that cries out for bold tacos. Keep this sealed in a jar in your refrigerator and it will keep for at least a month.

MAKES 1/3 CUP (IT CONDENSES DOWN QUITE A BIT)

2 cups fried chiles de árbol
3/4 teaspoon coarse salt
2 teaspoons corn oil (use some of the oil you used for frying the chiles de árbol)
6 cloves minced garlic

1. Remove the stems from the fried chiles de árbol. Crush the chiles with your fingers or place them in a small food processor and pulse a few times until you have a rough chile powder. Do not grind this into a fine powder or you lose some complexity in taste. Transfer the crushed chiles to a bowl and stir in the salt.

2. Heat the oil in a small skillet over a medium heat. Add the garlic and sauté it for about 2 minutes. Stir the sautéed garlic to the chile powder.

NOTE: If you want to keep these as low fat as possible, roast the chiles de árbol by pressing them onto a hot griddle for 5 to 10 seconds and then grind them into a rough chile powder. Add the salt. Instead of sautéing the garlic, pan-roast the cloves and then smash them into a paste. Add this to the chile mix and then break up the clumps of roasted garlic and chiles with your fingers.

Taquería-Style Carrots Escabeche

These pickled carrots are popular additions to guacamole tacos, tacos dorados, and tacos de canasta. They should only be pickled for about two hours so that the carrots still have some crunch. There are plenty of variations of these, but the following is my favorite.

MAKES ABOUT 2 CUPS

1 large carrot, cut diagonally into 1/8-inch slices
1/2 large red onion, cut into 1/4-inch strips
2 jalapeño or serrano chiles, thinly sliced
8 whole cloves garlic
2 bay leaves
1/2 teaspoon Mexican oregano
1 teaspoon salt
White vinegar (enough to cover)
Juice of 2 limes

Combine all the ingredients in a jar with a tight-fitting lid. Seal the jar and set it aside at room temperature for about 2 hours to get the perfect texture. Refrigerate any leftovers.

MAKE IT QUICK: For a quick version, boil the garlic and the carrot and onion slices in a saucepan with enough water to cover for about 1 minute, then immediately remove them from the water and add them to the pickling jar. You'll have pickled vegetables in about 10 minutes. They won't be quite as flavorful, but you won't have to wait 2 hours, either.

Toppings Found at a Traditional Taquería

- Fried chiles de árbol
- Sliced radish
- Shredded cabbage
- Pickled onions
- Pickled chiles
- Minced or sliced jalapeño and serrano chiles
- Queso fresco
- Chopped cilantro
- Lime wedges

Fried Chiles de Árbol

These are incredibly easy to make, and they keep well. Frying the chiles de árbol activates their volatile compounds, making the flavor deeper and richer. These are relatively hot on their own, but the heat is mitigated quite a bit when they are added to a taco because the tortilla tones it down. If you don't want to fry these, you can still toast them by bringing a griddle to a medium heat and pressing them onto the griddle with a spatula for five to ten seconds per side. When you serve them, place them in a molcajete for a nice presentation and, before you add them to a taco, tear off the stem and very top of the chile. If you want to tone down the heat even more, shake out the seeds after tearing off the top. You can also use this technique on whatever dried chiles you have on hand.

MAKES 2 CUPS

Corn oil or other neutral flavored oil
2 cups dried chiles de árbol

Add about 2-inches of oil to a deep skillet, wok, or Dutch oven. (There needs to be enough oil to cover the chiles—if you want to make a lot of fried chiles, you can fry them in batches.) Heat the oil to 375°F. Add the chiles and fry them for one minute. They should turn a dark red color. Use a pair of tongs or a slotted spoon to remove the chiles from the oil. Place the fried chiles on a plate lined with paper towels to drain.

Note: I also make fried anchos, guajillos, and chipotles and then I crush them into flakes to use as a garnish. Save the oil used in this recipe to fry other chiles, as well. You can also use that chile-flavored oil for other dishes.

Preparing Fresh Vegetables and Herbs

Limes, cilantro, minced onion, minced chiles, cabbage, and radishes are standard fare at most taco shops. Typically, the taquero will add minced onion, cabbage, and/or cilantro to the appropriate taco for you while you are responsible for adding the lime and radish. When I am setting out a taco bar for my guests, however, I prefer to place all of those ingredients in bowls so they can choose what they want and garnish their tacos themselves. Typically, onion, cilantro, and lime go with most tacos while cabbage and radish are served with carnitas and any taco where you want to add crunch.

Limes: To make lime wedges, cut limes into eight sections.

Cilantro: Tear away the topmost part of the cilantro to avoid using the larger stem pieces. Bunch the cilantro together and mince it. I save the stems for blending into pureed salsas, since they have quite a bit of flavor.

Minced White Onion: Mince the white onion. Rinse the minced onion in a fine-meshed colander and then pat them dry as best you can. When onions are cut, there is an enzymatic reaction that causes the release of sulfurous compounds that gives the onion a harsh bite. Rinsing onions rinses away those compounds and mellows out the onion.

Minced Chiles: Minced serrano and jalapeño are the most common chiles served with tacos, though I also like minced habanero when I want something hot. Remove the stems, then cut the chiles in half. Remove the seeds and mince the chiles.

Sliced Cabbage: Purple and green cabbage sliced into thin strips about two inches long are fairly common taco adornments. If my sliced cabbage is going to be sitting out for more than twenty minutes, I like to keep it in cool water to keep the flavor fresh and to keep the cabbage from browning.

Sliced Radish: Sliced radish adds a spicy bite and crunch to tacos. Cut the top and bottom off of each radish. Slice the radish into very thin disks, no more than 1/8-inch thick. One radish will be enough for 6 to 8 tacos. If the radish is going to be out for more than 10 minutes, I keep it in cold water just like the cabbage.

Pickled Red Onions

Pickled onions are one of the most popular condiments at taco bars. They liven up a taco with their acidity and sweetness. They also happen to be incredibly easy to make. As a side note, you may see some recipes that call for sugar when pickling these onions, but you don't need it. They are sweet enough on their own, and the sugar detracts from the pure flavor of the onions. You can use either apple cider vinegar to make a mellower, slightly sweeter version of these, or lime juice to make pickled onions that pop. (See photo on page 140.)

MAKES 1 CUP

1 large red onion, cut into 1/4-inch wide strips
Apple cider vinegar or lime juice (enough to cover)

Place the onion strips in a bowl and add enough apple cider vinegar or lime juice to cover them. Marinate them for at least 1 hour. After an hour, they will be ready, but the longer they sit, the better they get. To store, simply keep them in the vinegar or lime juice in a sealed container and they will last for weeks in your refrigerator. Make sure you use a non-reactive bowl when pickling and storing these.

Pickled Chiles

. . . .

Pickled chiles are all about acidity and heat. They can be paired with just about any taco, and come in several varieties. The most popular pickled chiles are jalapeños, serranos, habaneros, and fresh chiles de árbol. Jalapeños and habaneros are typically sliced into very thin rounds, while fresh green chiles de árbol are usually left whole. Serranos are both sliced and left whole. I find it works best to snip the stems off the chiles that are left whole before I start pickling them. Pickled chiles are made exactly the same way as pickled onions. You can, of course, purchase these at most markets, especially pickled jalapeños, but they are so easy to make and they taste so much better, I strongly urge you to make your own.

There is a Yucatecan version of pickled onions and chiles that is spicy, sweet, and absolutely delicious. The pickling method is exactly the same as above, but you're going to slice one red onion and three habaneros. To the pickling liquid, add 1/2 teaspoon of salt and 4 whole allspice berries. This is best if it can pickle for a full day so the allspice can infuse the pickling liquid and infuse the onions and chiles.

Vegan Crema and Cheeses

Making vegan dairy alternatives merges the art and science of cooking. If you are just beginning to craft your own vegan cheeses, you are in for an exciting time in the kitchen! Be aware, however, that it is also a labor-intensive process requiring several steps and special components.

I find making vegan cheeses fascinating, and I hope you do, too. But if you don't want to make them from scratch, it's fine to skip them or use the substitutions I've indicated in the recipes. You'll find the crema fairly easy to make, but the *Queso Fresco* and *Queso Oaxaca* are quite involved.

Queso fresco ("fresh cheese") is a taco mainstay. It's a crumbly, salty cheese with a strong sour note that adds a nice accent to a taco. It's similar to feta but a little softer and not as sharp. Dairy queso fresco only takes a couple hours to make, but our vegan version will take about a day to properly develop.

Crema

Crema is kind of a cross between sour cream and crème fraîche. It has its sour notes, though not as prominent as in sour cream, but these are balanced by semi-sweet creaminess. The flavors help bring together the elements of a taco and provide a peppy top note to it. The process to make this is similar to making dairy crema, but it takes longer to get the flavor to properly develop. However, there is a cheat you can use if you want it right away and are willing to settle with a crema that isn't absolutely perfect, but still tasty.

MAKES 2 CUPS

1 1/2 cups raw cashews
Water for soaking
1/2 teaspoon granulated sugar
1/2 cup warm water
1/3 cup plain unsweetened non-dairy yogurt (my favorite is Whole Soy plain unsweetened soy yogurt, but any plain unsweetened non-dairy yogurt is fine)
1 capsule probiotics (to make it extra tangy), optional

1. Soak the cashews in water for about 4 hours, then drain and rinse them. In a small bowl, combine sugar and the warm water, stirring to dissolve the sugar. This is important because the sugar helps feed the culture already present in the yogurt, making the crema sour better. In a blender, puree the cashews, sugar water, non-dairy yogurt, and probiotic powder, if using.

2. Transfer the mixture to a glass bowl and cover it with plastic wrap or cloth, but don't seal it, as the mix needs to breathe. Set aside and let it sit for about a day and a half. Normally, dairy crema takes half a day to a full day to make, but it has more components for the culture to work on than this version does, which is why it takes longer. As it sits, the crema will sour and thicken. After this time, seal it and refrigerate it. When you are ready to use the crema, check the consistency. Add enough water to get it to a consistency that is a little thinner than sour cream. It should pour, but not run, off of a spoon.

3. The crema will last in your refrigerator for a couple weeks and will continue to thicken and sour. Add water to it as needed to get it back to the right consistency, or just let it be if you want a texture more like sour cream than crema.

MAKE IT QUICK: You can forgo the aging process and use it right away. If you do, you'll want to add 1/2 cup yogurt instead of 1/3 cup. The yogurt is already a little sour, so adding in more yogurt will add in sour notes without having to age the crema. The only drawback is the crema will taste more like yogurt and the flavors won't integrate as well, but then you don't have to wait a day and a half.

Queso Fresco

The recipe starts by making sweetened cashew cream tofu. (See the alternative if you want to avoid soy.) This tofu is then marinated in the crema base to infuse it with a cheesy flavor. Finally, the cheese is suspended in cheesecloth to drain and tighten. For those used to dairy queso fresco, this will taste similar, but not as milky. You can get more of that milky flavor if you are willing to wait an extra day to develop more of a cheesy flavor. Read through the entire recipe to see how it works. It's a bit complex and you will want to be familiar with all the steps before you start. The soy milk you use should not contain thickening agents such as guar gum, tapioca starch, etc. Most brands of soy milk will work just fine. If it has added vitamins, sugar, or calcium, that's fine, too.

Note: To get a milky taste, we need to add sugar to the soy milk. I also put cashew cream directly into the soy milk so that when the soy milk coagulates, the protein in the soy milk will trap the fatty, milky-tasting cashew cream and bind it directly into the tofu. That way, we're not making tofu, we're on our way to making an actual non-dairy cheese. All we need to do now is culture it with vegan crema, and we'll have queso fresco.

MAKES 2 CUPS

3 cups raw cashews, soaked for 3 to 4 hours, then drained

7 to 8 cups soy milk (see Note above)

1/4 cup sugar

1 teaspoon salt

1/3 teaspoon citric acid or 5 tablespoons lemon juice

1 1/2 teaspoons granulated nigari combined with 1/4 cup of water

1/4 cup Crema (page 204)

Before you start making the sweetened tofu, soak the cashews and make the Vegan Crema if you don't have any already made.

Puree the soaked cashews with the soy milk. Add the sugar and salt to the mixture. This will make a rich, sweet, salty soy milk. Line another colander with cheesecloth and place it in the sink. Combine the nigari and water until the nigari dissolves. If you are using lemon juice, you do not need to use the water. Bring the soy milk mixture to a boil over a medium high heat and boil it for 5 minutes, stirring it the entire time. Remove the pot from the heat and let it sit for 2 minutes. Ideally, your soy milk should be between 170°F and 180°F when you add the nigari. Add 1/3 of the nigari water and quickly stir the soy milk a few times, then leave it alone for a few seconds. Add the next 1/3 of the nigari water and give it just one or two stirs. Cover the pot for three minutes. Add the final 1/3 of the nigari water and gently stir the top portion of the soy milk for 30 seconds. Cover the pot for another 3 minutes. By this time, the soy milk should have curdled. Pour it into the cheesecloth and drain thoroughly for 5 minutes. Fold the cheesecloth over the tofu cheese and place a weight on it, like a bowl. Let drain for about 20 minutes.

Finishing the Queso Fresco

Once the tofu cheese has drained, transfer it to a bowl and immediately mix it with the Vegan Crema. The warm, newly pressed tofu is very delicate, so be gentle when you stir the Vegan Crema into it. At this point, it will have a texture and flavor similar to a sour ricotta, but it will be a little beany. Let the cheese sit for about 12 hours. The beany taste will go away and the cheese will absorb much of the marinade. You can use it at this point but the texture is very soft. To firm up the cheese, wrap it in cheesecloth and hang it in a dry place for another 12 hours. Make sure to put something under the cheesecloth to catch the liquid as it drains. This will compact the cheese and give it a crumbly texture.

SOY-FREE OPTION: You can use peanut milk in this recipe exactly in the same proportion and manner as you would the soybeans. They have a similar protein and fat composition, which is the key to getting the right texture for the cheese. Just make sure to use unsalted, raw peanuts. For a master recipe on making your own soy milk and peanut milk, go to The Vegan Taste website.

Quick-and-Easy Queso Fresco Alternatives

• •

That's a whole lot of work for queso fresco, but I wanted to give you a good vegan rendition of this classic cheese. There are other versions out there that are simply crumbled tofu marinated in oil and some sort of acid, and while they are far easier to make, they also taste like tofu marinated in oil and acid. My version puts a milky flavor directly into the tofu and cultures it with Vegan Crema to create a real cheese flavor and texture.

If you don't want to take the time to make this, don't worry. You can use salted pepitas, pine nuts, or even chopped avocado dressed with salt and lime in place of queso fresco in any of the recipes. The job of queso fresco is to add a shot of saltiness, sourness, and fat to a taco and you can do that with any of the options I just outlined. Most of the time, that's exactly what I do, until I get the bug to make queso fresco.

Queso Oaxaca

Queso Oaxaca, named after the state that made this cheese famous, is a stringy cheese similar to mozzarella. Not surprising, considering that both milk and the method to make cheese was introduced into Oaxaca by European cheesemakers. Unlike mozzarella, which is made with buffalo milk, queso Oaxaca uses the same methods, but with cows' milk. This version, while not stringy, serves the same purpose on a taco as dairy queso Oaxaca. That is, it's a thick white cheese that melts. Only a few of our tacos use it, but it's indispensable for making tacos vampiros and it works best if you add it to the tortilla first and then place hot ingredients on top of it. The heat from the ingredients will become trapped in the cheese, causing it to soften and melt if they are hot enough. This cheese is based heavily on Miyoko Schinner's meltable mozzarella cheese, but I modified to give it the flavor indicative of queso Oaxaca, which is more buttery and less lemony than mozzarella. You may also see queso Oaxaca called queso asadero ("roasting cheese"), which is the cheese of choice for melting in the oven.

MAKES 2 CUPS

1 cup slivered almonds, soaked and ground into a smooth paste
1/4 cup Crema (page 204) or 1/4 cup vegan yogurt
1/3 cup canola oil
2 teaspoons sugar
1/2 teaspoons salt
Large bowl of ice-cold water
6 tablespoons tapioca flour
1 tablespoon carrageenan powder
1/2 teaspoon xanthan gum

1. Soak the almonds for about 4 hours. Drain, then grind into a smooth paste with the vegan crema, oil, sugar, and salt. Do not let this sit for more than a couple hours before working with it because queso Oaxaca does not have much of a sour taste and the vegan crema will culture the mix too much if it sits for more than a couple hours.

2. Get a big bowl of ice water ready. Combine the wet mix with the tapioca flour, carrageenan powder, and xanthan gum. Transfer this to a pot and bring it to a simmer over a medium heat. Whisk it for about 3 to 5 minutes. It should thicken and turn glossy.

3. This next step is optional, but it will fashion the thickened cheese in the pot into the traditional rope shape of queso Oaxaca. Take a big chunk of the cheese, form it into a ball, and then quickly roll it out into a 1-inch thick rope by rolling the ball and pressing down on it with your palm. The mix will be hot, so you may want to wear gloves. As soon as you have the rope, drop the cheese in the bowl of ice water for about 30 seconds, and then remove it. Repeat this until you have used your entire mix.

4. To store this, form a coil with the rope, place it in a sealed container, and use when you need it. If you are going to keep it for more than a couple days, store it cover in water.

Mango Salsa (page 220)

CHAPTER

Salsas and Guacamoles

"Authentic salsas, guacamoles, and hot sauces."

Salsas enliven and brighten the flavors of tacos. Complex on their own, salsas add even more texture, heat, and acidity, giving them pop and zing. They are one of the four essential food groups of the taco. Some taco connoisseurs claim that a taco isn't a true taco without salsa. There are a few exceptions to this, but for the most part, they are right. For me, choosing the right salsa for a taco is like choosing the right wine.

There are typically several good matches, but a bad match can ruin the experience. Most salsas use tomatoes and tomatillos to carry the salsas' flavors, though fruit, such as mango or pineapple, is sometimes used. Though salsas are simple to make and rarely use many ingredients, they can be as complex as the cooks that make them. Some are straightforward and bold; some have an undertone of restless smoke; some dance across the tongue; and some are searingly hot.

Hot sauces are also included in this taco food group, and the line between a salsa and a hot sauce can be quite blurry. On second thought, that may be caused by the tears affecting your vision from eating so many smoking hot chiles. Even so, I don't place too much differentiation between hot sauces and salsas, save that a hot sauce is always thin, spicy, and highly acidic. Hot sauces typically focus more on a straight chile and vinegar combination rather than on the tomatoes and tomatillos.

Guacamoles are also included as a saucy topping for tacos, especially the type of guacamole found at most taquerías, which is thin to the point where it is almost a sauce. Even though it may not be the thick chip-dipping kind you are used to seeing, it is aptly designed to be saucy enough to drip down into the taco and pull all the elements of the taco together. The thicker ones can be used as fillings on their own, but I included them in this section to keep all the guacamoles together for ease of reference.

The Pentad of Salsas

These first five salsas are the classic taquería salsas. They encompass the primary styles of salsa, a roasted smashed salsa, a thin chile-based salsa, a green salsa, a fresh salsa, and a saucy guacamole. Together, they form the core of the taco bar. I like to call them the Pentad of Salsas.

Crushed Red Salsa

Salsa Roja de Molcajete

This is the classic crushed salsa. It has a robust sweetness from the roasted chiles, tomatoes, onions, and garlic and a nice rustic texture. A molcajete speeds the process of making this salsa up greatly, but you can easily make this in a mixing bowl with a potato masher or heavy wooden spoon.

HEAT LEVEL: 4 | MAKES: 2 CUPS

3 plum tomatoes, roasted
2 jalapeños, roasted or chipotles in adobo
1 medium white onion cut into 3/4-inch thick disks
4 cloves garlic
3 tablespoons chopped cilantro
1/2 teaspoon salt
Juice of 2 limes

1. Preheat the oven to 450°F. Place the tomatoes and jalapeños in a baking dish and roast them for 15 minutes. (If you are using chipotles in adobo instead of jalapeños, you do not need to roast them, just the tomatoes.)

2. In a skillet over medium heat, pan-roast the onion and garlic until they are partially blackened. Chop the roasted onion and garlic and transfer it to a molcajete (or mortar and pestle). When the tomatoes and jalapeños are done roasting, remove the stems from the jalapeños. Remove the seeds and veins if you want to tone down the heat.

3. Chop the jalapeños, but leave the tomatoes intact. You don't want to break the tomatoes until they are in the molcajete so you can keep all the tomato juice in the salsa. Add the jalapeños, tomatoes, cilantro, salt, and lime juice to the molcajete and smash them to make a rough sauce. Give it a stir to make sure everything is evenly incorporated.

Green Salsa with Avocado

Salsa Verde Cruda con Avocado

Salsas verdes are tomatillo based salsas, but the ones for tacos are typically pureed with avocado to make the salsa creamy. I particularly enjoy the balance of tart and creamy as it helps pull together all the elements of a taco.

Note: When cutting the vegetables for this recipe, don't worry about getting them precise. You will puree everything, anyway.

HEAT LEVEL: 5 | MAKES 2 CUPS

1/4 cup coarsely chopped white onion

6 large tomatillos, husked removed and quartered

1 chile verde or poblano chile, coarsely chopped

2 serrano chiles, stems removed (remove the seeds and veins to tone down the heat)

1 cup coarsely chopped cilantro

1/4 teaspoon salt

Juice of 1 lime

1 avocado, pitted, flesh scooped out

Puree all the ingredients in a blender or food processor.

MAKE IT QUICK: Combine the flesh of an avocado with a jar of your favorite salsa verde in a blender or food processor and blend until well combined.

Using a Molcajete
• • • • • • • • • • •

To get the most out of your salsa, I suggest using a molcajete for crushed salsas and thick guacamoles and a high speed blender for your smooth salsas, hot sauces, and taquería-style guacamole. However, if you don't have a molcajete or mortar and pestle, don't worry. You can easily crush your salsas using a large mixing bowl and a potato masher or heavy wooden spoon. A strainer will help you make the smoothest hot sauce, though it's not necessary.

Guacamole Salsa

Guacamole Taquero

This is one of the five classics served at taquerias — it's a borderline between a guacamole and salsa. Guacamole for tacos, while still thick, is much saucier than guacamole for dipping chips. This spicy, tart guacamole is spooned over the taco and oozes down the ingredients, spreading its creamy goodness throughout the taco. Unlike the other salsas, this one only keeps for a few hours, so only make as much as you will need. Keep it very cold to lengthen its life, and if you need to store it for some reason, press plastic wrap directly onto it to minimize its contact with the air.

HEAT LEVEL: 3 | MAKES: 1 1/4 CUPS

4 medium-size tomatillos, husks removed and quartered

1/4 cup roughly chopped white onion

2 serrano chiles or jalapeños, roughly chopped (I like mine ripe and red for this recipe)

1/4 cup chopped cilantro

2 cloves garlic

1 tablespoon chopped fresh epazote, optional but recommended

Juice of 2 limes

1/2 teaspoon salt

1 large avocado

In a blender or food processor puree the tomatillos, onion, chiles, cilantro, garlic, epazote (if using), lime juice, and salt. You may need to press on these with a stick to force them onto the blender blades so they puree. Once the ingredients are pureed, pit the avocado, scoop out the flesh, and add it to the blender. Puree until smooth.

Pico de Gallo

Salsa Mexicana

You probably know salsa Mexicana by its other name, pico de gallo. This is the salsa my mom always made for parties or to go along with her enchiladas when I was growing up. As a child, I wouldn't have anything to do with it, but as an adult, I crave it. My mom's version uses salsa inglesa, also known as Worcestershire sauce, instead of lime juice. The key to this recipe is toning down the onions by rinsing them and using fresh, in-season tomatoes. The tomatoes will make or break this recipe.

HEAT LEVEL: 3 | MAKES 2 CUPS

1/2 cup minced red onion, rinsed
3 plum tomatoes, roughly chopped
1 to 2 jalapeño chiles, minced
1 clove garlic, minced
1/4 cup chopped cilantro
Juice of 1 lime or 1 tablespoon of salsa Inglesa (vegan Worcestershire sauce)

Note: If you do not have a molcajete or mortar and pestle, simply cut the ingredients, combine them in a bowl, and allow them to rest for 15 minutes before serving.

After rinsing the minced onion, smash it two or three times in a molcajete or with a mortar and pestle. Add the chopped tomatoes to the molcajete and crush them just once or twice. You should still have mostly whole chunks of tomatoes. Stir in the jalapeño, garlic, cilantro and lime juice, mixing until they are combined. Let the salsa rest for at least 10 minutes before serving to allow the flavors to meld.

Guajillo Chile Salsa

Salsa Roja de Guajillo

This salsa is the epitome of the smooth, chile-based salsa. The predominant chile flavor is melded with garlic and held together with apple cider vinegar. For a more decadent version with a deeper flavor, you can fry it in oil to caramelize the pureed guajillos.

HEAT LEVEL: 4 | MAKES 1 CUP

8 guajillo chiles
1 plum tomato
2 cloves garlic
1/2 teaspoon salt
1 tablespoon apple cider vinegar
1/3 cup water (I use the rehydrating liquid from the chiles)
Optional: 2 tablespoons olive oil (to make the fried variation)

Remove the stems from the guajillos. Toast the guajillos in a dry pan over a medium heat by pressing a spatula down on them for about 10 seconds per side. Pour steaming water over them, enough to cover them, and let them sit for about 20 minutes. In a blender or food processor, puree the rehydrated guajillos, tomato, garlic, salt, vinegar, and water.

VARIATION: For a fried version, omit the apple cider vinegar and water when you puree the other ingredients. Heat the oil in a skillet, over medium heat. Add the paste and fry it, slowly stirring, for 6 to 7 minutes. Slowly add the water and apple cider vinegar, stir, and remove it from the heat.

Working with Chiles and Avocados
• •

When working with chiles, both fresh and dried, it's important to remove all the stems before using in these recipes. If you need to tone down the heat, you can remove the seeds and veins, or simply use fewer chiles.

When you are working with the avocados, cut them in half, remove the pit, and scoop out the soft green avocado flesh and discard the hard skin.

Más Salsas

In addition to that core pentad of salsas, these rank among my favorites. By switching between them, you can radically change the same taco into very different creations. They range from cooked salsas to fresh salsas to thin salsas and chunky salsas. After making tacos, I typically find that I have salsa left over, so I keep a few empty jars handy to quickly jar the remaining salsas to have on hand for next time. Because the salsas have so much acidity and capsaicin, they will last at least a month or longer if kept sealed in your refrigerator.

A Note about Equipment: A molcajete and tejolote (mortar and pestle) are very helpful when making smashed salsas, but you can get away with a mixing bowl and potato masher, too. More important is a good blender so you can get the best puree or grind on the chiles and some of the other ingredients. A citrus reamer will also help since many of the salsas use limes or oranges, but the reamer is not absolutely necessary.

Salsa Verde
Salsa Verde Cocida

This is a simple cooked salsa verde. Cooking the tomatillos removes much of their tartness and sweetens the overall salsa. It's not only great for tacos, it's perfect for jarring and for setting out as a dip for chips.

HEAT LEVEL: 3 | MAKES 4 CUPS

5 chiles verdes or poblano chiles, pan roasted, stems removed and discarded
8 large tomatillos, husks removed and chopped
1/2 medium-size yellow onion, minced (just under 1/2 cup)
2 cloves garlic, minced
2 cups chopped cilantro
1/4 cup chopped epazote, optional but recommend
3/4 teaspoon salt
1/4 cup water

Chop the pan-roasted chiles and set them aside. In a saucepan over a medium heat, combine the tomatillos, onion, garlic, cilantro, epazote (if using), salt, and water and simmer this for 7 to 8 minutes. As the tomatillos soften, press on them with a heavy wooden spoon or masher to get them to release more of their juices. Add the reserved chiles to the saucepan and simmer this 2 minutes longer.

Peanut Chile Salsa

Salsa de Cacahuate

This thick peanut chile salsa is excellent for tacos that have a heavy, robust flavor. It gives a strong depth to grilled tacos and tacos with pan-seared ingredients. I have a fondness for chiles and peanuts, so I use this on tacos even when it's not the best choice just to have an excuse to eat the salsa. You can also thin out this salsa and turn it into a soup base. There are plenty of variations on this salsa, but one of my favorite versions are Chef Hugo Ortega's recipe and my own variation of Chef Ortega's.

HEAT LEVEL: 5 | MAKES: 1 1/4 CUPS

1/3 cup olive oil

8 chiles de árbol

2 guajillo chiles

14 cloves garlic

2 tablespoons sesame seeds

1/2 cup Spanish peanuts

1 teaspoon dried Mexican oregano

1 teaspoon salt (or 1/2 teaspoon salt if using salted peanuts)

1 tablespoon apple cider vinegar

Heat the oil in a small deep skillet or saucepan over a medium-high heat. Add the chiles, garlic, sesame seeds, and peanuts and fry for 2 minutes. Transfer the mixture to a blender, including the frying oil. Add the oregano, salt, and vinegar and puree this until smooth.

Cocida y Cruda = Cooked and Raw

• •

Salsas crudas are salsas made with fresh, uncooked ingredients, and *salsas cocidas* are salsas made with cooked ingredients.

Mango Salsa

Salsa de Mango

Mango salsa is a lively addition to Baja-style tacos and lighter flavored tacos. Its sweetness contrasts nicely with searing chile heat and it lends a nice peppy feel to tacos dorados and even on top of guacamole. This is one of those salsas that should only be made when mangoes are in season. Otherwise, it will taste very lackluster.

HEAT LEVEL: 4 | MAKES 1 1/4 CUPS

1/4 cup finely diced red onion
1 cup diced fresh mango
1 serrano chile, minced
3 tablespoons minced cilantro
Juice of 2 limes
Pinch of salt

Rinse the onion, then transfer it to a bowl. Add the mango, chili, cilantro, lime juice, and a pinch of salt and stir it all together. Let this rest for about 10 minutes before serving.

Chiles de Árbol Salsa

Salsa de Chiles de Árbol

This salsa is made from pure chiles de árbol, white vinegar, and just a couple of spices. It is searing hot, but perfect for those addicted to super piquant salsas. It works well on just about any taco and will keep forever in the refrigerator. If you want a version that is a little more decadent, but has a more complex, deeper flavor, you can fry the chiles before grinding them.

HEAT LEVEL: 8 | MAKES 1 1/4 CUPS

30 chiles de árbol
2 cloves garlic
1 teaspoon dried Mexican oregano
1/2 teaspoon ground cumin
3/4 teaspoon salt
1/2 cup white vinegar

Briefly toast the chiles by pressing them down on a griddle over a medium heat for about 5 seconds. If you prefer, you can fry these instead, just like you were making Fried Chiles de Árbol (page 201). In a blender or food processor, grind the chiles, garlic, oregano, cumin, and salt until you have a fine powder. Add the vinegar and give it a few more pulses to incorporate everything. Doing it this way helps the chiles grind into a finer powder than if you just pureed them using the vinegar right from the start.

Mule Driver Salsa

Salsa Arriera

I first heard about this salsa in Diana Kennedy's *Recipes from the Regional Cooks of Mexico,* and I became fascinated by it, so I tracked down as many recipes for it as I could. This salsa is basically a massive amount of roasted chiles serranos mashed with a few other ingredients. Its name is based on the fact that it was a favorite amongst mule drivers, or so the story goes, and its primary flavors are hot and hotter followed by roasted. I couldn't decide between my two favorites, so I provided both. The only difference between them is the use of salsa Inglesa, also known as Worcestershire sauce.

HEAT LEVEL: 8 | MAKES: 1 1/4 CUPS

20 serrano chiles, roasted
1/4 medium white onion, minced (about 1/4 cup)
2 cloves garlic
2/3 teaspoon salt
3 tablespoons water or 2 tablespoons water and 1 tablespoon salsa Inglesa
   (vegan Worcestershire sauce)

While the chiles are roasting, mince the onion and rinse it, then smash the onion, garlic, and salt into a paste in a molcajete or mortar. Otherwise, puree the ingredients in a blender. Once the chiles are done roasting, smash the chiles and add them to the onion and garlic paste. Add the water into the salsa to thin it.

¡Agua! ¡Agua, Por Favor!
• • • • • • • • • • • • •

The first cry of many people after eating spicy food is for water, but if you need to cool that burn, water won't do the trick. Capsaicin is not water soluble, so water will just spread it to other parts of your tongue, and that means even more heat. Very, very cold water helps a little, but that's because the cold deadens the nerve endings. Oily or fatty foods, like coconut milk can help, as they create a barrier between capsaicin molecules and the nerve endings. Alcohol dissolves capsaicin, so beer and tequila are your friends in this situation. Plus, it's a good excuse to have beer or tequila. Finally, sugar partly neutralizes capsaicin and also gives the mind another strong flavor to focus upon. It's one of the primary reasons that cultures that have a lot of spicy food also have a lot of sugary food.

Drunken Salsa

Salsa Borracha

Salsa borracha, or drunken salsa, is a fun salsa of pasilla or ancho chiles, fresh orange juice, and dark beer. Some recipes for salsa borracha also call for tomatoes and tomatillos, but I prefer the unmitigated taste of the chiles, orange juice, and beer. It's got a mix of sweet and bitter tastes with a little heat, making a complex salsa perfect for some of the heavier-tasting tacos.

HEAT LEVEL: 3 | MAKES 2 1/2 CUPS

6 pasilla or ancho chiles, toasted
1 dried chipotle chile
1 clove garlic
1/2 cup dark beer
1/4 cup fresh orange juice
1/2 teaspoon salt
1/2 medium white onion, minced (just under 1/2 cup)

1. Place the toasted chiles in a bowl and pour steaming water over them. Let them rehydrate for about 15 minutes.

2. In a blender or food processor, puree the rehydrated chiles, chipotle, garlic, beer, orange juice, and salt. Transfer the mixture to a bowl. Add the minced onion and let it rest for about 10 minutes so the orange juice can mellow out the onion.

Dog Nose Salsa

Salsa Xnipec

Salsa xnipec is a specialty of the Yucatán. Its name means "dog's nose" in Mayan, ostensibly because it is so hot, your nose will get wet like a dog's. I'm not sure if that story is true, but the salsa is certainly hot enough to make your nose run. It is made with habaneros and onions marinated in sour orange juice. This is one of those salsas that you should only eat if you are used to eating spicy foods. If you are, it is absolutely delicious.

REGION: YUCATECAN | HEAT LEVEL: 9 | MAKES 3 CUPS

3 habanero chiles, seeds and veins removed, minced

3 plum tomatoes, diced

1 small red onion, minced, then rinsed

1/4 cup chopped cilantro

1/2 cup sour orange juice or 2 tablespoons orange juice and 2 tablespoons lime juice

1/2 teaspoon dried Mexican oregano

1/4 teaspoon ground black pepper

1/2 teaspoon salt

In a bowl, toss together the habaneros, tomatoes, onion, cilantro, sour orange juice, oregano, pepper, and salt. Let this rest for about 45 minutes so all the flavors can mingle.

Green Salsa with Chiles de Árbol

Salsa Verde con Chiles de Árbol

This is a classic taco salsa of Central Mexico. It's got a sweet undertone from the roasted tomatillos and plenty of heat from fried chiles de árbol. Even though it's not one of the Pentad of Salsas, it's one of my personal favorites.

HEAT LEVEL: 6 | MAKES 1 1/2 CUPS

5 large tomatillos, fire-roasted or pan-roasted
Olive oil, for frying
8 chiles de árbol, fried or toasted
1 guajillo chile, fried or toasted
3 cloves garlic
1/4 cup water
3/4 teaspoon salt

While the tomatillos are roasting, add about 1/2 inch of oil to a small saucepan and heat it to 375°F. Add the chiles de árbol and fry them for about 1 minute, then transfer to a paper towel. Repeat this with the guajillo chile. Remove the stems from the chiles, but keep the seeds. Once the tomatillos are done roasting, transfer them to a blender or food processor. Add the chiles, garlic, water, and salt and puree these until they are smooth.

MAKE IT LOW-FAT: For a low-fat version, toast the chiles instead of frying them. For a Jalisco-style salsa taquera, simmer the tomatillos until they are soft and toast the chiles instead of frying them. Puree all the ingredients. This will create a cleaner, sweeter salsa.

Using Storebought Salsa

. . . .

Because capsaicin is an anti-bacterial agent, salsa will keep in your refrigerator for a very long time. If you find one you particularly enjoy, make a big batch of it, seal it in a jar, and keep it in your refrigerator so you have it on hand. It will make the taco-making experience much quicker, and if you don't feel like making a salsa at all, keep a jar of your favorite salsa on hand. One of my staple favorites is Rick Bayless's Frontera brand salsas. They have good flavor, a nice variety, and are widely available. However, if I want the best of the five classics, my local Mexican market has incredible salsa that they make fresh every day, so I typically go there when I want one of the classic taco salsas. I urge you to visit your local Mexican or Latino market. Check the ingredients and make sure there aren't any filler ingredients, such as xanthan gum. Some markets will cheap out and stretch their salsa with such ingredients. You want to see just the straight, natural ingredients you would see if you were making your own salsa.

Salsa for the Brave

Salsa Macha

Macha means brave in Spanish, and, considering that this salsa is basically just pureed chiles and garlic, it is aptly named. It is more akin to a chile paste than a typical salsa. I find it interesting because it uses olive oil, a strong Spanish influence prevalent in the cuisine of Veracruz, where this salsa originated. It also happens to be fantastically delicious.

REGION: VERACRUZ | HEAT LEVEL: 8 | MAKES 3 CUPS

2 cups olive oil
15 chipotles morita (see below for variations)
1/4 cup slivered almonds
6 cloves garlic
2 tablespoons sesame seeds
1/4 teaspoon dried thyme
1 teaspoon salt
1 tablespoon white vinegar

Heat the oil in a saucepan to 375°F. Add the chiles and almonds and fry them for 2 minutes. Add the garlic and sesame seeds and fry these 1 minute longer. Remove them from the heat. Transfer the contents of the saucepan, including the oil, to a blender. Add the thyme, salt, and vinegar and process them until they are smooth.

VARIATIONS: Instead of just chipotles morita, you can use chipotles meco or chiles de árbol for a variation of equal spiciness or you can use guajillos or anchos if you want a very toned-down salsa macha. If you use these large chiles, just use five of them. You can also do a mix of different chiles. If you want a particularly brutal salsa, you can use 30 chiles tepin or pequin. I like to call that version of this recipe Salsa Loca because you have to be insane to eat it.

Yogurt Sauce

Salsa de Jocoque

Jocoque is basically identical to the standard Lebanese yogurt mint sauce. Typically, this salsa is used on top of Tacos Árabes, but it can also be combined with rajas or even on top of enchiladas. Try cooking it with some greens for a tangy, creamy taco filling. Make sure you get an unsweetened yogurt when making this salsa or it will taste a little weird. That's why I prefer to use unsweetened plain soy yogurt instead of coconut yogurt because the coconut one is always too sweet.

HEAT LEVEL: 0 | MAKES 2 1/4 CUPS

2 cups plain unsweetened vegan yogurt
1 clove garlic
Juice of 1 lemon
1/2 teaspoon salt
1/4 cup minced fresh mint

In a blender or food processor, puree the yogurt, garlic, lemon juice, and salt. Transfer this to a bowl. Smash the minced mint with the back of a knife. Stir the smashed mint into the yogurt sauce. This is best if it can sit for about 10 minutes before serving.

Hot Sauces

Hot sauces are simply very thin salsas that tend to have very high acidity content. The acidity makes them pop with flavor, and it heightens the other components of the sauce. When I make these, I usually make them in double or triple batches and then pour them into clean used bottles. These will generally keep in your refrigerator for at least six months and sometimes more. You can also do the formal canning process, keep them in your pantry for years, and give them away as gifts.

A Note about Equipment: You will be well-served by having a high-speed blender when making the hot sauce recipes, but even if you only have a standard blender, you can still make them, they just won't be quite as smooth. Other than a measuring cup, a measuring spoon, a knife, a cutting board, and a skillet for the occasional roasted or toasted ingredient, that will be all you need.

Roasted Garlic Pequin Chile Sauce
Salsa Picante de Chile Piquín y Ajo Asado

This recipe is one of the first hot sauce recipes I ever created and it also happens to be one of my favorites, still. It packs a powerful punch, not just from the heat of the tiny chiles piquin, but from the garlic and vinegar as well. It is best used by the spoonful and not poured on your tacos in large amounts. Otherwise, it will completely overwhelm the flavor of the taco instead of acting as an accent to it.

HEAT LEVEL: 7 | MAKES 1 CUP

12 to 15 cloves peeled garlic
15 to 20 pequin chiles
3/4 teaspoon salt
3/4 cup raw apple cider vinegar
1 tablespoon olive oil

1. Pan-roast the peeled garlic until it blackens slightly. Using the peeled garlic will add a slight charred flavor to the garlic, making the sauce more interesting and complex.

2. Transfer the garlic to the blender. Once the garlic is out of the pan, toast the pequin chiles in the same pan for about 30 seconds and quickly transfer them to the blender. Don't worry about removing the stems or seeds. All of that will get blended into the sauce.

3. Add the vinegar and oil and puree until it is smooth. Transfer to a jar with a tight-fitting lid. This will keep jarred in your refrigerator for several months.

Note: The oil is used to smooth out the acidity of the vinegar, but you can omit the oil if you wish.

Garlic Sauce

Salsa de Ajo

This is a simple garlic sauce, but it doesn't need that many ingredients to be outstanding. It's basically, garlic, vinegar, and salt, with more garlic. I love using this sauce on just about all of my tacos and it makes a nice sauce to put out for guests that can't handle a lot of heat. I strongly suggest using garlic that is already peeled, but not already minced. Once a garlic clove is cut open, it will start to go bad within just a couple of hours, but as long as it remains uncut, it remains as fresh as if it were still in the garlic paper.

HEAT LEVEL: 0 | MAKES 1 3/4 CUPS

20 cloves of garlic
1 cup apple cider vinegar
1 teaspoon salt
1/2 teaspoon ground black pepper
2 tablespoons chopped fresh epazoten optional, but recommended:

In a blender or food processor, puree the garlic, vinegar, salt, pepper, and epazote, if using. Transfer this to a jar with a tight-fitting lid. This will keep for at least six months.

Habanero Tequila Hot Sauce

Salsa Picante de Tequila y Chile Habanero

I enjoy the balance of sweet and spicy with this sauce. The pineapple is the perfect accompaniment to the in-tense heat and fruit flavor of the habanero. You can also make this with chipotles in adobo in-stead of habaneros for a fun variation on this recipe. I use water in this recipe to allow the unadulterated tastes of the pineapple and habanero to shine and the tequila lends a fun back note.

HEAT LEVEL: 8 | MAKES 2 CUPS

3 habanero chiles
2 cups chopped fresh pineapple (if your pineapple is not that sweet, add 1 tablespoon agave nectar)
Zest of 2 limes
1/2 cup water
3/4 teaspoon salt
2 1/2 tablespoons tequila blanco

Remove the stems, seeds, and veins from the habanero. In a blender, puree all the ingredients until they are smooth. Transfer the sauce to a jar with a tight-fitting lid. This will last about three months.

Chipotle Hot Sauce

Salsa Picante de Chipotle

This main flavor in this hot sauce comes from the smoky, tobacco-colored chipotles meco. I add a touch of agave to this recipe to balance out the heat of the chipotles and a little cumin to give a subtle bass note to the sauce. You can make this with other dried chiles to alter the heat level, or do a mix if you want a more complex flavor, but I adore the pure chipotle.

HEAT LEVEL: 6 | MAKES 1 1/4 CUPS

5 chipotles meco
1/2 teaspoon cumin seeds
1 teaspoon salt
2 cloves garlic
1 cup apple cider vinegar
1 teaspoon agave nectar

1. In a dry skillet over medium heat, toast the chipotles for about 15 seconds per side. Remove the chipotles from the heat and set them aside. Add the cumin to the hot pan and toast the cumin for about 30 seconds to 1 minute. As soon as you can smell the cumin toasting, remove it from the pan.

2. In a small blender or spice grinder, grind the chipotles, cumin, and salt into a powder. If you are used a spice grinder, transfer the powder to a blender. Add the garlic and about 2 tablespoons of the apple cider vinegar to the blender. Puree this until you have a smooth paste, adding an extra tablespoon of apple cider vinegar as needed.

3. Using this small amount of apple cider vinegar first is important for creating a smooth sauce. Add the remainder of the apple cider vinegar and agave and puree until smooth. Transfer to a jar with a tight-fitting lid. This will last six months to a year.

Guacamoles

At its heart, a guacamole is just a thick sauce of avocadoes with salt and lime. Everything else is bonus. In fact, the word itself stems from the Nahuatl word ahuacamolli, which is a conjunction of ahuacatl (avocado) and molli (a thick sauce). I find that interesting because the word mole is also a derivative of molli. Etymology aside, I add guacamole to nearly all my tacos. I find the creaminess of the avocado and acidity of the lime pulls all the other ingredients together. Given how quickly it disappears when I have guests over for dinner, I am guessing they feel the same way.

I strongly suggest making guacamole at the last minute, but if you need to make it ahead of time, press a piece of plastic wrap directly onto the guacamole to minimize its exposure to the air, which is what browns it. You may also consider adding in the juice of one more limes since a high acid content will also keep it from browning. Store it in the back of your refrigerator so the cold can further slow the browning process.

A Note about Equipment: A molcajete and tejolote will not only make producing guacamole quick and easy, it makes for a fine presentation. If you don't have them, don't worry. You can easily make it in a mixing bowl and smash the avocado with a heavy wooden spoon. A small citrus reamer will help, too, so you can get the most juice from the limes, but is not necessary.

How to Choose and Cut an Avocado

• •

I always use Hass avocados in my recipes. They have the perfect amount of fat versus water content and the best flavor of any of commercially available avocados. I look for a dark green skin, and I give the avocado a gentle squeeze. There should be a slight give, but the skin should not feel like it is collapsing. Also, check for anything that looks off at the top where the stem was attached.

To cut the avocado, make an incision along the spot where the stem was attached and press down until you hit the seed. Then rotate the avocado along the blade of the knife, not the other way around, until the avocado is sliced in half. Twist the two halves opposite each other until one of the halves pops off the seed. Next, place the seed half on a cutting board (don't do this in your hand!) and thunk the knife into the seed. Twist the knife and lift out the seed.

Toasted Pepita Sun-Dried Tomato Guacamole

I first tasted a version of this guacamole in Chicago at Rick Bayless' Frontera Grill, and I fell in love with the crunch of the pepitas and the tangy intensity of the sun-dried tomatoes over the backdrop of creamy avocado. Naturally, I had to make my own version. This goes great with pretty much any taco, but use it sparingly, because the sun-dried tomatoes are intense and you don't want them to overwhelm the other flavors of the taco. (See photo on page 233.)

HEAT LEVEL: 3 | MAKES 3 1/4 CUPS

3 avocados
Juice of 2 limes
1/2 teaspoon salt
2 cloves garlic, minced
1 serrano chile, minced
1 teaspoon fresh chopped marjoram or oregano
4 to 6 sun-dried tomatoes, sliced
3 tablespoons pepitas, toasted and salted (you can buy them already toasted and salted, if desired)

Pit the avocado and scoop out the flesh into a molcajete or bowl. Add the lime and salt and mash the mixture, but don't make it completely smooth. Stir in the garlic, serrano, marjoram or oregano, and sun-dried tomatoes. Top with the pepitas.

Chopped Guacamole
Guacamole Picado

This is the quintessential, unadorned guacamole. It only has three ingredients because that is all that it needs. I actually prefer this over the guacamole taquero and I can easily eat tacos with just corn tortillas and chopped guacamole. I like using a coarse, flaky sea salt with this recipe because it lends a nice texture to the guacamole and since salt is such a predominant flavor, you can taste the minerals in the salt. If you want a spicy version of this recipe, add a minced serrano to the finished dish.

HEAT LEVEL: 0 | MAKES 2 CUPS

2 avocados
Juice of 2 limes
1/2 teaspoon coarse salt or 1/3 teaspoon fine salt

Pit the avocados and scoop out the flesh. Give the avocado a few chops one way and then the other, then slide it into your serving bowl. Add the lime juice and toss to coat the avocado. Sprinkle on the salt and give the avocado a few more gentle tosses.

Roasted Poblano Guacamole

This guacamole is my secret weapon, a food ambassador for avocados everywhere. It has complexity and depth from the roasted poblano garlic paste, creaminess from the avocado, and brightness from the fresh lime. Whenever I serve this as part of a guacamole bar, it is always the first to go.

HEAT LEVEL: 2 | MAKES 3 1/2 CUPS

1 poblano chile, pan-roasted or fire-roasted
6 cloves garlic, pan roasted
1/2 teaspoon coarse salt
2 tablespoons chopped cilantro
Juice of 2 limes
3 avocados
1 small firm tomato, diced

1. Peel off the blackest parts of the skin from the roasted poblano. Remove the stem and seeds and discard them, then chop the poblano. Peel the roasted garlic.

2. In a molcajete (or a mixing bowl if you don't have one), mash the poblano, garlic, salt, cilantro, and lime juice into a paste. Pit and chop the avocado (this makes it easier to mash). Add the avocados to the molcajete and mash it. Don't worry about getting it perfectly smooth. The avocado should still have some texture to it. Gently stir the paste, which should be mostly sitting at the bottom of your molcajete, into the mashed avocado. Top the guacamole with the diced tomato. I serve this directly in the molcajete.

CHAPTER

Sides

"Zesty rice, beans, potatoes, and other taco go-withs."

Most tacos are served by themselves, though occasionally they may come as part of a meal with a small set of sides. The one most commonly found at taquerías is fresh fruit, whatever is in season, dressed with chile, lime, and salt. It's a popular snack all over Mexico, regardless of whether or not one is at a taquería.

Of course, it's hard to talk about Mexican food without talking about rice and beans, which are popular sides at taquerías where one sits down to eat, as opposed to a grab and eat taco stand. This is especially true in the U.S. at many of the fancier taquerías. I've provided a few sides to make your taco experience into more of a plated meal experience instead of a taco bar or taco stand experience. Of course, you can always get away with making simple rice and beans, but I really like these twists on the classics. One last note. You can use the pintos borrachos from Tacos with Pintos Borrachos (page 100). It makes a wonderful side all on its own.

Ancho Garlic Beans

Anchos and garlic create the sauce for these beans, which is fried and then mixed and stewed with pintos to make a side flavorful enough to stand alongside any taco. If you like the ancho garlic paste, you can make an extra-large batch and then store it in your refrigerator for later use.

MAKES 4 CUPS

6 ancho chiles
12 cloves garlic
1 teaspoon dried Mexican oregano
1/2 teaspoon ground cumin
2 tablespoons olive oil
1 1/2 cups dried pinto beans
1 teaspoon salt

1. Rehydrate the anchos by pouring steaming hot water over them. Don't forget to snip the stems off first. Let them sit for about 20 minutes, then remove them, but keep the rehydrating liquid. In a blender or food processor, puree the anchos, garlic, oregano, and cumin.

2. Heat the oil in a large saucepan over a medium heat. Add the ancho garlic puree and cook, fry this, slowly stirring it, for about 5 minutes. Add five cups of liquid using the rehydrating liquid from the chiles and enough water to make up the remainder until you have 5 cups total. Bring this to a simmer and add the pinto beans. Simmer for about 1 1/2 hours, until the beans are soft. Gently mash the beans until they are roughly textured. You should end up with about half the beans mashed. Stir in the salt and serve hot.

Achiote Rice

By cooking achiote paste into the rice, it infuses it with a myriad of aromatic and earthy flavors and gives it an inviting deep red color. I am also sharing my secret to making fluffy, delicate rice with you. You can use this to cook any sort of rice to keep the grains from sticking. You can substitute smoked paprika for achiote paste for a rustic flavored variation on this recipe. For a low-fat version, simply omit the olive oil.

MAKES 3 1/2 CUPS

8 cups water
Juice of 1 lime
2 cups long-grain brown rice
2 tablespoons achiote paste
1/2 teaspoon salt
2 tablespoons olive oil

Preheat the oven to 325°F. In a large saucepan, combine the water and lime juice and bring it to a boil. Add the rice and boil it for 10 minutes. Drain well. Transfer the rice to a baking dish. Add the achiote paste, salt, and olive oil, and toss to combine. Cover the baking dish with foil and bake for 20 minutes.

Mojo de Ajo Potatoes with Fried Guajillos

This is a simple fried potato recipe using one of my favorite kitchen staples in the world, mojo de ajo. The potatoes are kicked up with sprinkles of crispy chile guajillo bits and a coarse sea salt. Just a few ingredients for absolutely divine potatoes.

MAKES 4 SERVINGS

4 waxy potatoes like Rose or Yukon Gold, cut into 1/2-inch dice
3 tablespoons Mojo de Ajo (page 62)
1 guajillo chile
3/4 teaspoon coarse sea salt

1. Steam or boil the potatoes for about 8 minutes. While they are cooking, bring the mojo de ajo to a medium high heat in a small wok. Remove the stem and seeds from the guajillo and crush it in your hand. Add the guajillo bits to the oil and fry them for about 1 minute. Use a slotted spoon to remove them from the pan and set aside on a small plate.

2. Drain the cooked potatoes or remove them from the steamer and add them to the hot wok. Fry the potatoes, gently and slowly stirring them, until they start to lightly brown, about 5 minutes.

3. Remove the wok from the heat and sprinkle the potatoes with with the salt. After you plate the potatoes, top them with the crispy guajillo bits.

Fruit with Chile, Lime, and Salt

Fast and simple belies how incredibly delicious this snack is. It rides on the quality of the fruit you use, so choose an in-season fruit when you make this. My favorite fruits to use are watermelon and mango, but you can use pineapple, apples, papaya, and even coconut. Also, you can vary the heat and flavor of the snack by using different types of chile powders. I prefer grinding my own chiles guajillo and combine it with a touch of chipotle powder. Of course, you can also just use a storebought chile powder.

MAKES 4 SERVINGS

4 cups cubed or thickly sliced fruit (I like watermelon and mango)
Juice of 2 limes
2 tablespoons chile powder
1/2 teaspoon salt

Cut the fruit and toss it in a bowl with the lime juice. In the same bowl, add the chile powder and salt and toss it all together. Serve immediately.

Note: Anchos, guajillos, chipotles, chiles de árbol, and dried New Mexico chiles all make great choices for chile powders, or you can simply use a store bought chile powder. For fruit, my first choices are watermelon and mango. You can also use dehydrated fruit with this recipe, too. The flavor will be more intense and sweeter.

Taquerías, Puestos, and Taco Bars
• •

Taquería used to refer to a taco cart, but as tacos gained in popularity, the word is now used for any movable cart or establishment that specializes in tacos. In some parts of the U.S., a taquería can be a place that actually specializes in burritos. That drives me a little crazy, but it is what it is. A *puesto* is a permanent establishment that specializes in tacos. It could be a taco truck that is *always parked* in the same spot or a small restaurant. You always know a puesto will be in the same spot. Taco bars are generally more upscale U.S. restaurants dedicated to turning tacos into a casual fine dining experience and feature full bars that showcase tequila and mezcal. In Mexico, some *fondas,* which are small restaurants, are actually taco bars.

Oaxacan Peanuts

Cacahuates Oaxaqueños

This snack is found at taquerías and bars across Oaxaca. In a way, it's the Oaxacan version of beer and pretzels, but far more interesting! It is very important that you let the peanuts cool once they are done cooking or else they will have a damp feeling.

MAKES 2 CUPS

4 chiles de árbol, partially crushed
1 tablespoon olive oil
5 cloves garlic, minced
2 cups roasted Spanish peanuts
1/2 teaspoon salt (omit if you use salted peanuts)

Crush the chiles de árbol a few times. You want to end up with each chile in several pieces. Heat the oil in a skillet over medium heat. Add the garlic and chiles and sauté for about 2 minutes. Add the peanuts and salt and sauté for another 6 to 8 minutes, slowly stirring while they cook. Remove from the peanuts the heat and allow them to cool for about 10 minutes before serving.

A Nogales street vendor sells Horchata (page 251), Pineapple Agua Fresca (page 253), and popular local snacks.

CHAPTER

Bebidas

*"Aguas frescas and other
refreshing drinks."*

Drinks are an important component of rounding out the taco experience. More so than rice, beans, or sweet treats, drinks are the true companions to the taco. Most taquerías and puestos offer a line of aguas frescas. These are drinks meant to be served cold or are naturally refreshing on their own and always at least a little sweet.

At taco bars, alcohol-based drinks like margaritas and various tequilas are more common, while _cerveza_ (beer) is served just about everywhere tacos are found. I happen to have a few other favorites that I serve with my tacos, but I don't limit these to just times when I am serving tacos. They're great any time of the day and pair well with most Mexican meals.

Blackberry Atole

Atole de Mola Negra

An atole is a drink thickened with a little masa harina. Some are chocolate based, some are fruit based, and some are berry based, like this blackberry atole. This sweet drink is perfect after dinner and will do just fine as a substitute for dessert.

MAKES 6 CUPS

2 cups blackberries
5 cups water, divided
1 piloncillo (about 3 ounces) or 1/4 cup brown sugar
1/2 cup masa harina combined with 1 cup of water

1. In a saucepan, combine the blackberries and the 1 cup of water and bring it to a simmer. Simmer for about 5 minutes, stirring to turn the blackberries into a sauce. Press the blackberry sauce through a strainer into a small bowl and set it aside.

2. In a saucepan, bring the remaining 4 cups water and the piloncillo to a boil, stirring until the piloncillo dissolves.

3. Combine the masa and water mixture in a bowl or blender and stir or blend it until it is smooth. Add the masa mixture to the boiling water along with the blackberry puree and quickly stir it. Reduce the heat to a simmer and simmer it for 5 minutes. Serve hot.

MAKE IT SIMPLE: Puree the blackberries, all the water, and the masa harina, then press it through a sieve into a pot. Add the piloncillo or brown sugar and bring the drink to a low simmer, slowly stirring it until the masa thickens and the piloncillo or brown sugar dissolves.

Spicy Cinnamon Almond Coffee

Café de Olla Picante con Almendras

Going to Italy turned me into an espresso drinker, but when my wife purchased me a fine Chemex® coffee pot, she turned me into a full-fledged coffee drinker. I immediately set about making flavored coffees and this one turned out to be my favorite. It's a smooth coffee sweetened with piloncillo with hints of almonds and cinnamon. I like having this around to sip while I make all the components for my tacos. It's a fun drink to share while everyone waits for lunch or dinner to be made.

MAKES 4 CUPS

4 cups water
1/2 cup coarse ground coffee
3 tablespoons slivered almonds, toasted (see Note)
2 (2-inch) pieces cinnamon stick
1 (5-ounce) piece piloncillo (1 large cone) or 4 tablespoons brown sugar

For all methods: The water should be 200°F. You can do this without a thermometer by bringing the water to a boil in a saucepan, removing the saucepan from the burner, and then letting it rest for about 15 seconds before pouring it over your coffee. Or, you can use an infrared thermometer, if you have one.

French Press Method: Add all the non-water ingredients to the bottom of your French press. Bring the water to 200°F and pour it into the press. Let the coffee sit in the press for about 4 minutes. If you use this method, use 4 small 1 to 1 1/2-ounce piloncillos instead of one large piece and place each one in its own cup. Once the coffee has brewed, pour it into each cup and stir until the piloncillo dissolves. If you have a small French press, you may need to do this in two batches, so split the ingredients accordingly.

Chemex® Method: The order in which you add your ingredients to the filter matters quite a bit when using the Chemex system. You need to give the coffee grounds room to bloom and not clog the filter. Place the piloncillo at the bottom of the Chemex pot. If it won't fit through the neck, you can break it up or use smaller piloncillos. Next, add your filter to the pot. Add your coffee grounds to the filter first, then the cinnamon, and then the slivered almonds. If you add the almonds to the filter first, the filter gets clogged. Bring your water to 200°F and slowly pour it into the filter. Once the coffee has brewed, remove the filter. Give the coffee a stir to break up any of the undissolved piloncillo.

Café de Olla Method: In a saucepan, combine the almonds, cinnamon sticks, piloncillo, and water and simmer this for 5 minutes before adding the coffee grounds. As soon as you add the coffee grounds, remove the pot from the heat. Let this steep for 4 minutes, then serve the coffee by pouring it through a fine-mesh strainer into the cups.

Note: Toast the almonds in a dry pan over medium heat, for about 2 minutes, until you see them brown a bit.

Aguas Frescas

Aguas frescas are light, sweet drinks made with fruits, berries, flowers, grains, and anything else that can be made into a sweetened refreshing drink. These should not be confused with *refrescos*, which are soft drinks. You can easily make your own agua fresca creations at home by pureeing in seasonal fruits with water and sweetening them to taste. Serve them over ice or refrigerate them to finish them off. I love experimenting with different flavor combos when making aguas frescas. There are so many you can try, you could have a different one every day of the year! The ones I've detailed here are taquería classics and some of my favorites.

Go to any taquería or puesto and you'll be able to find these three classic aguas frescas:

* horchata
* agua de jamaica
* agua de tamarindo

Be aware, though, that most places add milk to their horchata, so stick with the *agua de jamaica* or *agua de tamarindo*.

Hibiscus Tea

Agua de Jamaica

Pronounced huh-MY-ih-cuh, this is a tart and sweet hibiscus tea ("jamaica" is the Spanish word for hibiscus). It will definitely wake up your taste buds and the brilliant reddish purple color of the tea is beautiful to behold. It's also incredibly easy to make, so it's one of my go-to drinks whenever I am hosting a taquiza (a taco party). For an aromatic version of this tea, add 1 stick of cinnamon and 10 allspice berries to the flowers.

MAKES 5 CUPS

5 cups water
1 cup dried hibiscus flowers (labeled jamaica in Mexican markets)
6 tablespoons sugar

In a saucepan, bring the water to the point where it is almost boiling. Remove the pot from the heat and add the hibiscus flowers. Stir the sugar into the hot water until it dissolves. Let this sit for about 1 hour, then pour through a strainer into a pitcher. Serve over ice.

Horchata

Horchata is, at its heart, sweetened cinnamon rice milk. It's often flavored with vanilla, too. Most horchata has milk added to it to make it creamy (sadly, I didn't know this when I first started drinking it a few years ago), but in the south of Mexico, coconut milk is sometimes used to replace the dairy milk. Almonds are also a popular additive in the south, and I happen to love almonds and coconut, so this is my favorite version of horchata. It can be a little labor intensive to make, so if you don't want to go through the entire process of soaking rice and squeezing it, use the cheat at the end of the recipe. (See photo on page 244.)

MAKES 5 CUPS

1 cup long-grain white rice
6 tablespoons slivered almonds
4 1/2 cups hot water
2 (4-inch) cinnamon sticks, or 1/2 teaspoon ground cinnamon
1 vanilla bean pod, split open, or 1/4 teaspoon vanilla extract
1 (13-ounce) can unsweetened coconut milk
3/4 cup sugar
Ice

1. Grind the rice in a blender, then add the almonds and continue to grind this until you have rice and almond pulp. Don't over-grind the almonds or it will turn them into almond butter!

2. In a saucepan, bring the water to the point where it just starts to steam. Take it off the heat and add the rice/almond mixture, the cinnamon sticks, and the vanilla bean pod. Once the water cools, cover the pot and let it sit in your refrigerator for at least 6 hours.

3. Remove the cinnamon sticks and vanilla bean pod. Blend the rice/almond/water mixture until it is completely smooth. Line a strainer with cheesecloth and set it over a bowl into which you can pour the mix. Pour the mixture into the cheesecloth and wrap it closed once most of the liquid has percolated through the cheesecloth and strainer. Squeeze the cheesecloth to get even more horchata goodness out of the pulpy mix. You can even go another step further, re-blend this mix, and squeeze it one more time.

4. Heat the coconut milk in a saucepan over a medium-low heat until it is warm. Add the sugar, stirring to dissolve it. Pour the coconut milk mixture into to the bowl with the horchata and stir. Serve over ice.

MAKE IT SIMPLE: In a bowl or pitcher, combine 3 cups rice milk, 1 cup almond milk, 1 1/2 cups coconut milk, sugar, the vanilla extract, and the ground cinnamon. Stir everything together and serve it over ice.

Sweet Tamarind Tea

Agua de Tamarindo

I love the interplay of sweet and sour with this agua fresca. Tamarind imparts a powerful flavor, so this agua fresca is very potent. The sugar balances that sour note out so well, though, I find I keep sipping on this drink well past the point where I have had my fill. You can find tamarind pods at most Mexican and Asian markets.

MAKES 4 CUPS

1 cup tamarind pods (about 6) or 1/4 cup tamarind paste
4 cups water
1/4 cup sugar

Remove the shells from the tamarind, revealing the pulp and seeds. Skip that part if you are using tamarind paste. In a saucepan, bring the water to a boil and add the tamarind pulp and seeds. Boil this for about 2 minutes. Remove from the heat and stir the sugar into the pot until it dissolves. Let it steep for 2 hours. Press the tea through a fine-meshed sieve into a pitcher. The very soft parts of the pulp should move through the sieve while the seeds and more fibrous parts of the pulp should be left behind. For a richer flavor, use agave nectar or two large pieces of piloncillo instead of sugar.

Cantaloupe Agua Fresca

Agua Fresca de Melón

Cantaloupe is a popular melon used to make drinks and desserts. It's fairly sweet, so you don't need to add sugar. It was meant to be a fairly light drink, anyway. This is the perfect drink for hot summer days and spicy tacos.

MAKES 5 CUPS

2 cups water
4 to 6 tablespoons sugar (depending on the sweetness of the cantaloupe)
1 cantaloupe, cut, seeded, and peeled
Ice

Warm the water in a small saucepan over medium heat. Add the sugar, and stir to dissolve it. Remove from the heat. Coarsely chop the cantaloupe and place it in a blender. Puree the cantaloupe and sugar water. Serve over ice.

Mango Lime Agua Fresca

Agua Fresca de Mango y Limón

This recipe started out as a sorbet that I created several years ago, but I would find myself pureeing it with some water to thin it out into a drink. I love the pop of the lime and that lush sweetness that mango has. You can use frozen mango, but it tends to be a little tart, so you might want to add an extra teaspoon of agave. Serve this one chilled or over ice.

MAKES 4 CUPS

2 fresh ripe mangoes or 2 cups chopped frozen mango (use fresh when it's in season)
2 1/2 cups water
Juice of 2 limes
2 tablespoons agave nectar

If you are using fresh mangoes, cut down along the sides of the seed. Scoop out the inner yellow fleshy part with a metal spoon. If you are using frozen mango, it can go right into the blender. Puree all the ingredients. This is best if it is served slightly chilled.

Pineapple Agua Fresca

Agua Fresca de Piña

Fresh, ripe pineapple is one of the wonders of the world. If you have the perfect pineapple, you won't need any agave for this recipe. If it's not quite ripe or not quite in season, a little agave will add the remainder of the sweetness you might be missing. If the pineapple isn't ripe or is very much out of season, skip this recipe. It will be tart and lifeless, but if you have a good ripe pineapple, you will be in heaven. You can serve this one chilled or at room temperature.

MAKES 6 CUPS

1 fresh ripe pineapple
4 cups water
Agave nectar

Cut the top and bottom away from the pineapple. Cut down along the sides of the pineapple to remove the rough skin. Cut down around the core to easily remove the core. Coarsely chop the pineapple. You should have about 4 cups. In a blender, combine the chopped pineapple and water. Puree until smooth. Press the pineapple mixture through a fine-meshed sieve into a pitcher. Taste it and add agave to taste.

Piloncillo Water

Agua de Piloncillo

This drink was inspired by a popular Costa Rican beverage called *tapa de dulce,* which is hot water mixed with panela (unrefined whole cane sugar) and sometimes a touch of lemon. I wanted something a little simpler and quick, so when I got back from leading one of my vegan culinary tours in Costa Rica, I started mixing piloncillo with hot water for an easy morning pick me up. It also happened to be a natural pairing for spicy tacos. It's just sweet enough to offset some of the heat from the chiles, but refreshing enough to leave you feeling light. Serve this warm, but not steaming.

MAKES 1 CUP

1 cup steaming hot water
1 small piloncillo (about 1.5 ounces) or 2 tablespoons brown sugar

In a small saucepan or kettle, bring one cup of water to the point where it is steaming and pour it into a heatproof glass. Add the piloncillo and stir to dissolve it in the water. I sometimes can't find piloncillo that small, so when I can't, I just use a larger piece of piloncillo and make a larger batch, increasing the amount of water used by the same proportion as the increase in piloncillo.

Tequila, Beer, and Alcohol Drinks

Alcohol and tacos are like good friends having a night out on the town. It's a time of excitement and laughter that you don't want to end. When it does, it ends with a smile, and you can't wait until the next time you get together. I always feel like a good drink should have a bit of mystery and danger to it. Like I am with my friends, I am very choosy with what I drink. I think that comes from not being a big alcohol drinker. If I'm going to have alcohol, it has to be good. However, if I'm serving fifty people, it has to be cheap! That's just how it goes.

Alcohol is a good partner to tacos, not only because it acts as a social lubricant and can just be plain fun, alcohol also dissolves capsaicin, those tiny molecules that bring the heat. It means, basically, that you can eat spicier food and more of it. It soothes the savaged tongue. Beer is the most common alcoholic beverage served at taco carts and stands and puestos while the better tequilas, mezcals, and mixed drinks are available at taco bars.

You can make the drinks below with high-quality alcohol or more budget friendly alcohol, and they will still be good regardless. The more expensive ones will give you a slightly more complex-in-flavor drink, but don't splurge on the absolute best when you are mixing it with other ingredients. If I am just sipping tequila or mezcal or having a beer, I tend to go with the higher-end goods, because I can taste the nuance usually found in them. If I am mixing them into drinks, like you see with the recipes below, I typically go with a mid-grade alcohol, since the other ingredients will override some of that nuance.

I've listed some quality brands of alcohols that are vegan, but keep in mind that they are current as of the writing of this book. In a few years, those brands may change the way they process their products. I've also listed some of the more popular brands of vegan alcohol found at taquerías, like Negra Modelo. These are great options if you don't want to blow your budget, but still want a decent drink.

Cerveza (Beer)

Beer is a common part of the taco experience. I prefer darker beers that aren't very hoppy, so my tastes run toward lagers, stouts, and ales. These pair particularly well with heavier tacos, especially tacos de asador. For tacos that have a brighter quality, like many of the tacos from Baja, the tacos de canasta, and a few of the zestier tacos de comal, a lighter beer is usually more appropriate.

For dark beers, ales, and lagers, my favorite brands are Negra Modelo, Bohemia Obscura, North Coast Brewing Company's Brother Thelonious, Rogue Hazelnut Brown Nectar, Jack's Abby Smoke & Dagger,

Stone Oaked Arrogant Bastard Ale, and Gulden Draak. If you can find it, Noche Buena is a great dark beer with sweet, piney notes, that comes out of Mexico during the fall season. Negra Modelo is probably your best choice if you are looking for a good dark beer at a reasonable price.

For the lighter tacos, I go with Tecate, Dos Equis, Tripel Karmeliet, Blue Moon with a squeeze of orange and lime, Avery White Rascal, and Dogfish's 90 Minute IPA. For a budget-friendly beer, I go with Tecate, and if I want to make jokes about being the most interesting man in the world, I go with Dos Equis. Samuel Adams is also budget-friendly, easy-to-find, and vegan.

Tequila

When I first started drinking alcohol in my mid-twenties, I feared tequila. I had seen too many friends passed out on the floor. That's what happens when you slam down bad tequila. Don't do that. Good tequila is meant for sipping or mixing into drinks and is absolutely exquisite. Most tequila is produced in the state of Jalisco and is named after the town of Tequila, where it was first made by the Spanish not long after they arrived in Mexico in the early 1500s.

Most tequilas are vegan, but there are obviously some brands that are better than others. Casa Noble makes a very good line of organic tequilas that have a nice clean taste, but my favorite is the line made by Sol de Mexico. It's reasonably priced, especially for an award-winning tequila, and it has a beautiful flavor. Remember, *tequila añejo* (aged at least a year) is for sipping on its own, usually after tacos, and *tequila blanco* (unaged or aged very little) and *tequila reposado* (aged at least two months) are good for sipping while eating tacos.

Mezcal

Mezcal is the name of the distilled alcohol made from slow-roasted agave piñas (heart of the plant). Unlike tequila, there are well over forty different agaves from which mezcal can be made. There are far more mezcals that are vegan than those that aren't. One of my favorites is mezcal tobalá.

Because mezcal is made from fire-roasted agave, it has a smoky finish to it. Mezcal is almost always served by itself rather than being mixed with anything else. It also tends to have a sharper, more complex flavor than tequila. For me, it's the smokiness that draws me in and the reason why I broke the rule of serving it on its own in order to make my smoky Grilled Lime Margarita with Mesquite Smoked Salt. If you're still not sold on mezcal, consider this: drinking mezcal makes you a 10th level hipster; drinking good mezcal makes you a 15th level hipster; and drinking good mezcal while eating vegan tacos means you've hit the hipster level cap.

Be creative making your aguas frescas! Shown here in the foreground is a sliced cactus fruit with a glass of watermelon cactus fruit agua fresca and a shot of tequila añejo.

Desert Sage Spritzer

This drink is inspired by the Prizefighter drink at the Portland, Oregon vegan bar, The Bye and Bye. If you have a chance to visit the bar, you should. They are generous with their drinks, and the food is perfect bar food. What struck me about the Prizefighter was the muddled sage, so I had to create my own version of a sage drink. This spritzer is on the dry side, hence the name. It's refreshing with undertones of herbal notes and a bite of *tequila blanco*. I added a touch of agave to keep it from being too dry, but if you like your drinks particularly dry, omit the agave (and maybe add another shot of *tequila blanco!*)

MAKES 1 DRINK

4 to 5 sage leaves (preferably Berggarten sage)
3 tablespoons (1 shot) tequila blanco
1 teaspoon agave nectar
Juice of 1 lime
1/2 cup lightly carbonated water or plain filtered water
Enough ice to fill a glass

1. Muddle the sage leaves in a shaker (if you don't have a muddler, you can gently press on the leaves with a spoon). Add the tequila, agave, lime juice, carbonated water, and ice. Give it only a couple of shakes. Pour it into your glass.

2. For a non-alcoholic version, skip the tequila and add an extra teaspoon of agave and a squeeze of lime for a very refreshing drink.

How to Muddle Sage
• • • • • • • • • • • • •

The trick to muddling sage, or any herb for that matter, is to avoid pressing on the large veins of the herb as much as possible, since most of the bitterness of an herb resides there. Place your sage at the bottom of your shaker or glass and press down lightly with your muddler, twisting the muddler as you do. This will juice the flimsy leaves without damaging the veins too much. If you don't have a muddler, tear the leafy parts off the large central vein as best you can and then press on the leafy parts with the back of a spoon.

Watermelon Cactus Fruit Agua Fresca with Tequila Añejo Shots

I don't need tacos to have an excuse to drink this incredible pairing. The sweet brilliance of the watermelon and cactus fruit are contrasted by the smooth burn of the tequila añejo. These are meant to be sipped in opposition to each other to get the best experience. One sip of the agua fresca, then one sip of the tequila, and back again between bites of taco. Make sure to get a good quality tequila añejo for this special treat.

MAKES 2 DRINKS

2 cups seeded watermelon chunks
2 cactus fruits
1 tablespoon agave nectar
4 ounces tequila añejo

1. Puree enough watermelon in a blender or food processor to get 1 cup of puree. You will usually need about 2 cups of watermelon, but the volume really depends on the size of your cut on the watermelon. Don't worry if you have extra left over.

2. Cut both ends off the cactus fruits. Cut a thin vertical slit along one side of the fruit. Gently ease your knife under the skin through the slit and use your knife to gently peel the fruits. Place the fleshy part of the fruit in a blender and puree it. Press the puree through a fine-meshed sieve until you have mostly juice. Mix this and the agave into the pureed watermelon. I typically serve this slightly chilled.

3. Pour the watermelon cactus fruit mixture into two small glasses and the tequila añejo into two large shot glasses.

How to Peel Cactus Fruit
• • • • • • • • • • • • • • • •

Most storebought cactus fruit (see photo on page 257) have had the needles removed, but check the fruit anyway. If needles remain, wear a pair of gloves to remove them. A ripe cactus fruit will have a dark burgundy color. It should have a little give like an avocado that has just turned ripe. To peel it, cut off the ends. Take a small knife and make an incision along the length of the fruit just deep enough to get through the skin. Pull the skin apart in both directions and it should peel away. The seeds are edible, but not pleasant to eat. Get rid of them by pureeing the cactus fruit and then straining the puree through a sieve. This will get rid of extraneous pulp and seeds.

Grilled Lime Margarita with Mesquite Smoked Salt

Margaritas are great when they are made with fresh lime and good alcohol. It's a classic drink that's now part of the Mexican experience. I wanted to change things up a bit and make something a little darker, a little more mysterious and alluring. That's what the mezcal and the smoke are to me. It permeates the entire drink, from the char of the grilled limes to the smoky mezcal to the shot of smoked salt on the rim of the glass. You can, of course, forgo grilling the limes and just use regular salt and good tequila blanco to make the classic margarita, but I hope you find the smoky version I created here to a sultry companion to your tacos.

MAKES 4 DRINKS

8 large limes, cut in half diagonally (see note)
1/4 cup agave nectar
4 shots mezcal or tequila reposado or añejo
6 tablespoons (2 shots) Cointreau or other good quality orange liqueur
Mesquite smoked salt
Sprinkle coarse sugar
Option: Make it spicy by placing a dried chipotle meco at the bottom of each
  glass

Note: I cut limes in half diagonally because it exposes more surface area of the lime to be grilled and it also makes them easier to juice.

Grill the limes until they develop blackened char lines. This will take about 5 minutes. Ideally, you should do this over a wood fire, but you can still do it with a gas grill. Flip the limes over and grill the round sides of the lime halves. This will further cook the lime and mellow out the flavor. Juice the limes into a pitcher or a bowl. Keep the lime rinds Stir the agave into the lime juice until they are thoroughly combined. Mix in the shots of mezcal and Cointreau. Take the inside of the juiced lime rinds and rim 4 margarita glasses. Sprinkle mesquite smoked salt and just a touch of sugar around the rim of the glasses. Add the margarita mix to the glasses and serve. This should be served at room temperature and not over ice, which does not play well with the smoky components.

Guajillo Chile Tawny Port

I was inspired to make this recipe while shopping in Trader Joe's. I kept thinking about including a wine recipe, but wine doesn't seem to fit tacos very well. Then I stumbled upon the aged port sitting on the shelf, and I immediately thought a little added guajillo flavor would make a simple, outstanding drink. I am infatuated with the ruddy guajillo paired with the sweet, deep flavor of the port. Now that is a wine I can serve with tacos.

MAKES 4 DRINKS

  2 guajillo chiles
  2 cups water
  2 cups tawny port

1. Remove the stems and seeds from the chiles. Over a medium heat in a dry pan, toast the chiles for about 15 seconds per side.

2. Bring the water to a boil in a kettle or pot. Place the chiles guajillo in a small bowl and pour the water over them. Let them sit for 15 to 20 minutes, until they are completely soft. Remove the chiles from the water and let them cool for about 5 minutes. Transfer the chiles to a blender, along with 1/2 cup of the port, and puree until smooth. Press the mixture through a fine-mesh sieve into a small bowl. Combine the smooth puree with the rest of the port. Serve at room temperature.

Sangrita

Sangrita, not to be confused with sangria, is a spicy citrus chaser meant to be sipped between sips of tequila blanco. It was originally created in the state of Jalisco, the state of origin for tequila, and was made from the juice left over at the bottom of a popular fruit salad made with Seville oranges, limes, pomegranates, and chiles. Cholula hot sauce is a popular addition to the blend, and it's essential for my favorite version of sangrita.

MAKES 4 SMALL SERVINGS

1 cup fresh orange juice (preferably from Seville oranges)
1/4 cup fresh pomegranate juice
Juice of 1 lime
2 tablespoons Cholula hot sauce

Stir all the ingredients together in a bowl and let it sit for 5 minutes before serving.

Shopping in Nogales, Mexico

Resources
Glossary
Acknowledgments

Resources

Shopping Online

Shopping for ingredients online is easier than it's ever been. The best place to find your ingredients and equipment is at a Mexican-oriented market, but if you need to source either of those online, the following websites are good places to start. None of these companies endorsed me, these are just my recommendations.

MexGrocer.com. This site has equipment like tortilla presses, corn grinders, metal comales, and molcajetes. It's also sells ingredients like piloncillo, achiote paste, and dried chiles. It's a gathering of all the major Mexican utensils and ingredients in one place. www.mexgrocer.com

Bob's Red Mill. A good place to find organic masa harina (corn "flour" for tortillas) and organic whole wheat flour. www.bobsredmill.com

Frontera Fiesta. Chef Rick Bayless' salsas are some of my favorite commercial salsas. If you don't want to make your own salsas, these are a great option with a wide range of heat levels and styles. www.fronterafiesta.com

Penzey's. Specializes in spices and is a great source for dried epazote and good quality chile powders. www.penzeys.com

La Tienda. Focuses on Spanish goods, but their cazuelas are among the best I've used and it's one of the few brands that don't use lead in their glaze. www.latienda.com

My Toque. Another seller of good quality cazuelas under the brand La Chamba. They also have other clay cooking items, including the elusive clay comal. www.mytoque.com

Lodge Manufacturing. The website of Lodge Logic, a prolific, good-quality brand of cast iron cookware. Cast iron skillets, grill pans, and griddles are excellent for pan-roasting. www.lodgemfg.com

Epicurean. If you purchase a good knife, you need a good cutting board to go along with it. Not only will a good cutting board make your prep time quicker, it will also protect the edge of your knife. My favorite brand is Epicurean. www.epicureancs.com

Chemex®. These are my favorite coffee pots for brewing a smooth, flavorful coffee. Make sure to get the special filters that go with the coffee pot as they are designed to filter out more of the bitter components in coffee than traditional filters do. www.chemexcoffeemaker.com

A Note on Amazon and eBay

Amazon.com has all of the above items listed on their site, although their standard free shipping offer only applies to a select few of them. You can also visit www.ebay.com for some of the equipment. I was able to get my corn grinder relatively inexpensively that way.

Glossary

The following is a glossary of Spanish terms used throughout this book.

Albañil, Tacos de – Bricklayers' tacos.

Achiote – A small red seed also called annatto.

Achiote Paste – A spice mix made primarily from achiote with several fragrant seeds added to the mix.

Adobo – A marinade, but which is often used as a sauce or a component of a sauce.

Aguas Frescas – Refreshing sweetened drinks, usually served chilled.

Ajo – The Spanish word for garlic.

Al Carbon – Cooked over an open flame.

Al Gusto – A phrase that can mean to taste, or as you like.

Ancho Chile – The dried form of the poblano. Ancho means "wide" in Spanish.

Añejo – Aged for a prolonged time. It can refer to aged alcohol, cheese, and other foods.

Aquí – A Spanish word that means "here."

Árbol, chile(s) de – This means "tree chiles." They are small, hot chiles and can be found fresh or dried.

Asador – tacos with fillings charred over an open flame

Bebidas – Drinks.

Blanco – White, though sometimes it is translated as silver.

Café de Olla – A pot of coffee.

Calabacín – Zucchini.

Caldillo Durangueño, Tacos de – Tacos with a Durango-style stew.

Carnitas Michoacánas – Carnitas Michocán-style.

Cascabel Chiles – Bell-shaped dried red chiles so named because they sound like a rattle.

Cazuela – A glazed clay cooking vessel ideal for stewing ingredients and keeping them warm.

Cebolla – onion

Cebollita – small onion

Cerveza – beer

Champiñones – Mushrooms, usually wild mushrooms

Chipotles – Smoked, dried jalapeños.

Chorizo – A marinated spicy Mexican ground sausage.

Codex Mendoza – A text commissioned by Antonio de Mendoza in the 16th century detailing the history of Aztec kings and the lives of the Aztecs.

Comal(es) – A metal or clay "pan" ideal for sautéing ingredients and cooking tortillas. Metal comals are flat and oblong and more common than clay comals. Clay comals are slightly curved and are excellent for cooking tortillas.

Cortés, Hernán – The Spanish conquistador who conquered part of Mexico.

Crème Fraîche – A type of thin sour cream.

Díaz, Porfirio – A dictator who ruled Mexico until he was overthrown in 1911.

Epazote – An herb with a bright, acidic flavor.

Estilo – A Spanish word meaning "in the style of."

Frijoles – The Spanish word for beans.

Guajillo chile – A long red chile used as the base for quite a few chile sauces.

Güero(s) (chiles) – Hot, medium-size yellow chiles.

Guisado – A dish of stewed or slow-cooked ingredients.

Habanero – A small, fat orange or yellow chile with very high heat.

Hatch chiles – A unique variety of chile grown in the Hatch Valley of New Mexico.

Hongos – A common word for mushrooms.

Huitlacoche – A fungus that grows on corn and is eaten as a delicacy.

Jalapeño – A very common, thick medium-length green chile with medium heat.

Limón – Lime

Maíz – Corn. This spelling reflects the Taíno use of the word, while "maize" is the Spanish. Maíz is typically used when referring to it in a historical sense.

Maguey – Another name for agave.

Mañana – The Spanish word for "morning," or "tomorrow."

Masa – The Spanish word for dough. In Mexico, it almost always refers to corn dough.

Masa Harina – Dried and ground corn that has been specially treated so it can be mixed with water to make corn dough.

Mezcal – An alcohol derived from fire-roasted agave cores.

Mineros – Miners

Mixiote – The outer film of agave leaves. This is used to wrap ingredients so they can be lightly steamed.

Molcajete – A rough mortar traditionally made from lava rock, though some are made from other material like concrete.

Mojo de Ajo – Olive oil that has been roasted with a large amount of garlic and citrus juice.

Mole – A thick sauce that develops over low heat for a long period of time.

Molina – A corn grinder.

Nahuatl – The language spoken by the Aztecs. Nahuatl is an umbrella term for quite a number of different dialects.

Napolitos – Cactus pad strips (see nopales).

Nejayote – The leftover liquid from making nixtamal.

Nixtamal – Corn that has been specially treated in an alkaline solution and partially cooked. This treatment makes the components of the corn more bioavailable and allows the corn to be ground into masa.

Noche – The Spanish word for "night."

Nopales – Whole cactus pads or strips from the prickly pear cactus.

Otros – A Spanish word that means "other."

Pasado Chiles – Dried long green chiles.

Pepitas – Green, shelled pumpkin seeds.

Piquín Chiles – Small, oblong orange chiles that are very hot.

Piloncillo – A cone of hard unrefined sugar.

Plancha – A very large, flat metal cooking surface usually found in restaurants or at large taco stands.

Poblano Chile – A large green chile frequently roasted for sauces or for turning into strips called "rajas."

Pozole – Corn that has been nixtamalized and fully cooked.

Puesto – A permanent establishment that specializes in selling tacos.

Quelites – Edible field greens.

Queso – cheese

Queso Fresco – fresh cheese

Rajas – strips of roasted green chiles

Reposado – aged for a short time

Rojo – red

Serrano Chile – A medium-length thin green chile that is hot, but not incredibly hot.

Sin – The Spanish word for "without."

Sólo – The Spanish word for "only."

Soya de Carne – Spanish for TVP or "soy meat."

Sudados – A Spanish word that means "sweated." Tacos de Canasta are sometimes called Tacos Sudados.

Tacos Árabes – Arabic-style tacos similar.

Tacos de Asador – Tacos with grilled fillings.

Tacos de Canasta – Tacos lightly steamed in a basket and wrapped in cloth (canasta means "basket"). Typically eaten in the morning.

Tacos de Comal – Tacos with sautéed fillings.

Tacos de Discada Norteña – A style of mixed "meat" tacos from northern Mexico.

Tacos Dorados – Fried tacos.

Tacos Dulce – Sweet tacos, or dessert tacos.

Tacos de Guisado – Tacos with stewed fillings.

Tacos Mañaneros – Breakfast tacos.

Tacos Rápidos – Quick-to-make tacos.

Tacos al Vapor – Tacos cooked over a steamer.

Taquería – A cart or establishment that specializes in selling tacos.

Taquero – A person who makes tacos.

Taquiza – A taco party.

Tejolote – The pestle for the molcajete, used to bash and grind ingredients.

Teosinte – A type of grass and the genetic predecessor to corn.

Tequila – Alcohol distilled from agave syrup. The syrup is typically extracted from the agave plant by steaming or pressure cooking it.

Tortilladora – A tortilla press.

Tortillero – A tortilla warmer. Also the name for someone who makes tortillas.

Vegano – The Spanish word for "vegan."

Vegetariano – The Spanish word for "vegetarian."

Verde – "Green."

Verdolagas – Purslane.

Verduras – The Spanish word for "vegetables."

Acknowledgments

My humble gratitude and many thanks go out to my wife Madelyn Pryor for not only supporting me writing this book and shouldering a lot of extra work for our business because of it, but for actively encouraging me to research the topic, write it, and make lots of tasty tacos! I would also like to thank my family for sharing our family history, our folklore, and our recipes. Learning how much food was ingrained in my family history was eye opening. Very many thanks go to the taqueros on the street who shared their outstanding recipes and just plain good eats with me. These are the true caretakers of the ever-changing world of Mexican food. *¡Muchas gracias!*

I want to thank Jon Robertson and everyone at Vegan Heritage Press for publishing this book. Thanks also to Susan Richey-Schmitz of A Dog's Life Photography and Art for help with the photos, and Cynthia Lozada for additional research.

Many thanks to my friends, who were extra supportive on recipe-testing days. To the chefs who inspired me to set foot on my journey into the beauty of real Mexican cuisine. To you, for reading this book and for being motivated to make compassionate choices without ever compromising on the quality of your food. Finally, to my great uncle Hector for winning that contest so many years ago. *¡Buen provecho!*

Jason Wyrick

Eat Healthy | Eat Compassionately | Eat Well

About the Author

Chef Jason Wyrick is the executive chef of The Vegan Taste. In 2001, Jason was diagnosed with diabetes in his mid-20s and was told he would have to be on medication for the rest of his life. Instead, Jason became vegan, reversed his diabetes in eight months, and lost over 100 pounds over the course of two years. Along the way, he learned about factory farming, which cemented

his decision to become vegan. He also learned that food had to be outstanding, or no one was going to eat it! He then left his job as the director of marketing for a computer company in order to become a chef and help others learn how to eat healthfully, compassionately, and well. Since then, he has co-authored the *New York Times* Bestselling book *21 Day Weight Loss Kickstart* with Neal Barnard, M.D., and has taught alongside Dr. Barnard, Dr. John Mc-Dougall, and Dr. Gabriel Cousens. Jason became the first vegan culinary instructor in the world-famous Le Cordon Bleu program through the Scottsdale Culinary Institute, founded the world's first vegan food magazine, *The Vegan Culinary Experience,* has presented for the American Dietetic Association and the American Diabetes Association, Humana, The Wellness Community, Farm Sanctuary, and is a regular guest at the Scottsdale Culinary Festival.

He has catered for prestigious organizations, including Google, the Frank Lloyd Wright Foundation, PETA, and Farm Sanctuary, and has been featured in the *New York Times,* and on both local and national television. He has taught hundreds of vegan cooking classes across the United States and has taught internationally in both Costa Rica and Italy. His recipes have appeared in *Vegetarian Times* and have been featured in several of Dr. Barnard's books. Most of all, Chef Jason loves good food and sharing it with others.

Find Chef Jason Wyrick online at:
  Website: www.thevegantaste.com
  Facebook: www.facebook.com/thevegantaste
  Twitter: www.twitter.com/thevegantaste - @thevegantaste
  Instagram: www.instagram.com/thevegantaste

Index